PAGEMAKER in easy steps

Scott Basham

In easy steps is an imprint of Computer Step
Southfield Road . Southam
Warwickshire CV33 OFB . England

Tel: 01926 817999 Fax: 01926 817005
http://www.computerstep.com

Fourth edition 1998
Earlier editions 1996, 1994, 1993

Notice of Liability

Every effort has been made to ensure that this book contains accurate and current information. However, Computer Step and the author shall not be liable for any loss or damage suffered by readers as a result of any information contained herein.

Trademarks

Adobe and PageMaker are registered trademarks of Adobe Systems Incorporated. All other trademarks are acknowledged as belonging to their respective companies.

Printed and bound in the United Kingdom

ISBN 1-84078-002-9

Contents

Chapter One

The Basics

This chapter gets you started with PageMaker. It shows you how to open the application, and make sense of its screen layout.

Covers

Introduction

This book covers versions 6.5, 6.0, 5.0, 4.0 and 3.x of PageMaker. These are denoted next to the Headings when appropriate throughout the book, otherwise the features are present in all versions.

Although most screenshots in this book are taken from Windows, Mac users should have no trouble following the examples as PageMaker is now virtually identical across both platforms.

Desktop Publishing can mean different things to different people. Back in 1984, the term DTP was first used to describe the newly released PageMaker version 1. In those days it meant the ability to combine text and graphics on the same page using a personal computer system.

Today many wordprocessors have this capability, while DTP has developed and expanded to cover a much greater range of features and accuracy of control. Systems based on PCs are now being used to create virtually any kind of document previously associated with traditional publishing: from novels and technical manuals to glossy magazines and marketing flyers.

PageMaker version 6.5 has a rich array of facilities to import text and artwork from other computer application packages, as well as allowing you to generate these directly from within PageMaker itself. It allows precision alignment, sizing and orientation of elements either by using the Mouse or by working numerically with dialog boxes and an on-screen Control palette. There is a high level of typographical control, as well as a host of features to help with the organisation and management of long documents.

More recently, PageMaker has developed features which allow you to design Web pages, for publication on the Internet rather than printed on paper.

In this guide you will be taken through all the essential features of the various versions of PageMaker for Windows/Mac. To get the most out of this book, it is recommended that you are firstly familiar with the Windows/Mac operating environment (i.e. using a Mouse, icons, menus, dialog boxes etc.). The objective of this guide is to show you PageMaker using pictures and concise explanations rather than endless pages of technical detail. Remember that it is also important to experiment using your own examples; like many things you will find that practice is the key to competence.

Starting PageMaker

If You Are Using Windows 95/98

Use the Start button to access the Programs menu, and select the PageMaker icon, usually located within the Adobe entry (Aldus for earlier PageMaker versions).

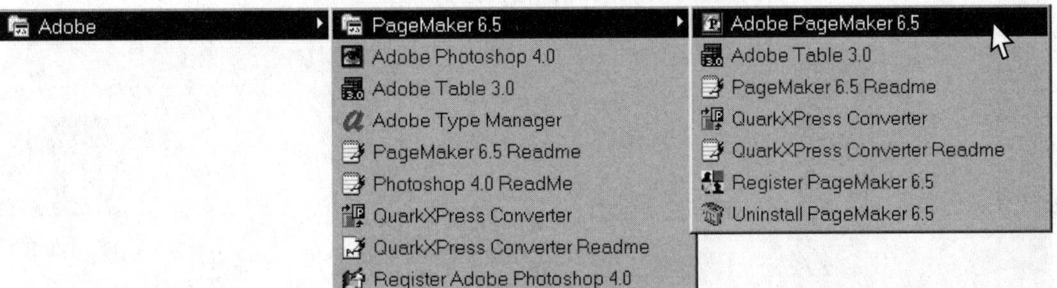

Alternatively, if a shortcut has been set up, then you can activate PageMaker by double-clicking on this icon:

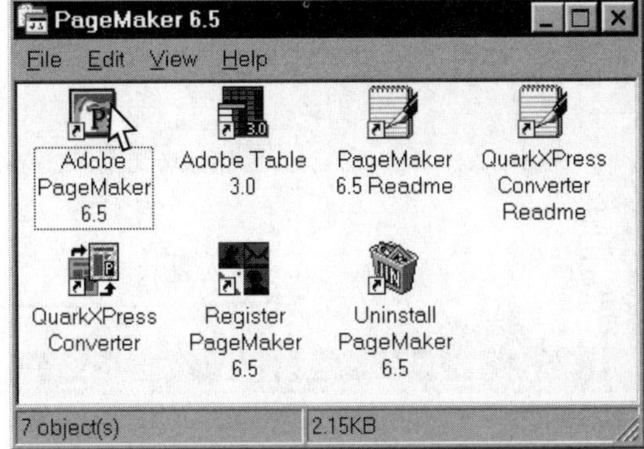

If You Are Using a Macintosh

Locate the PageMaker icon on your desktop and double-click. Alternatively you may be able to access PageMaker from the Apple Menu.

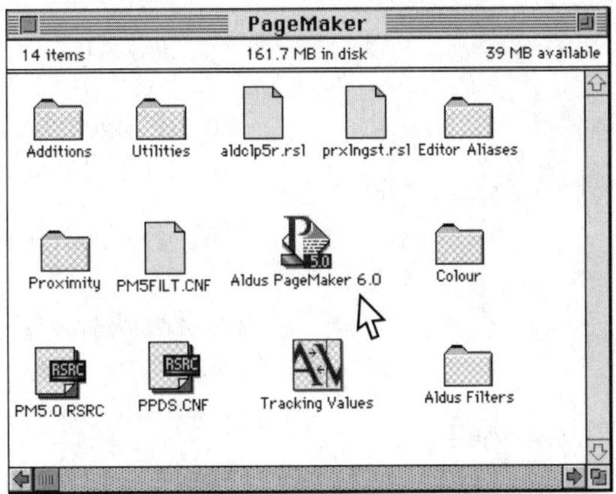

You can double-click on a PageMaker file to open the file and start the program.

Katharine's Title.p65

The PageMaker Screen

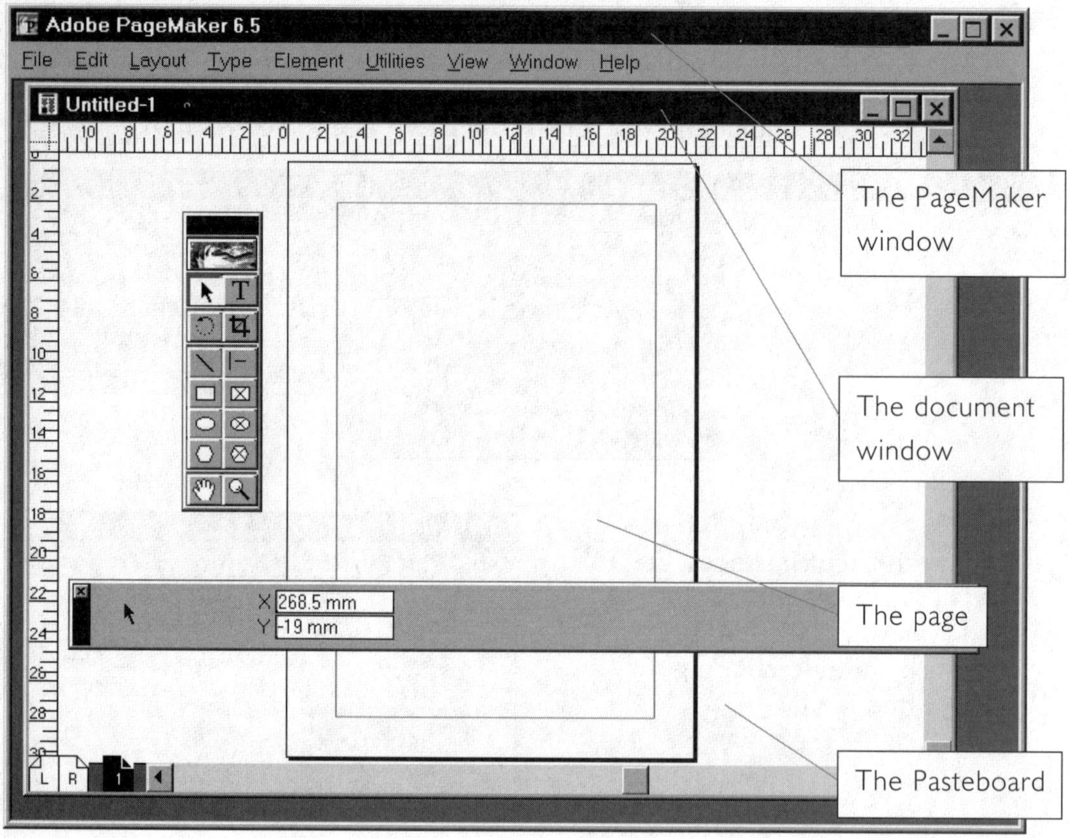

The PageMaker window

The document window

The page

The Pasteboard

1 Choose **New...** from the File menu

2 Click **OK**. The screen is arranged as follows:

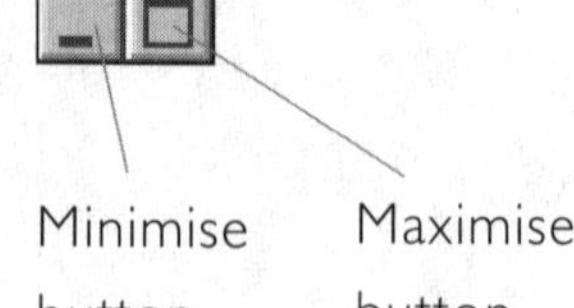

Minimise button   Maximise button

In Windows 3.1 these buttons look like this: 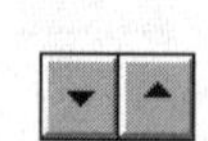

The PageMaker Window

Note: Clicking on the Close box will close PageMaker.

The Document Window

You can work on more than one document at a time using PageMaker, each with its own window. Note the Maximise and Minimise buttons will expand the window or shrink it to a single icon.

The Page and Pasteboard

All items positioned on the page will normally be printed. The surrounding Pasteboard is a working area.

Floating Palettes

In PageMaker 6.5, you can combine some palettes by dragging from the title tab of one palette into another. In this example Styles and Colours are combined. Simply drag outwards again to separate palettes.

These give you immediate on-screen access to tools and commands. You can move palettes to the most convenient screen position, or close them down altogether if not required.

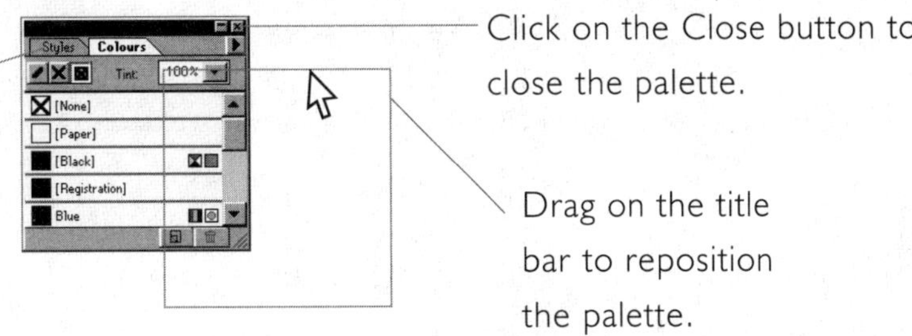

Click on the Close button to close the palette.

Drag on the title bar to reposition the palette.

Palettes can be turned on and off from the Window menu...

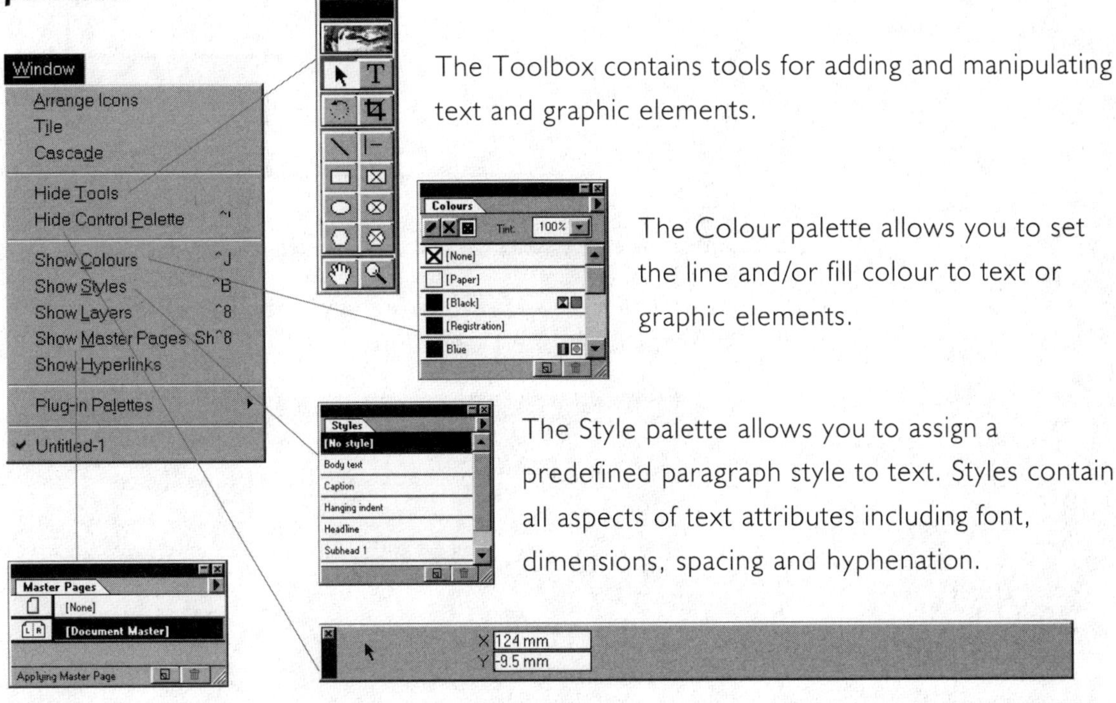

The Toolbox contains tools for adding and manipulating text and graphic elements.

The Colour palette allows you to set the line and/or fill colour to text or graphic elements.

The Style palette allows you to assign a predefined paragraph style to text. Styles contain all aspects of text attributes including font, dimensions, spacing and hyphenation.

The Master Pages palette lets you create and apply consistent page designs.

The Control palette gives you full numeric control over elements as an alternative to making adjustments manually with the Mouse or by dialog box. The controls which appear in the palette depend on the type of element(s) being edited.

The Rulers

The rulers help you make measurements on screen. Dotted line markers in each ruler indicate your current position.

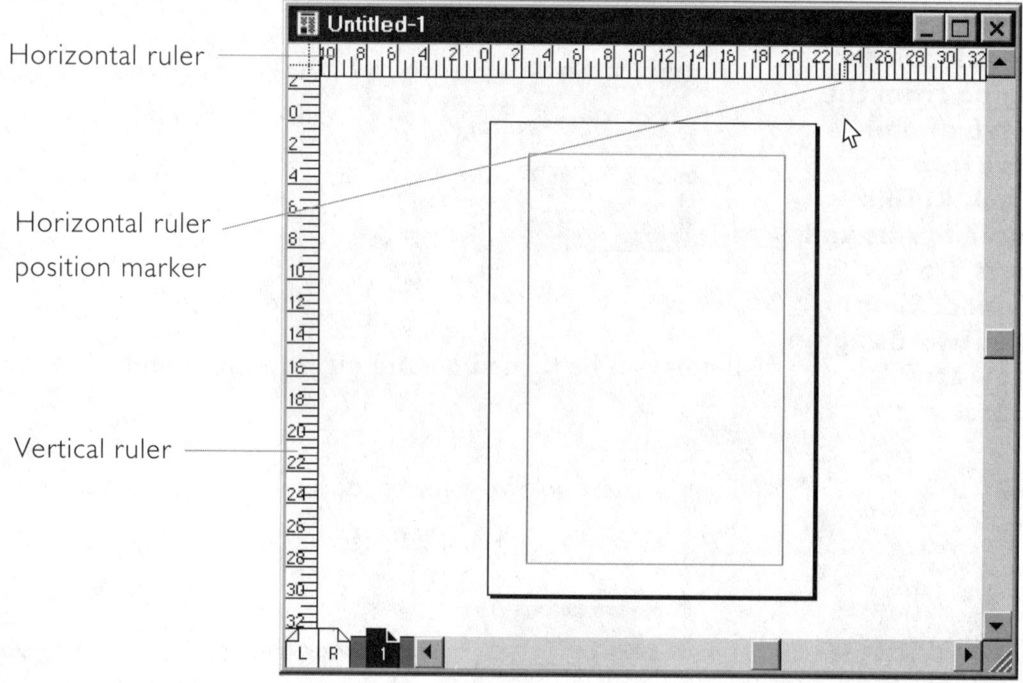

To change the units of measurement select **Preferences,** and **General** from the **File** menu.

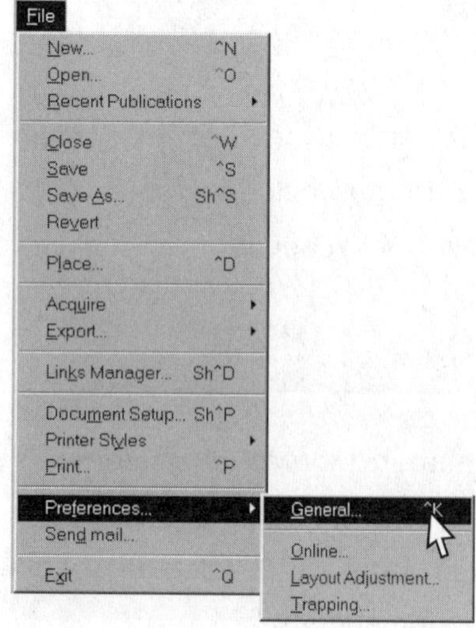

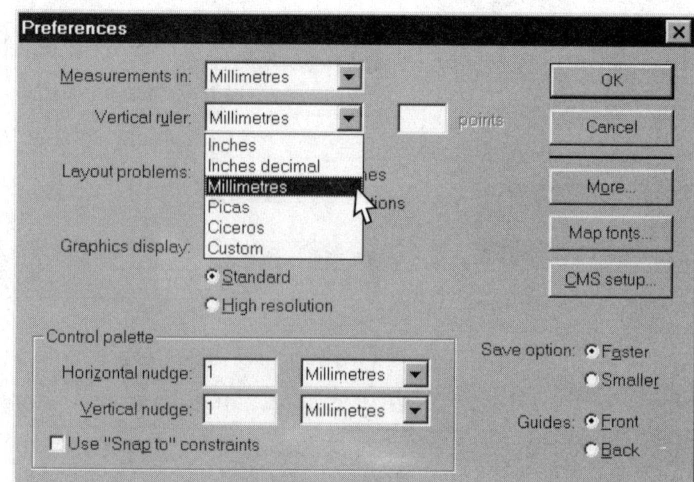

Repositioning the Zero Point

Initially all measurements are from the top left corner of the page. This can be changed by moving the Zero point.

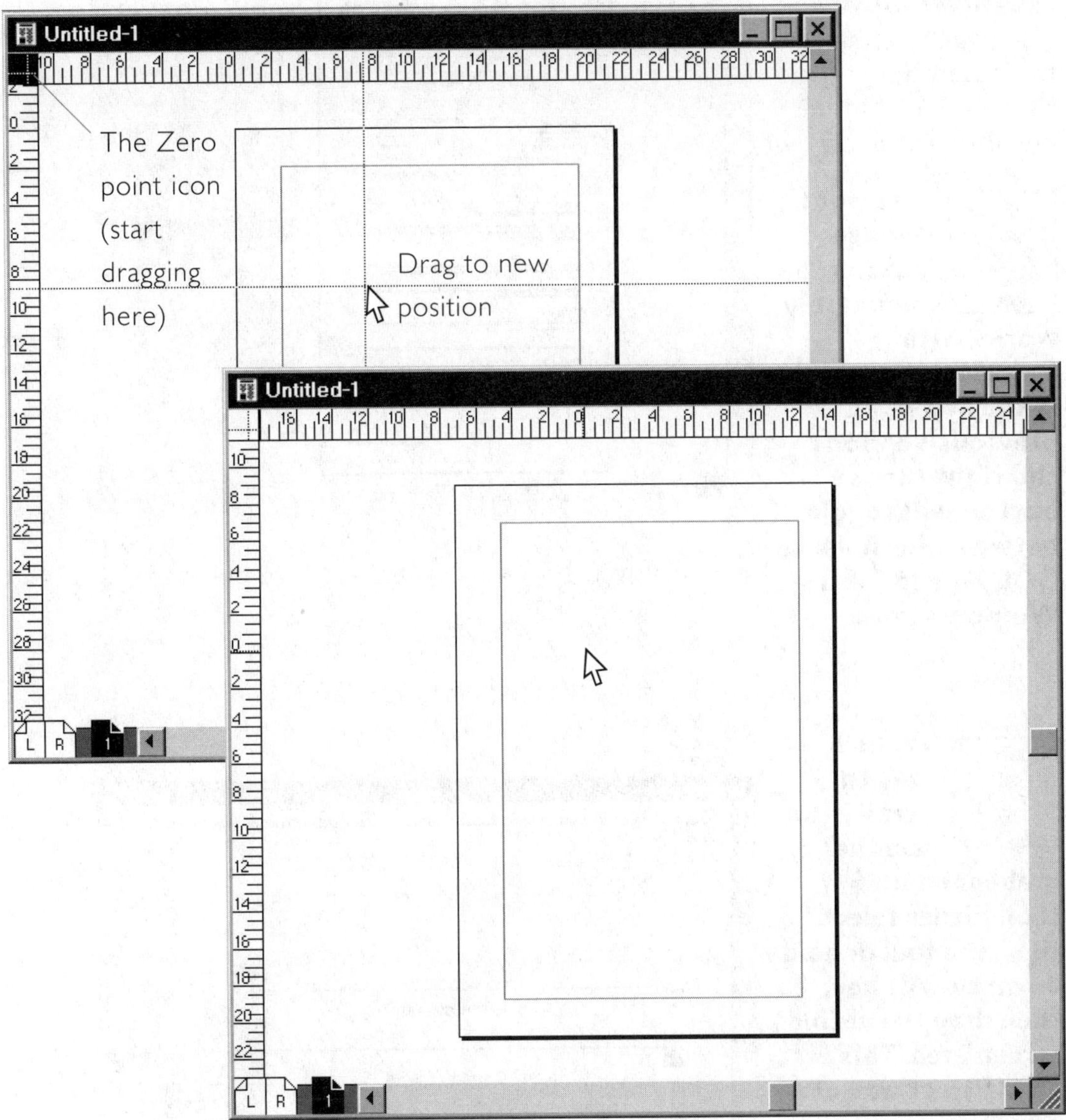

1 Move the Mouse pointer directly over the Zero point icon.

2 Drag downwards and to the right until you reach the desired position for the new Zero point.

Viewing the Page

There are eight levels of page magnification. Those used most often can be accessed directly with the Mouse.

Fit in Window

The page is reduced to a size where it will fit completely in the document window.

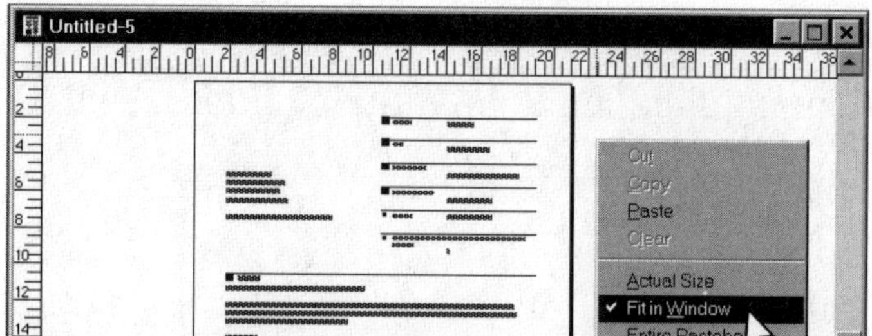

The right Mouse button menu only works with PageMaker version 6 and above. In previous versions the right Mouse button will toggle between Actual size (100%) and Fit in Window views.

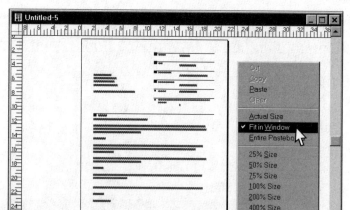

1 Point to the area of interest and hold down the right Mouse button. A context pop-up menu will appear.

2 Select the desired magnification.

A quick way to scroll is to use the grabber hand tool. Either select the hand tool or hold down the Alt key, then drag the visible screen area. This is an efficient way of scrolling, as redraw only occurs after you have released the Mouse button.

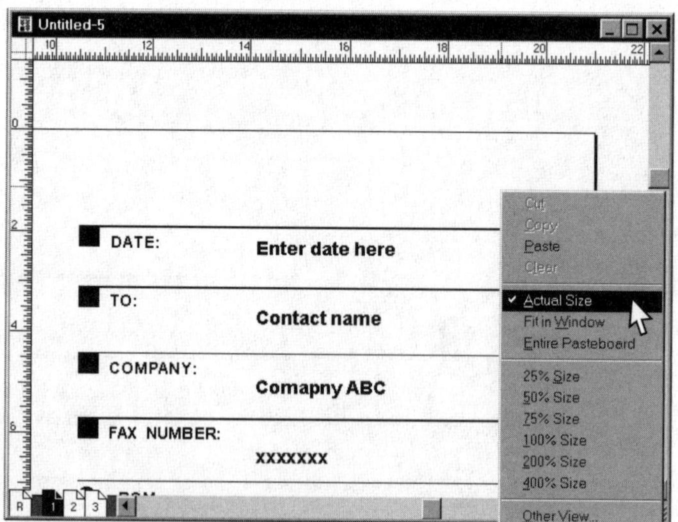

Other Page Views

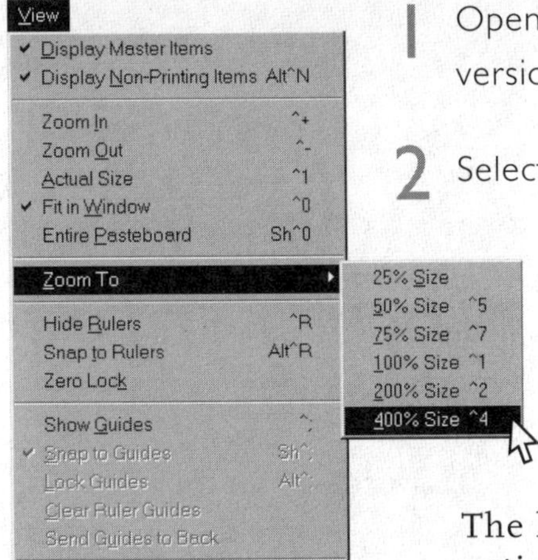

1 Open the **View** menu (or Layout menu if using a PageMaker version prior to 6).

2 Select the **Zoom To** submenu.

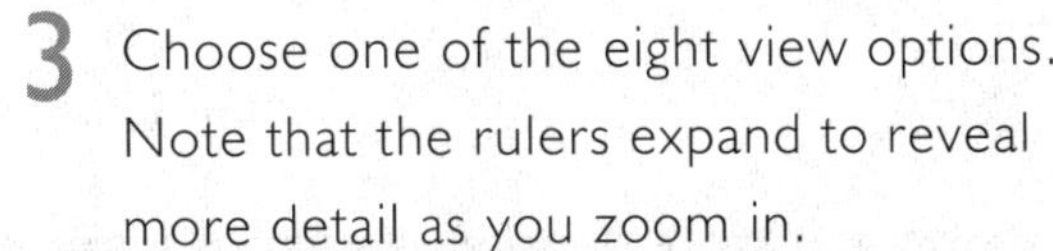

3 Choose one of the eight view options. Note that the rulers expand to reveal more detail as you zoom in.

The keyboard shortcuts are listed next to each menu option. The ˆ symbol means "hold down the Control key". For example, holding down the Control key while pressing "2" will switch the view to 200% size.

Show Pasteboard

This zooms out to reveal the entire pasteboard area. The area beyond its perimeter is out of bounds.

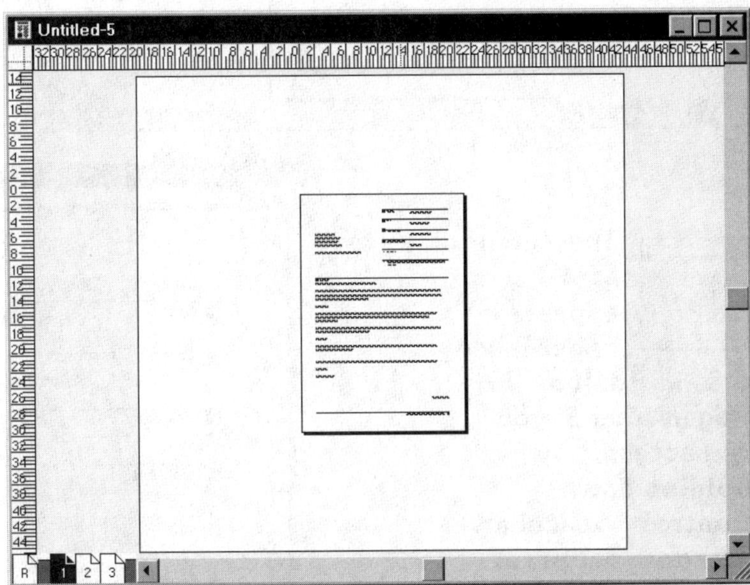

In all views you have access to all PageMaker's layout editing features.

Many keyboard shortcuts have changed with the advent of PageMaker version 6. Watch out for "Fit in Window" which has changed from ^W to ^O. ^W now closes your document down completely, a problem for PageMaker veterans who have developed a reflex action of frequently hitting ^W as they work.

The Zoom Tool 

Double-clicking on the zoom tool returns you to 100% view.

1. Select the zoom tool.
2. Position to the area where you want to zoom in and click.
3. Alternatively, use the tool to draw a rectangle area (drag with the Mouse). When you release the Mouse button PageMaker will zoom in to fill the screen with this area.

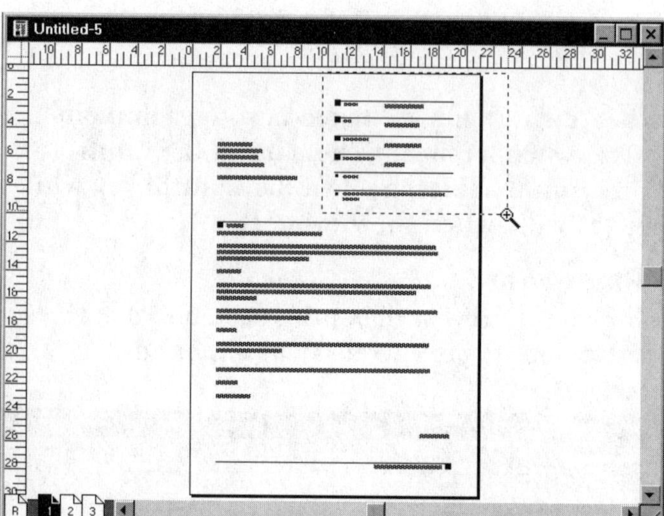

Using the zoom tool, you can magnify the page up to 400% actual size.

To zoom out, hold down the Control key as you click or drag.

The Zoom tool appears in PageMaker 6 & 6.5 toolbox. In PageMaker 5, you can access it by holding down Control + Spacebar. To zoom out press Alt + Control + Spacebar.

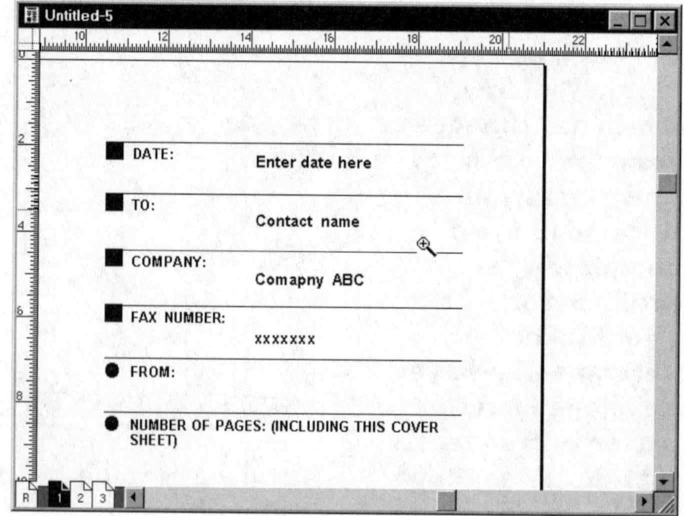

Chapter Two

Working with a Publication

This chapter shows you how to store and retrieve your documents from disk. It also deals with navigation between pages within a publication.

Covers

New Publication

1 Choose **New...** from the File menu to display the initial Document Setup dialog box.

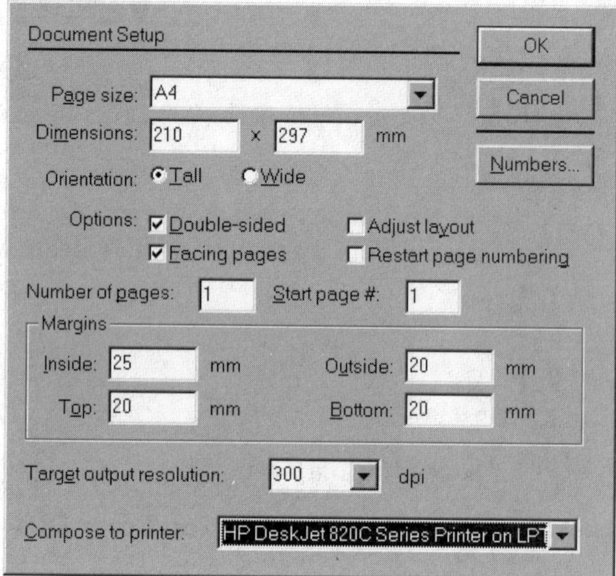

2 Choose from one of the preset page sizes in the **Page size** drop-down menu, or enter values directly into the **Dimensions** boxes (this allows you create a custom page size).

Tall orientation

3 Click on the **Tall** or **Wide** radio button to choose Page orientation (note this affects the entire document).

Wide orientation

4 The starting page number will normally be 1, but you may change this by entering a value in the **Start page #** box.

5 If you know how many pages you require, then enter this value in the **Number of pages** box. However, it is easy to add or remove pages later on.

...cont'd

You can view your pages as thumbnail images using the Sort pages command from the Layout menu (PageMaker 6 or above), or the "Sort Pages" addition (PageMaker 5).

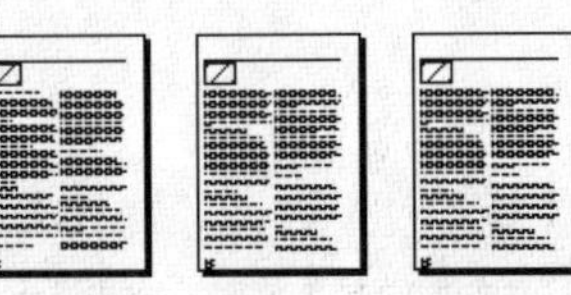

Single pages

Page 1 Page 2 Page 3

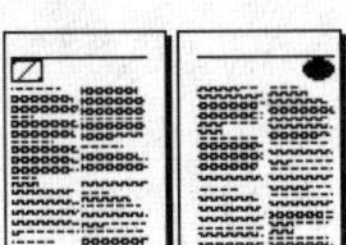

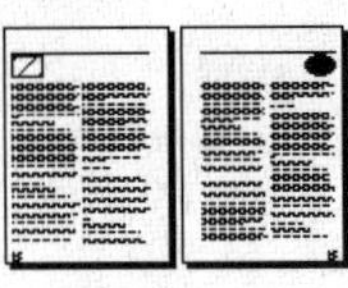

Facing pages

Pages 4 & 5 Pages 6 & 7

6 If your document is to be single-sided (printed on only one side of the paper) then remove the cross from the **Double-sided** checkbox. If the Double-sided option is active then you have a further choice to display **Facing pages**. This causes PageMaker to show you pages as "spreads" with left and right pages next to each other.

7 If your document is part of a larger Book list (see Chapter 12), then you have the option to **Restart page numbering** from this point.

8 Enter your page margins. Note that if your document is double-sided then you can set inner and outer margins (the inner margin is at the spine of a bound publication).

9 Choose your target printer from the **Compose to printer** drop-down menu. This will give you a list of printers installed in Windows. It is important to specify from the outset the printer used for your final, not draft, output if these are different. This gives PageMaker information about the text capabilities, graphics and printable page area which can be used.

10 The **Target printer resolution** will normally be set automatically according to your choice of printer, but you can alter this manually.

You can return to the Document Setup dialog box by choosing Document Setup from the File menu. In this way you can alter settings even once you have begun work on a document.

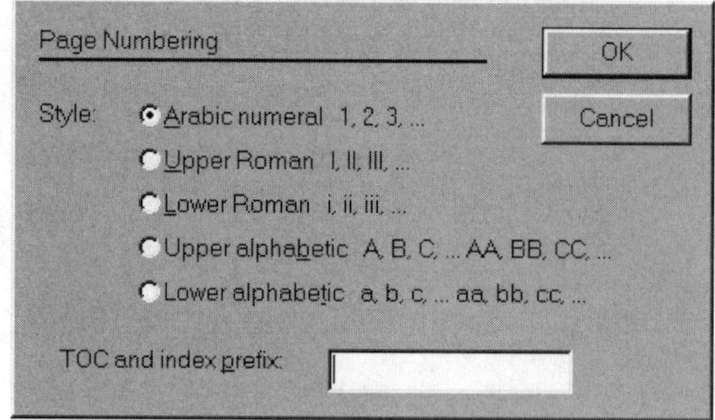

11 Click on the **Numbers...** button to alter the style of page numbering. Options include Roman numerals and alphabetic numbering.

Opening a Publication From Disk

1 Go to the **File** menu and choose **Open**.

If you are using a version of PageMaker prior to 6.5, then by changing this option to "Older PageMaker files" you can open untitled copies of files which were created using an older version of PageMaker. (Version 6.5 does this automatically.)

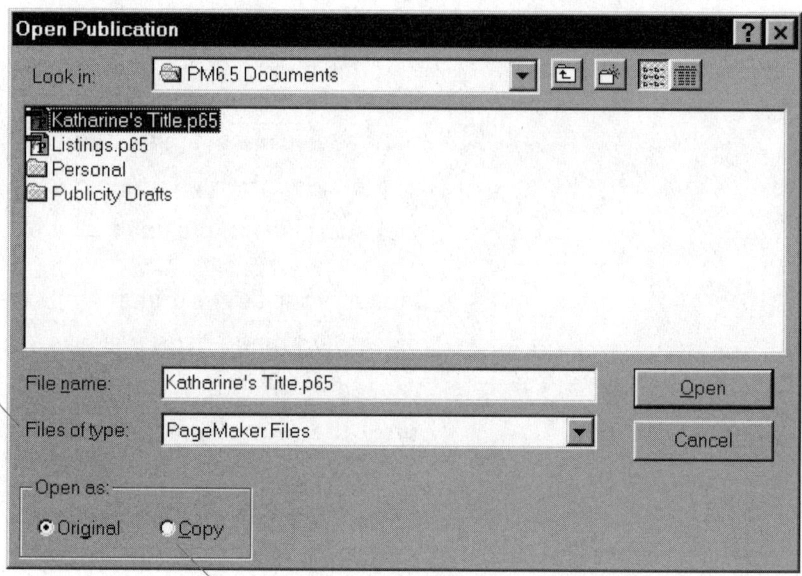

You can open an untitled copy of an existing document by clicking on the **Copy** radio button.

You can open as many publications as memory will allow. Each can be activated either by clicking on a visible part of its window or via the Window menu.

2 The dialog box displays all valid PageMaker files in the current directory. If necessary change directory by typing its path in the File name box or by clicking on items in the Directories box.

3 Type or select the file name of the document you wish to open. Click OK.

The Page Icons

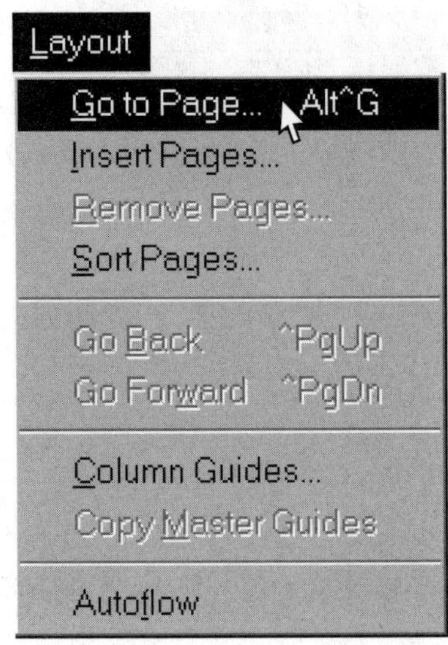

The page icons appear at the bottom left corner of the document window. The currently active page is highlighted.

To move to another page simply click on its icon, or use the **Go to Page** option from the Layout menu.

Master Pages

These are labelled **L** and **R** (**R** only if the document is single-sided). These do not print but can act as a background for the "real" pages in your publication (see Chapter 8). In PageMaker 6 or above, you can use the Master Pages palette to switch between different Master Page designs.

Every time you move to a new page, PageMaker performs a mini-save as a security measure. If your machine crashed during use, you should be able to recover your document. If your document is currently untitled, the mini-saved version will be on disk as a .TMP file, within your Windows temporary directory.

If you rename this as a .P65 file (or whichever extension is appropriate to your PageMaker version), you can open it within PageMaker. After this you should immediately save to another file name.

Inserting/Removing Pages

Inserting

1. Select the page either immediately before or after the place you want the new page(s) to go.

2. Choose **Insert Pages...** from the **Layout** menu.

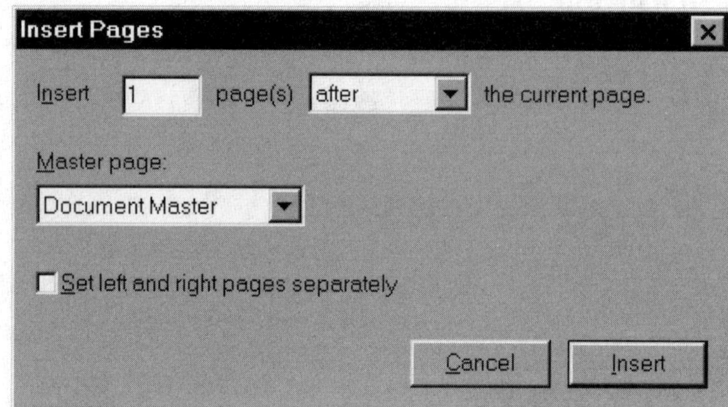

If you are using a double-sided document, there may be two current pages, and you will have a third option to add new pages between them.

3. Enter the number of pages to be inserted.

4. Select the position for the new pages, either before or after the current page.

Removing

The **Remove Pages...** option from the Layout menu works in the same way as Insert Pages...

There is an additional warning dialog box which asks you to verify the deletion:

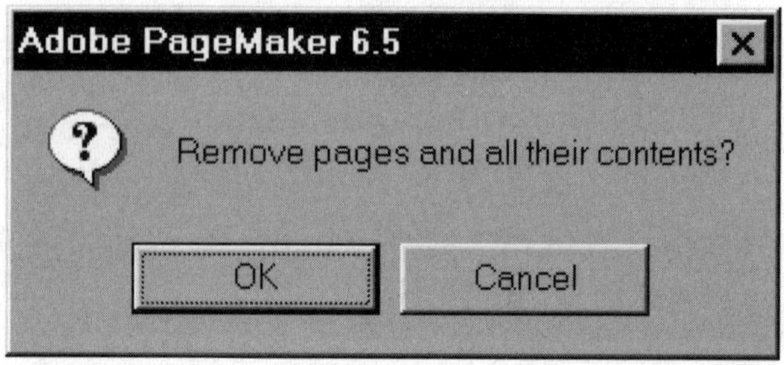

Saving a Document

An untitled document window indicates that a file has not yet been saved.

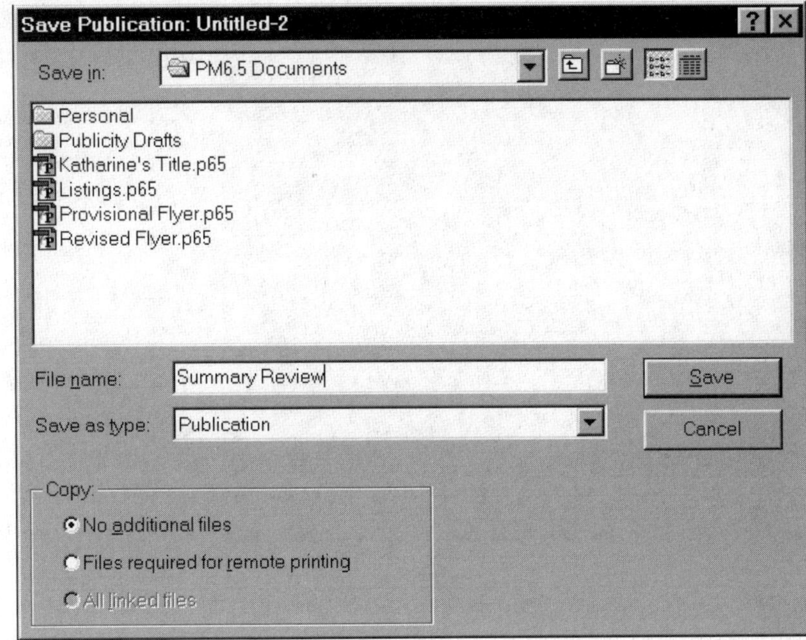

If you are using PageMaker 6 or above with Windows 95/98, then you can move, rename or delete files from within any of the File dialog boxes (e.g. Save, Open or Place) – just right-click on a file. With previous versions, use the Windows file-managing system(s).

1. If you have more than one publication open, then make active the one you want to save by clicking in its window (or selecting from the **Window** menu).

2. Choose **Save** from the **File** menu. If your document already has a name then the save action will be automatic.

3. If you are saving the document for the first time the Save Publication dialog box will appear. Make sure the correct directory is active (if necessary type in the path or navigate using the drop-down menu).

4. Type in a valid document name (8 characters or less, no punctuation if you are using Windows 3.1).

If you wish to save to a file name different to the current document, choose **Save As...** from the File menu.

Closing a Document

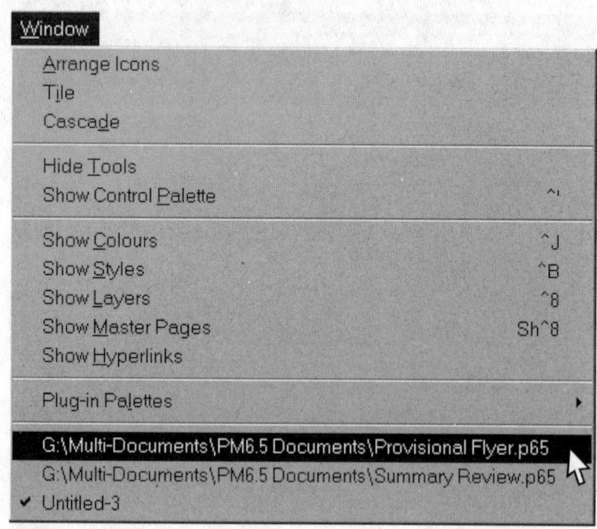

A document is closed when it is no longer required on screen.

1. If you have more than one document open, then make sure the one you want to close is active. This can be done by clicking on a visible part of the document window, or selecting the document name from the **Window** menu.

2. Either click on the document's Close box (Windows 95/98) or choose **Close** from the **File** menu.

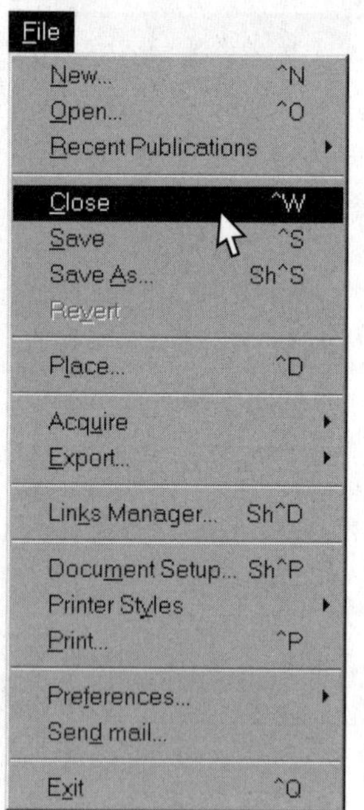

3. If the document has not been saved then the following dialog box will appear as a security measure:

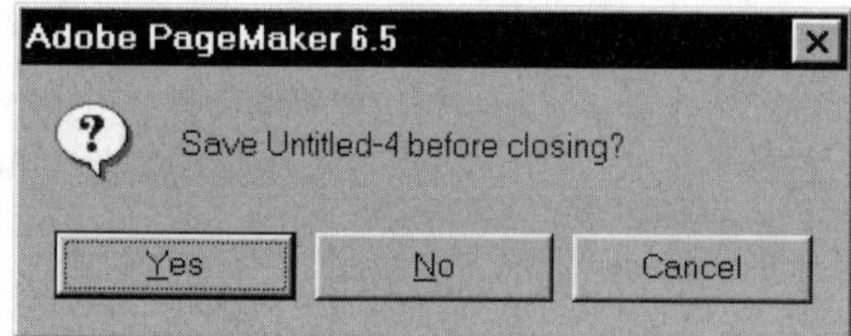

If you click **No** then the document will close without saving.

Clicking **Yes** will save your work (you may be asked for a file name if the document is currently untitled).

Cancel will abort the Close operation and return you to your document window.

Chapter Three

The Drawing Tools

This chapter covers PageMaker's built-in drawing facilities. In later chapters you will see that many of the techniques you learn here will apply equally well to text and elements imported from other packages.

Covers

Lines

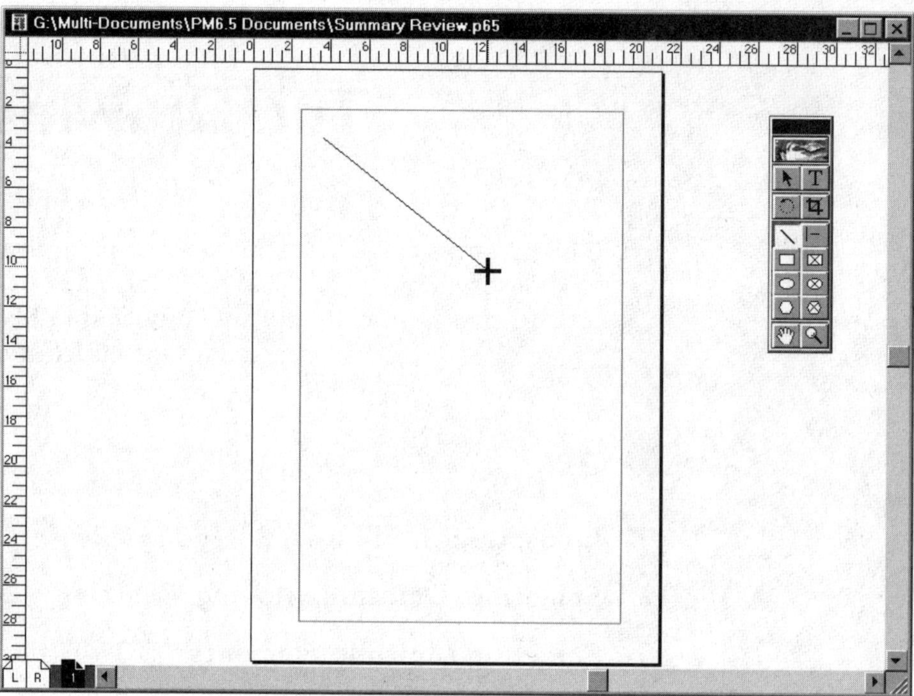

1. Select the line tool from the toolbox. The pointer will turn into a cross (to aid accurate drawing).

2. Drag from one end of the line to another.

The Constrained Line Tool

This will draw lines at 45 degree intervals, i.e. horizontally, vertically or diagonally.

You can achieve the same effect with the normal line tool if you hold down the Shift key while drawing.

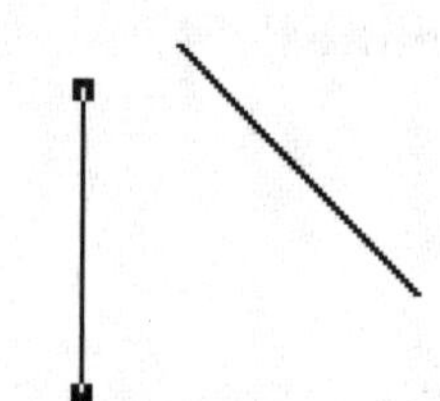

Boxes 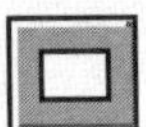

To draw a rectangle, select the box tool and drag from one corner to the other.

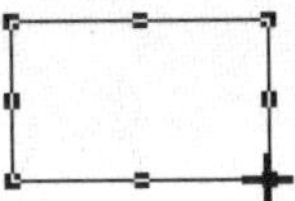

Ellipses 

To draw an oval shape, select the ellipse tool and drag diagonally.

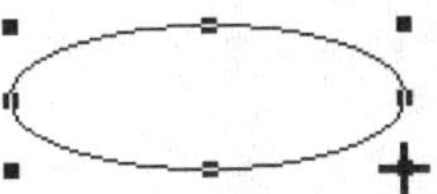

Polygons  **(PageMaker version 6 and above)**

To draw a polygon, select the polygon tool and drag diagonally.

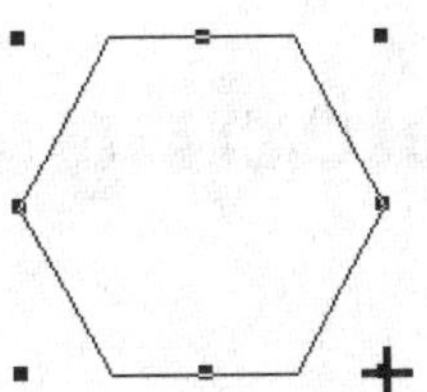

If you hold down Shift when drawing, all shapes will be made regular. Boxes will be kept square, and ellipses constrained as circles.

If you double-click on the polygon tool, the Polygon Settings dialog appears, allowing you to set the number of sides. You can also use the **Star inset** bar to change the shape gradually from a regular polygon to a wire-frame star.

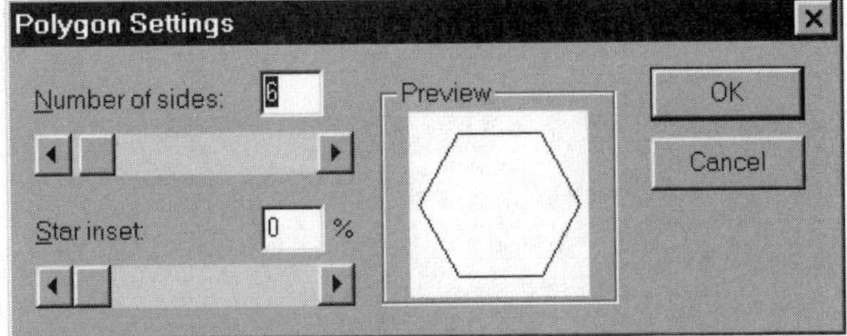

You can change settings to an existing polygon by selecting it, then choosing **Polygon Settings** from the Element menu.

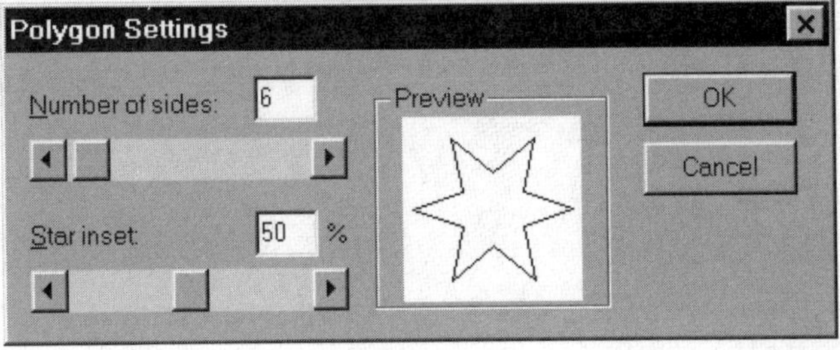

Selecting Elements

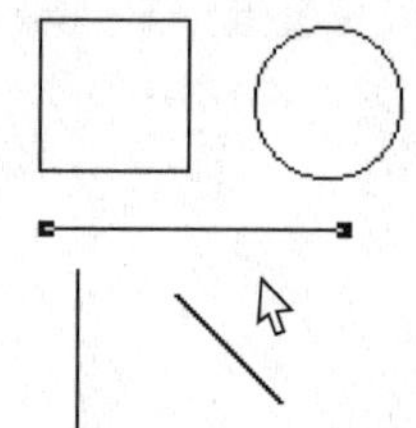

Normally, the element most recently drawn is selected.

You can tell that a shape is selected by the square handles (blocks) which appear at each corner.

To Select an Element

1. Choose the pointer tool. 
2. Click directly on the shape with the tip of the pointer.

Deleting Elements

1. Select the element to be deleted.
2. Press the Delete or Backspace key.

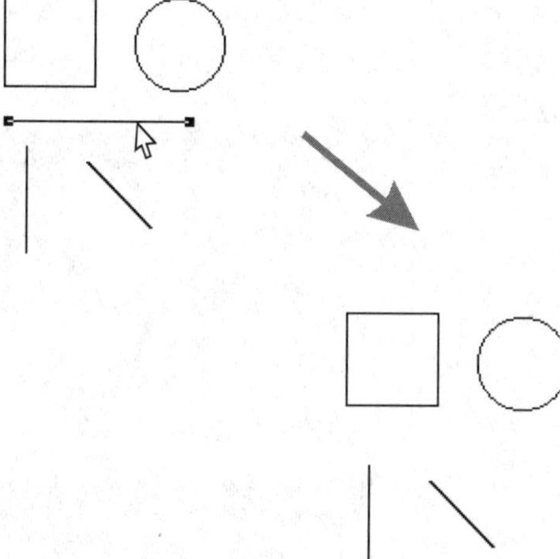

Moving Elements

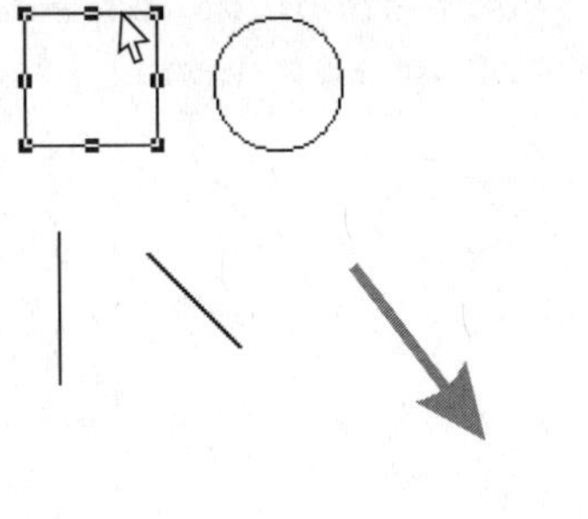

1 Select the element to be moved.

2 Drag to the new location.

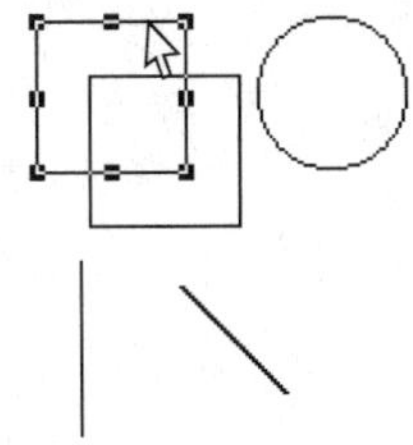

Resizing Elements

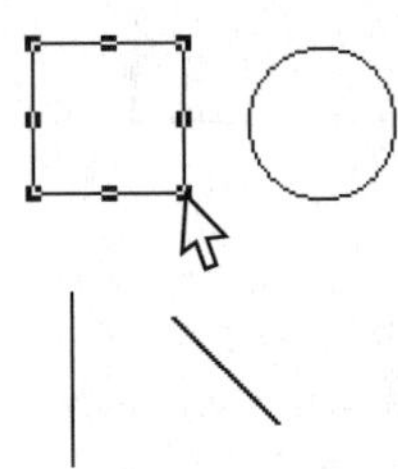

1 Select the element to be resized.

2 Drag directly on one of its handles.

Dragging on an edge handle will let you resize a shape horizontally or vertically, whilst dragging on a corner handle lets you stretch in both directions at once.

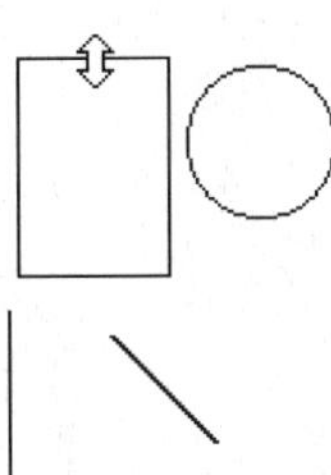

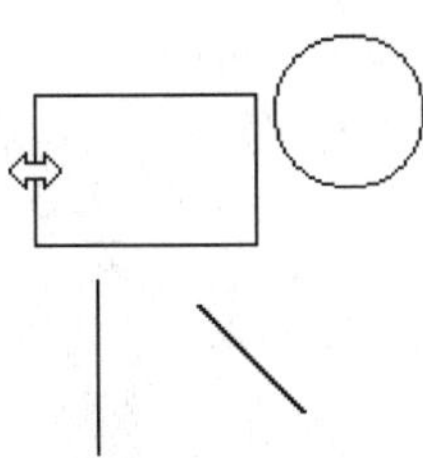

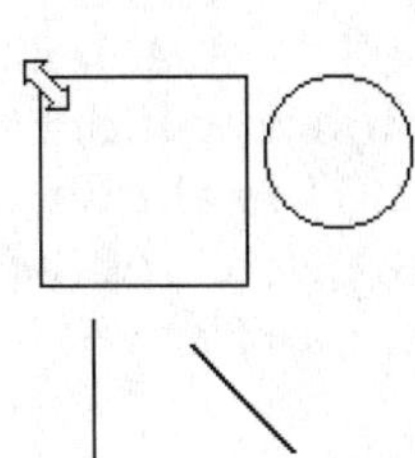

Selecting Multiple Elements

To select all elements on the page and pasteboard choose **Select All** from the Edit menu.

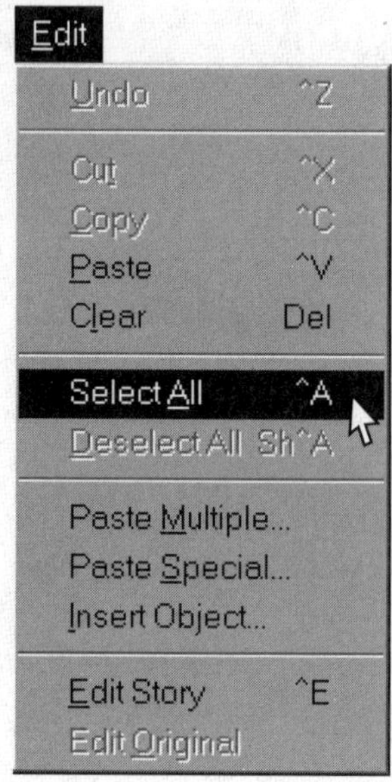

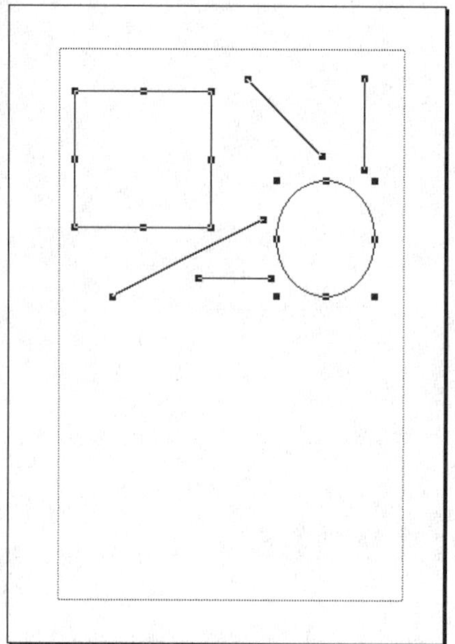

Shift-clicking

Normally when you click on an object any previously selected objects will be deselected.

If you hold down **Shift** while clicking successively on different objects, you can select as many as you wish.

Shift-clicking on an already-selected object will deselect it. This allows you to switch objects on and off at will.

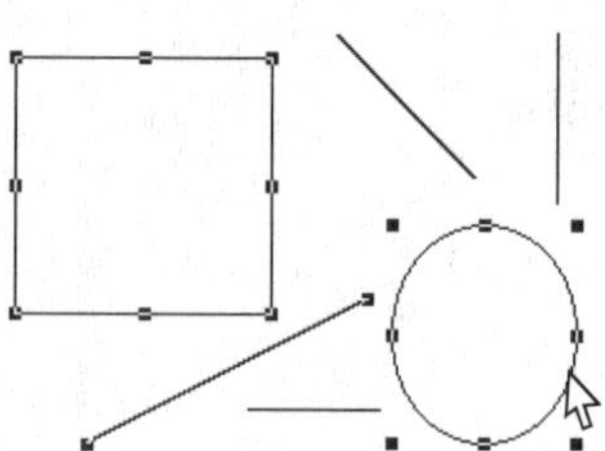

Creating a Selection Box

1. Select the pointer tool.
2. Move to a blank area of the page or Pasteboard.
3. Drag diagonally. As you drag, a box bordered by a dotted line will appear.

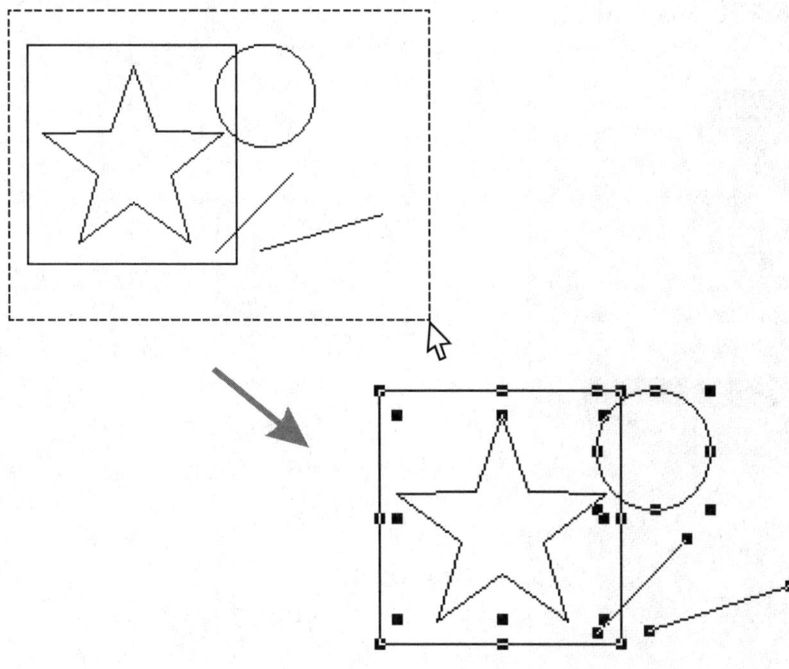

You can combine these techniques; e.g. Select All followed by Shift-clicking on one element (to deselect) will have the overall effect of selecting all elements but one.

4. When you release the mouse button, all objects *completely* enclosed by this box will be selected.

Summary

There are three ways to make multiple selections:

- Select All
- Shift-clicking
- Selection box

Grouping & Ungrouping Version 6 and above

Grouping is a feature new to PageMaker 6, although PageMaker 5 has a PostScript Group function in its Additions menu.

Grouping is useful because it allows you to create shapes using a combination of simpler shapes, thereafter treating them as a single object

To Group Elements

1. Select the elements to be grouped.
2. Choose **Group** from the **Element** menu, or type ^G. (In PageMaker version 6 Group is in the **Arrange** menu.)

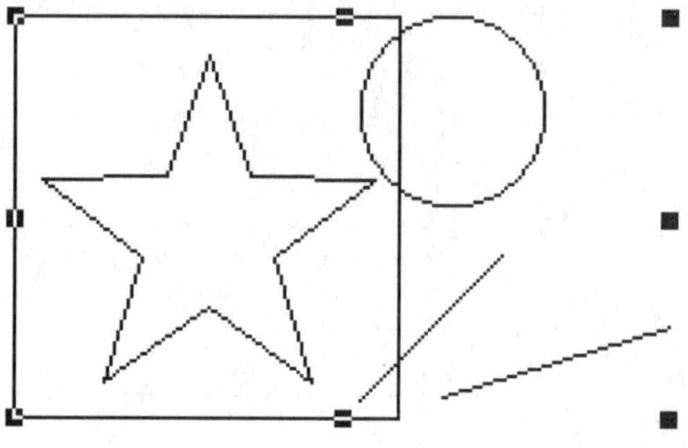

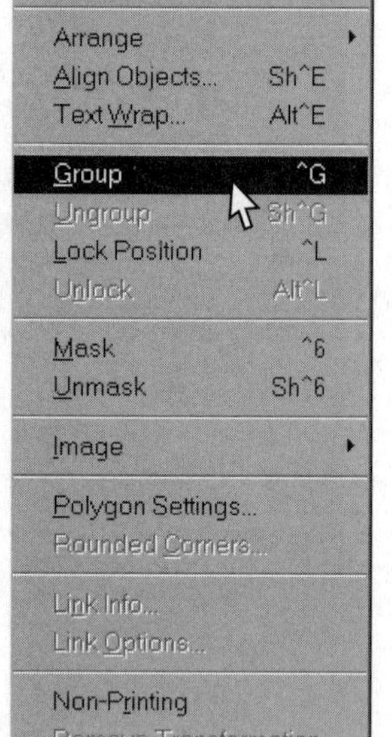

You can now move or resize the group as a single shape.

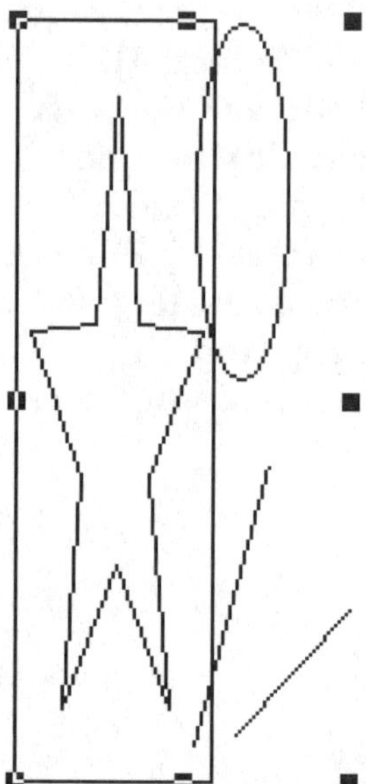

Ungrouping

To ungroup, simply select the group and choose **Ungroup** from the Arrange menu (or ^U). Element menu (or Sh^G) for V6.5 users.

It is possible to edit individual group elements without ungrouping. Simply hold down the Control key and click on the element you wish to edit.

Manipulating Elements using the Control Palette Version 5 and above

If the Control palette is not active, choose the Control Palette option from the Window menu.

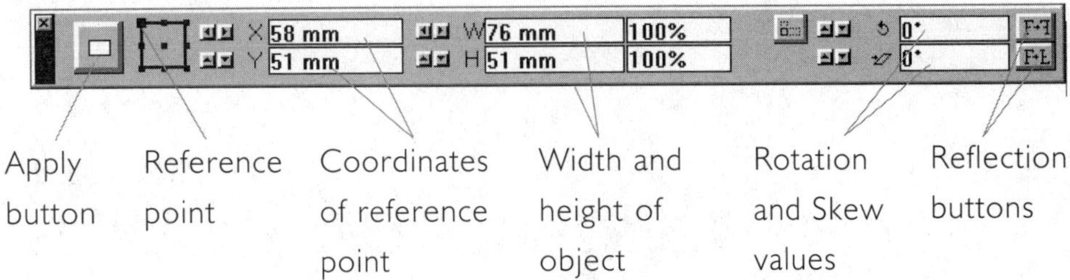

In PageMaker you have the choice to manipulate elements either visually using the mouse, or numerically with the Control palette.

The Control palette gives you the opportunity to specify the size, position or special effects applied to an object with complete precision.

Resizing an Element using the Control Palette

1. Select the element to be resized. The Control palette will display the object's attributes.
2. Edit the width and height values within the Control palette.

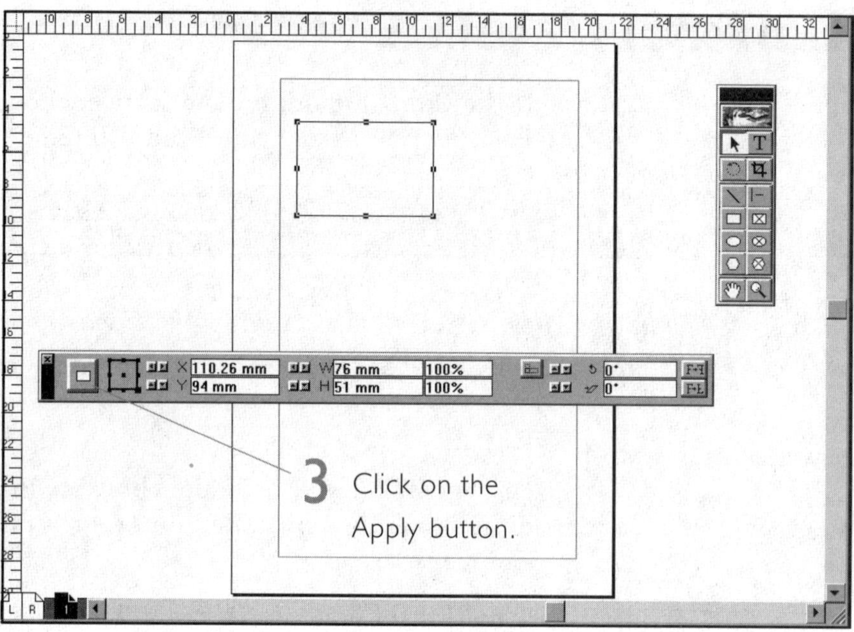

3 Click on the Apply button.

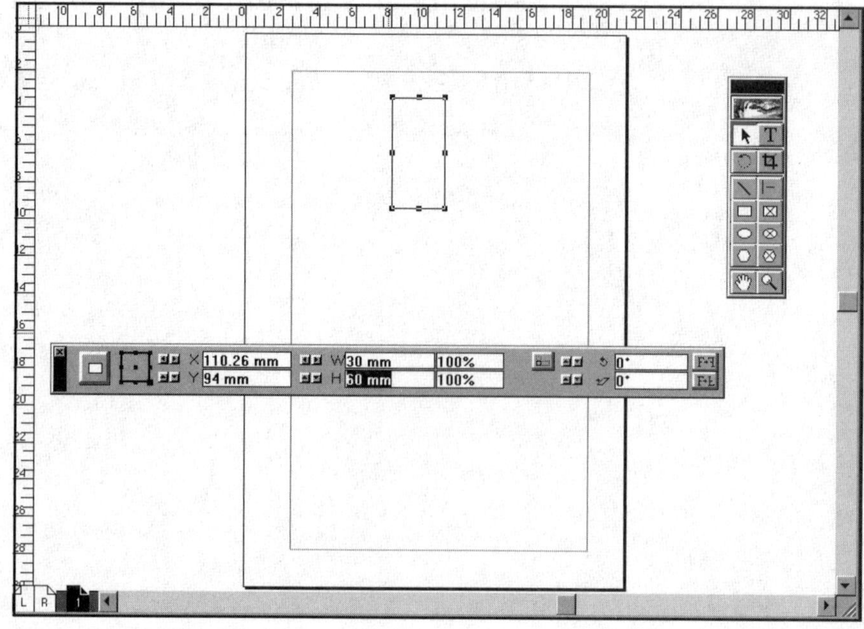

Moving Elements using the Control Palette Version 5 and above

When moving a shape using the Control palette, you can set the reference point by clicking on the symbol to the right of the Apply button.

Changing the Coordinates of the Top-left Corner of a Shape

1. Select the shape with the pointer tool.

2. Make sure the top-left reference point is active by clicking on its symbol in the Control palette. The point should be marked by a small square block (if it is marked by a double arrow then click once more on the point).

Click here to select the top-left reference point (repositioning mode).

3. Type in the new coordinates for this point.

4. Click on the Apply button. The shape will be moved so that its top-left corner has the specified coordinates.

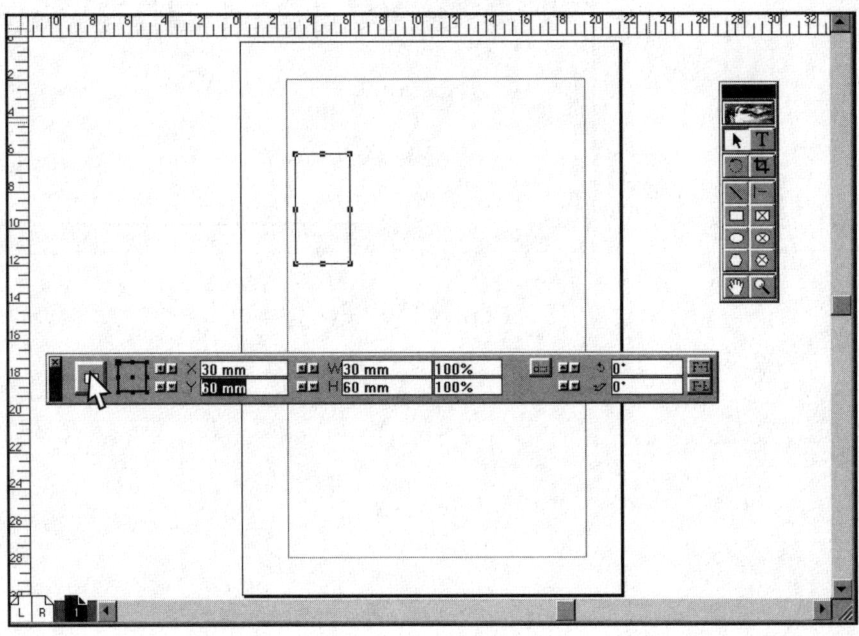

Resizing Elements using the Control Palette Version 5 and above

Lower-left reference point selected (resizing mode).

1 Select the shape to be resized.

2 Choose the reference point by clicking on the Control palette symbol. If necessary, click a second time to ensure that the point is marked by a double arrow. (This arrow indicates that resizing mode is active.)

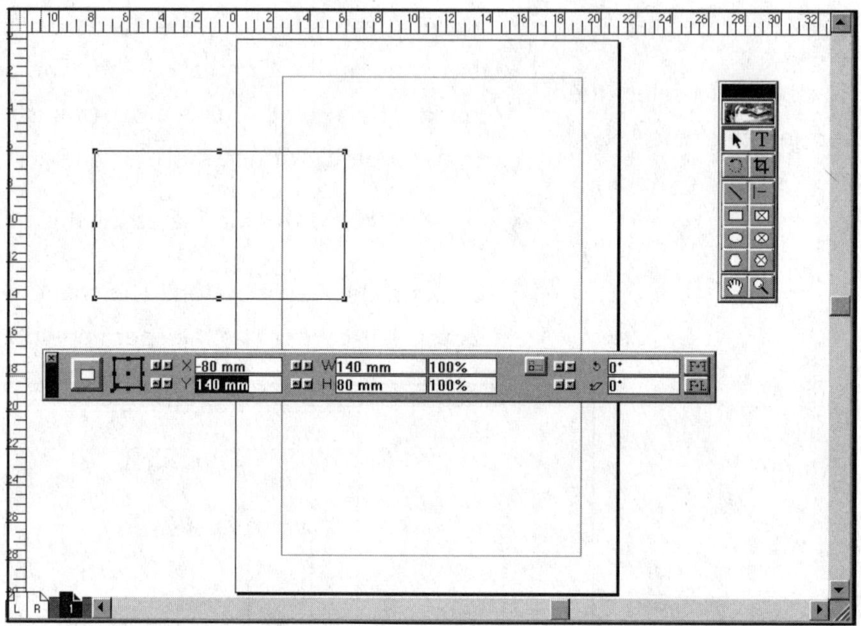

3 Enter the new coordinates for this point.

4 Click on the **Apply** button. The shape will be resized so that the required point has the given coordinates.

Aligning Elements using the Control Palette Version 5 and above

In this example we have two shapes we wish to align.

We would like to move the circle so that its centre has the same X coordinate as that of the rectangle...

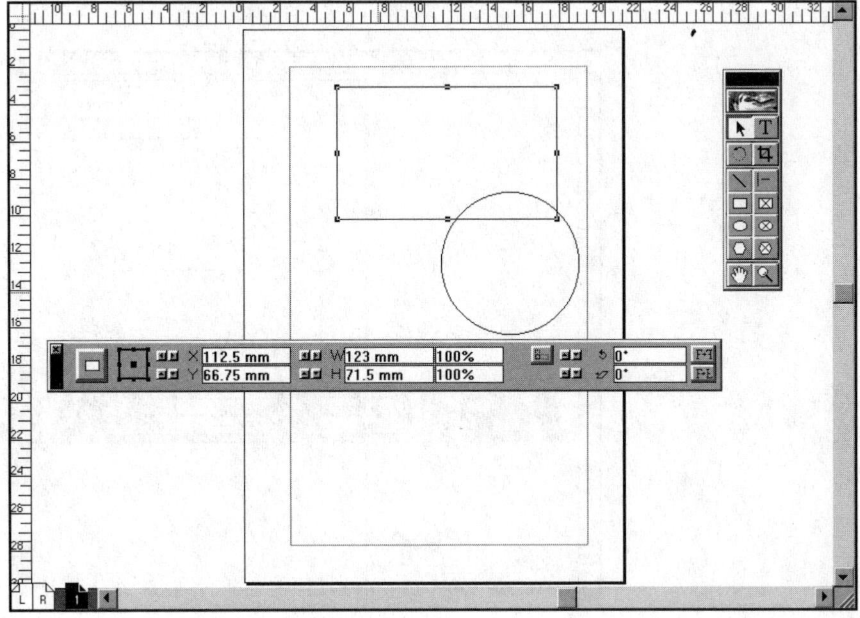

1 Click on the first shape (the rectangle) with the pointer tool and make the centre reference point active.

2 Note the X coordinate, in this case 112.5mm.

3 Click on the second shape (the circle).

4 Enter the same X value, 112.5mm.

5 Click on the Apply button. The circle's centre will now have the same X coordinate value as that of the rectangle.

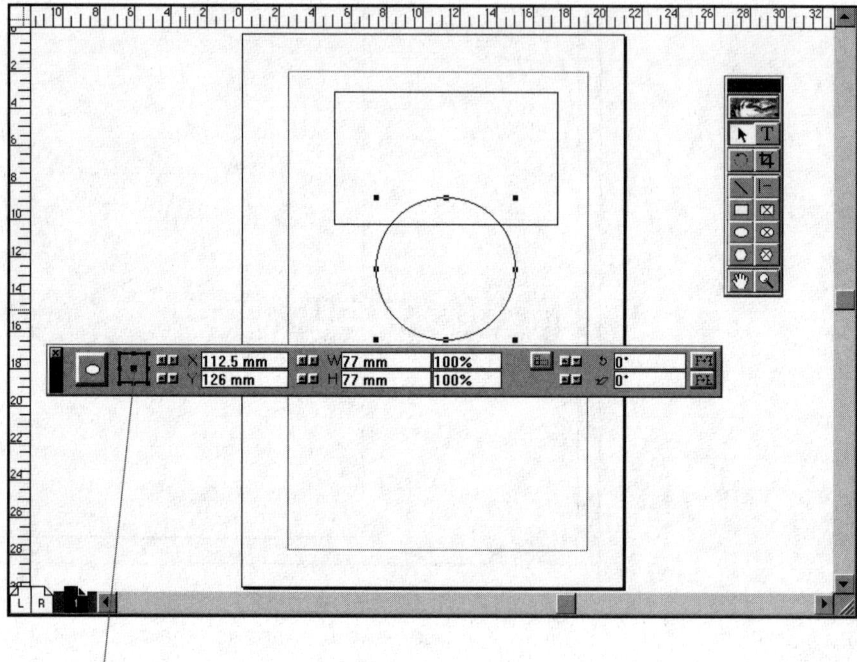

Centre point active. Note we are using repositioning (rather than resizing) mode.

Aligning Objects using the Align Dialog Version 6 and above

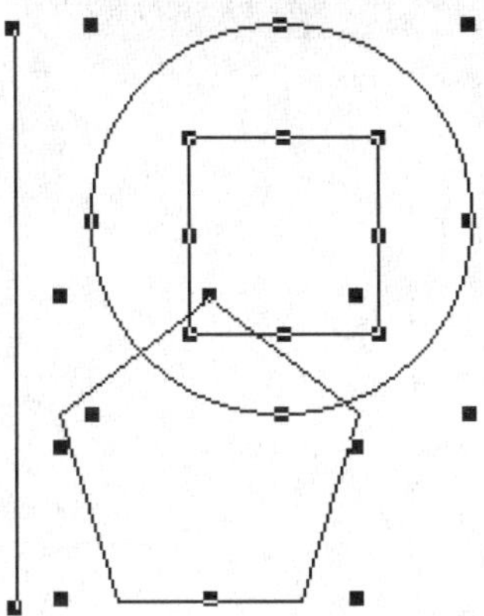

To align or distribute objects automatically in relation to each other, do the following:

1. Select the elements to be aligned.
2. Choose **Align Objects** from the Arrange menu.
3. Choose the appropriate Align or Distribute option for both the vertical and horizontal position of the elements.

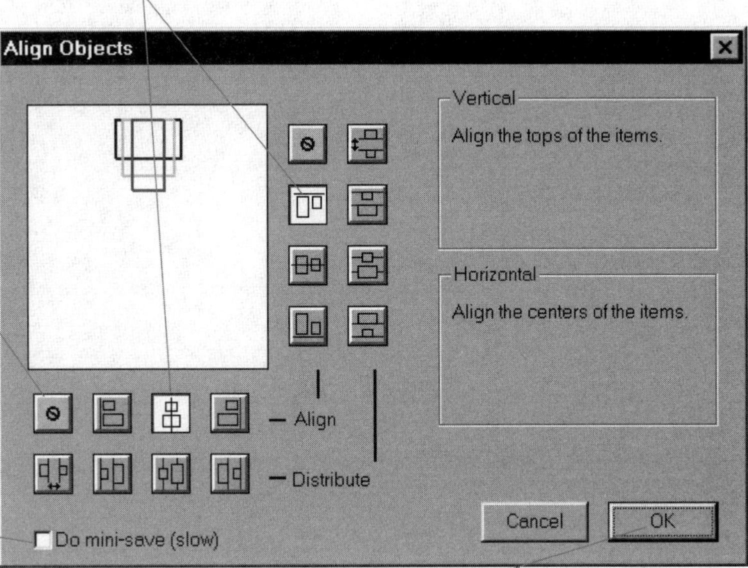

Select this button if no change is required.

If you select this option then you can use the Revert command (File menu) to undo the alignment once you've seen its effect.

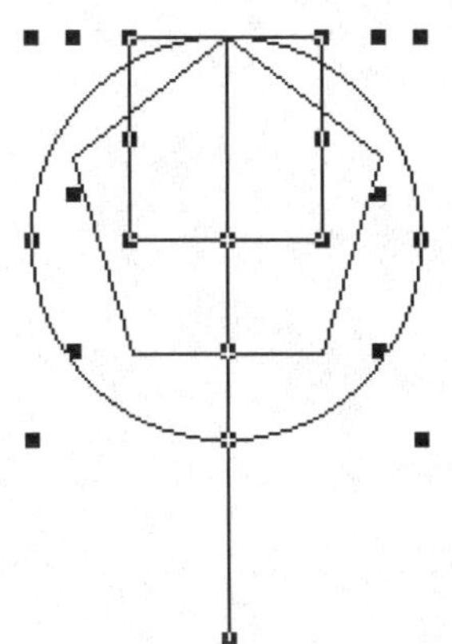

4. Click **OK**. The shapes will be aligned or distributed accordingly.

Using Fill and Line

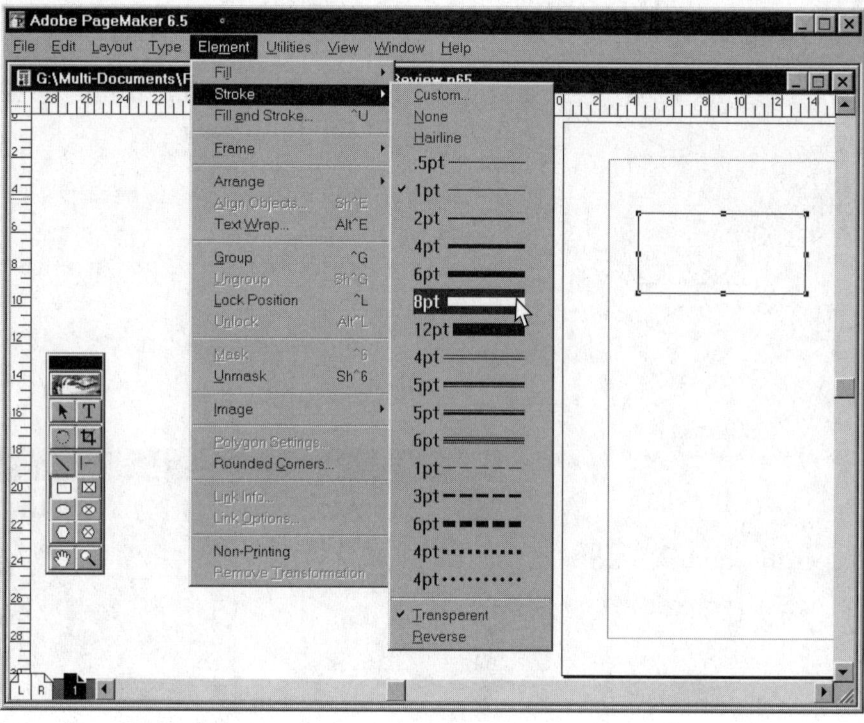

Changing Line Style

1. Select the element(s) to be changed.
2. Choose **Stroke** from the **Element** menu (this command is referred to a “Line” prior to PageMaker 6).
3. Select the desired line style.

You can control the line style more accurately by using the Custom option from the Stroke submenu of the Element menu.

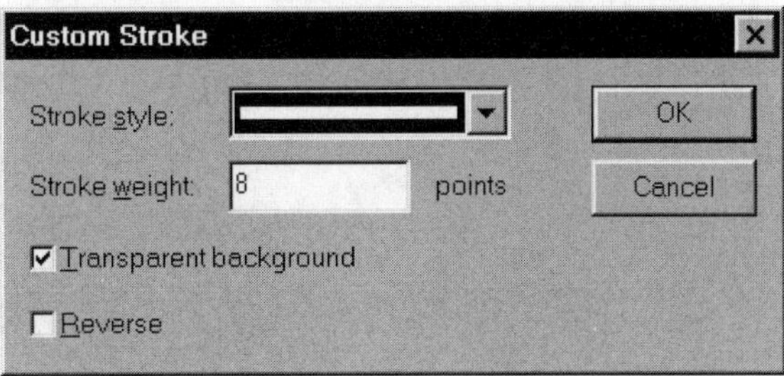

Here you can specify an exact line weight as well as style type.

Changing an Element's Fill

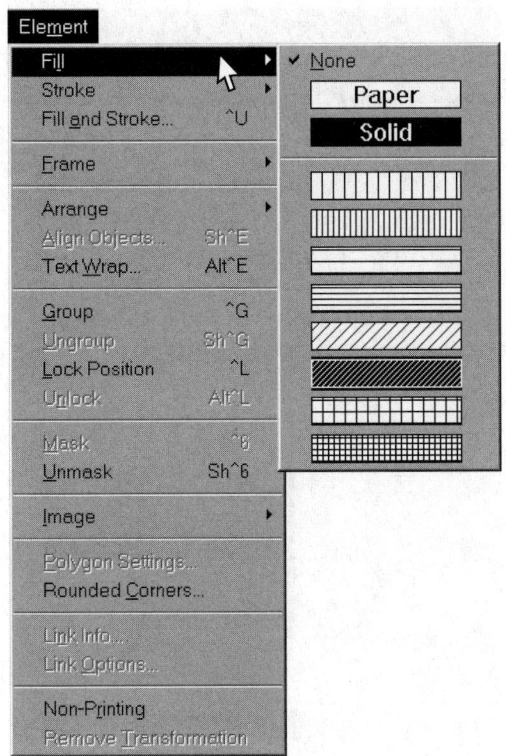

1. Select the element(s) to be changed.
2. Choose **Fill** from the **Element** menu.
3. Select the desired fill.

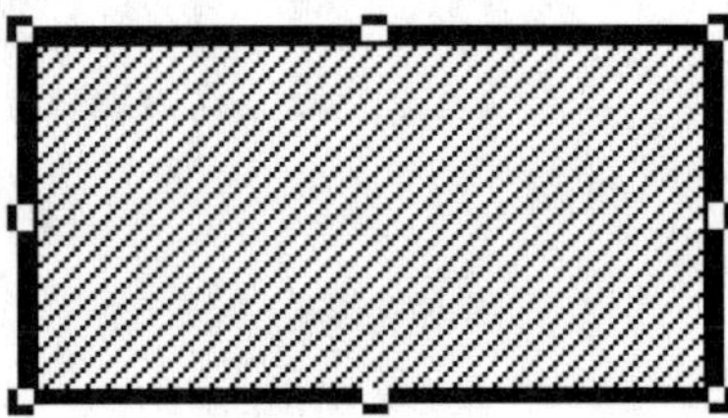

The Fill and Stroke dialog

The Fill and Stroke dialog box (Element menu) allows you to specify both colour and type of fill and line in one operation.

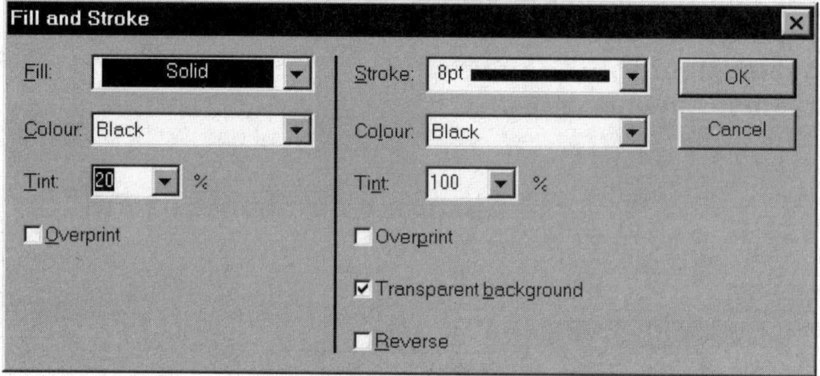

Note the subtle difference between a shape filled with "none", and another filled with "paper". The paper-filled shape is opaque – objects behind it cannot be seen.

The unfilled shape can only be selected from its perimeter, whereas a shape with any type of fill can be moved or selected from any point on its surface.

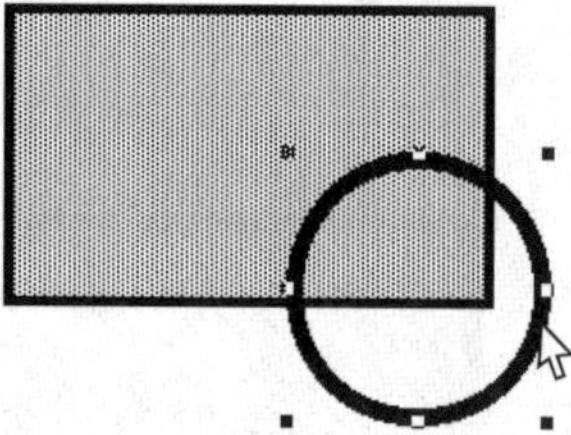

Select/move from edge only

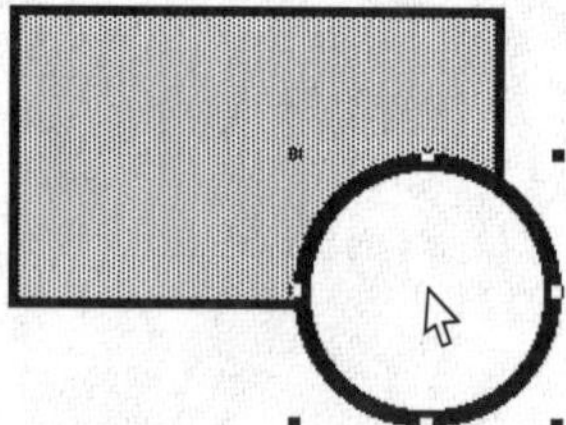

Select/move from any part of the object

Cut, Copy and Paste

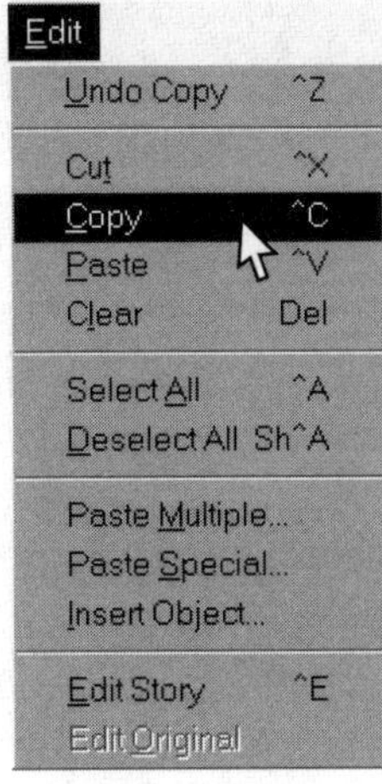

Copying

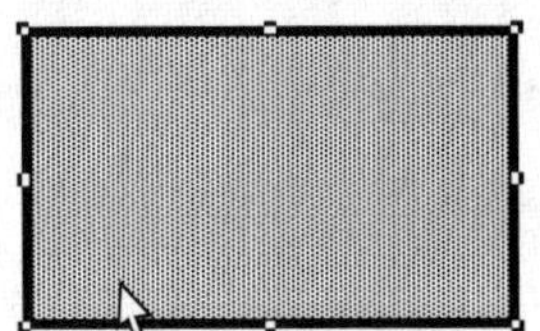

1 Select the Element(s) to copy.

2 Choose **Copy** from the **Edit** menu. A copy of the element(s) will be made and stored in the Clipboard.

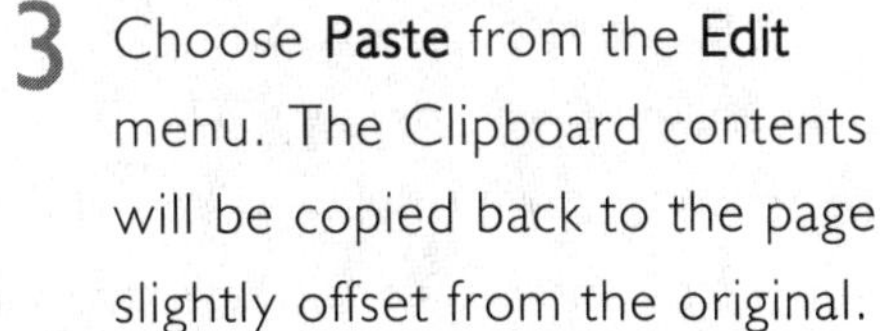

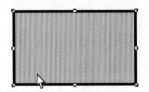

3 Choose **Paste** from the **Edit** menu. The Clipboard contents will be copied back to the page, slightly offset from the original.

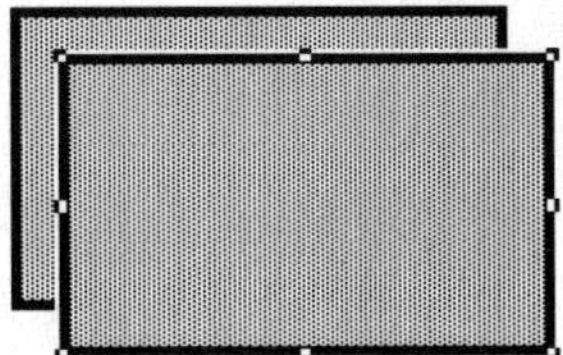

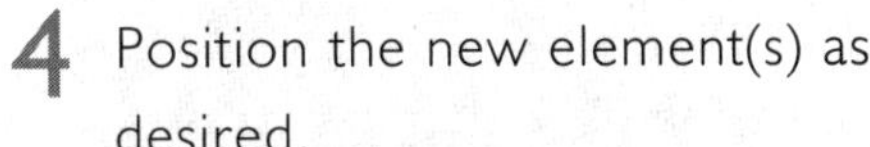

4 Position the new element(s) as desired.

Choosing Paste does not deplete the Clipboard contents, so pasting several times will give you additional copies.

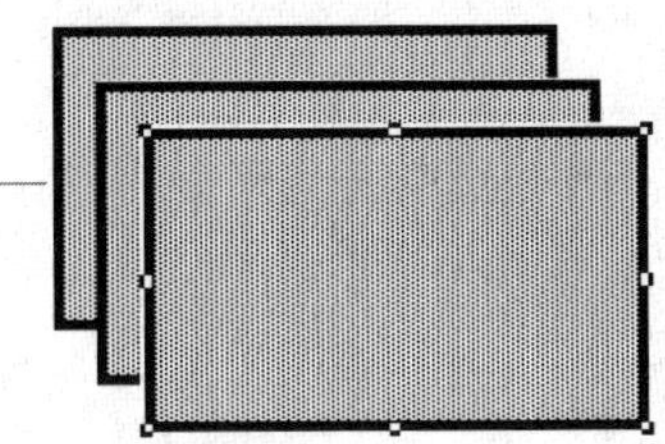

Cut

1 Select one or more elements.

2 Choose **Cut** from the **Edit** menu. The shapes will disappear from the page or pasteboard and are moved into the Clipboard.

3 To bring back the elements, choose **Paste**. This is useful when you want to move shapes from one page to another. For example, you may cut all elements from page 3, turn to page 7, and then paste them back.

Power Pasting

1. Select an element with the pointer tool.
2. Choose **Copy** from the **Edit** menu.

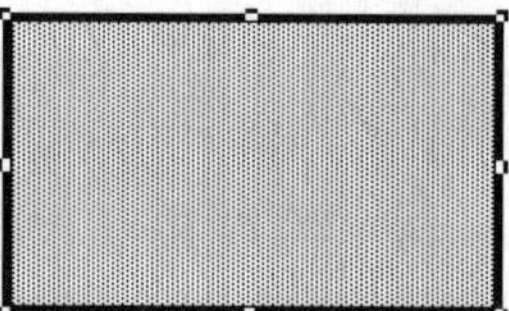

3. Instead of **Paste**, type **Control-Alt-V (Control-Shift-P on PageMaker 6 and below)**. The copy will appear positioned directly over the original. (This is useful if you want to copy items from one page to another whilst maintaining their exact position.)
4. Move the new element by dragging with the pointer tool. Make sure that you move it only once, and do not deselect

Instead of manually dragging the shape, you could adjust its position numerically with the Control palette.

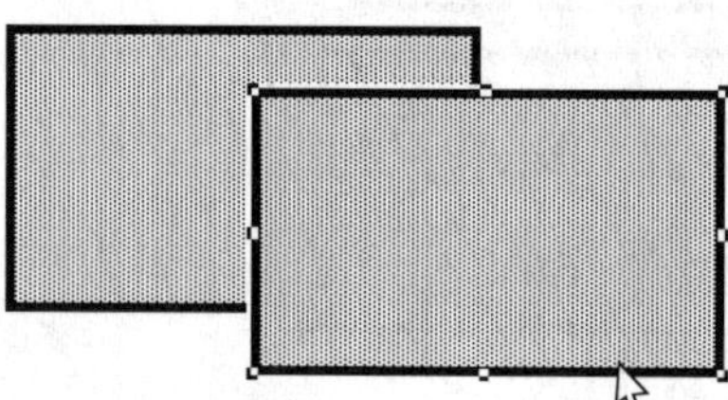

5. Type **Control-Alt-V** again. An additional copy will appear offset by the same distance as exists between the first two elements.

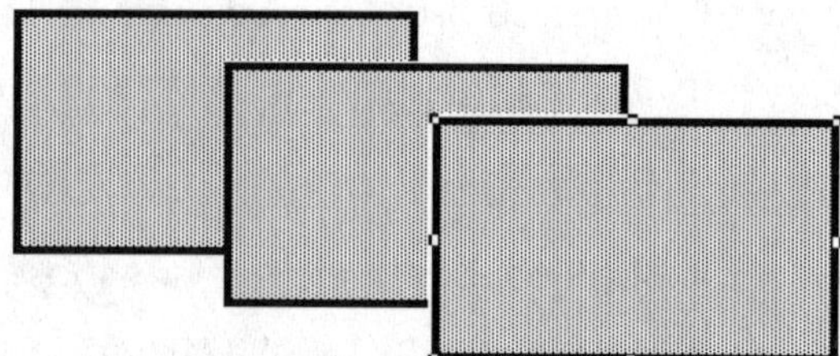

6. You can use **Control-Alt-V** to produce more copies at equal intervals. This technique is known as Power Pasting.

Paste Multiple Version 6 and above

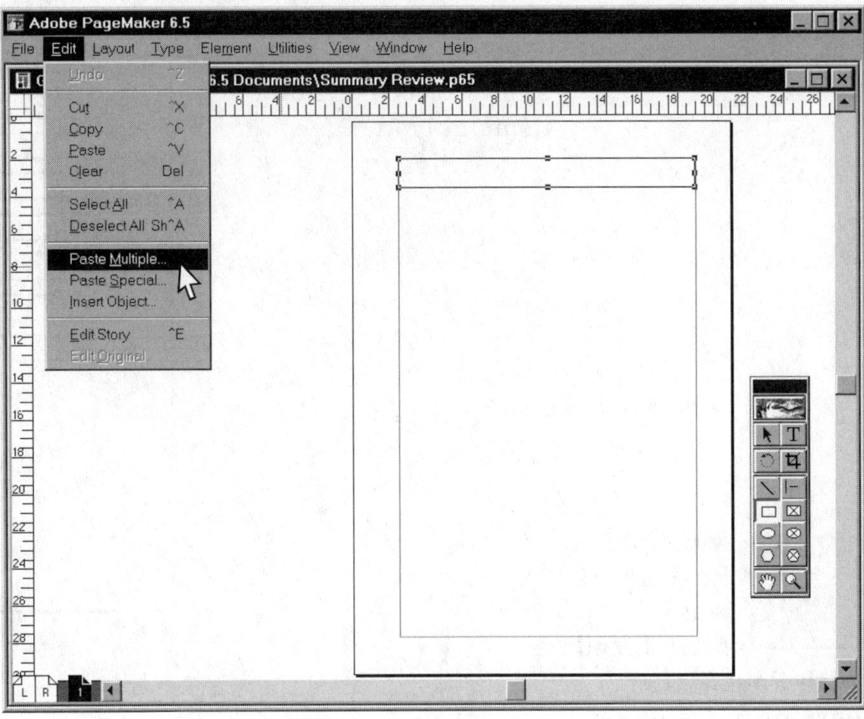

1. Select a shape with the pointer tool.
2. Choose **Copy** from the **Edit** menu.
3. Choose **Paste Multiple**, also from the **Edit** menu.
4. In the dialog box which appears, enter the number of copies required and the offsets (vertical and horizontal) for each successive copy, then click **OK**.

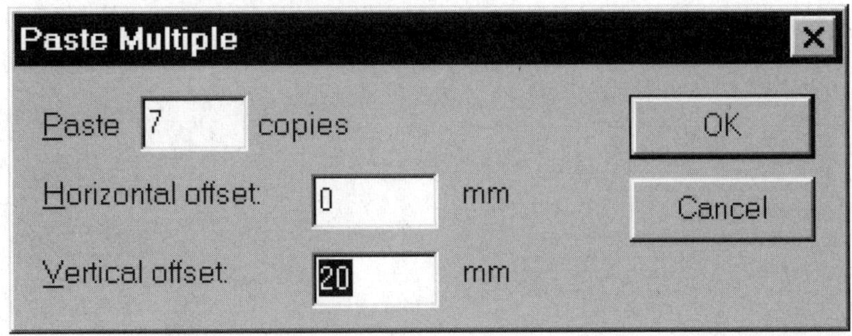

In this example seven copies are made, each 20mm directly below its neighbour.

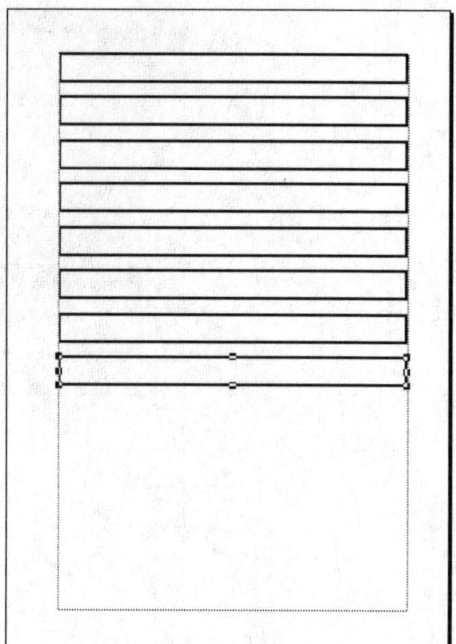

Multiple Pasting was introduced with PageMaker version 5. However, Power Pasting (see page 44) was present in earlier versions.

Magnetic Guidelines

Provided the **Snap to Guides** option is active (from the View menu), you will notice that the page margins are magnetic, i.e. elements tend to "snap to" the margin lines once within a certain distance. This makes it easy to align shapes.

Setting Your Own Vertical Guide Lines

1. With the pointer tool, move into the vertical ruler (the arrow should turn white).
2. Click the left mouse button and drag onto the page. A light blue vertical guideline will appear.
3. You can reposition this guide at any time, or delete by dragging it back onto the pasteboard.

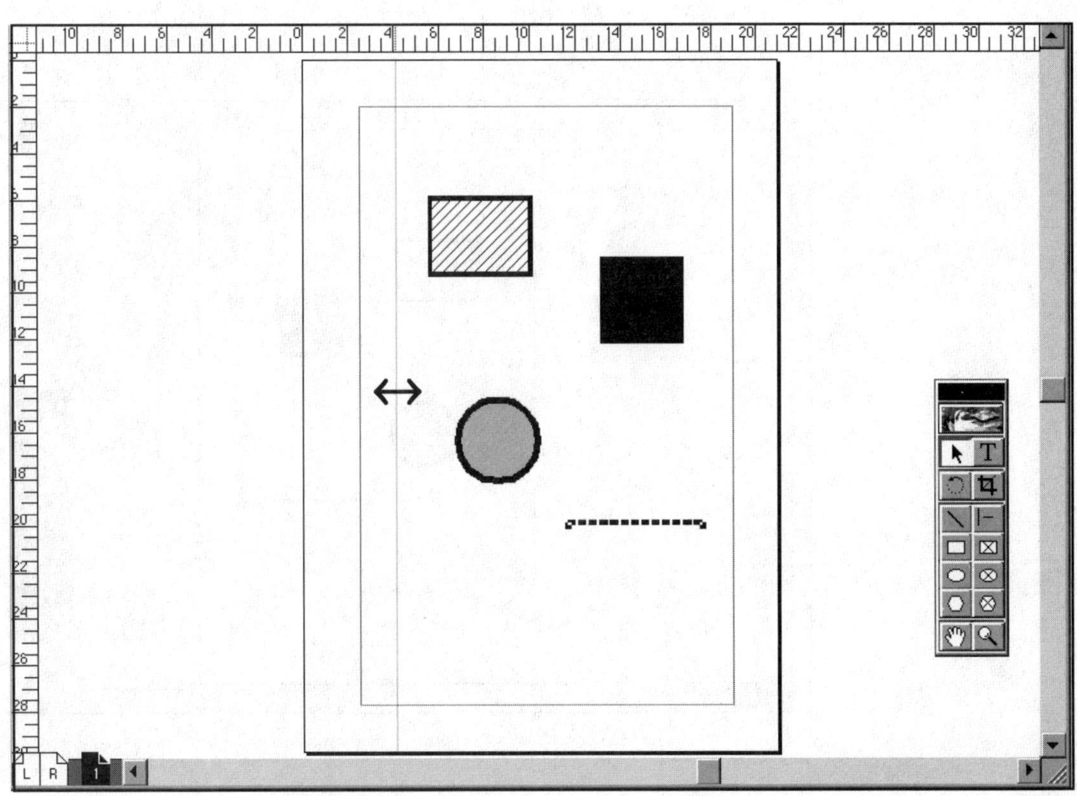

Creating Horizontal Guidelines

These are created in the same way:

1. Move into the horizontal ruler, and drag down onto the page.
2. You can repeat this process to create more guidelines, as long as the total count of horizontal plus vertical does not exceed 120 (in PageMaker 6 and above) or 40 (in PageMaker 5).

Guides normally appear in front of PageMaker elements. Sometimes this may make it difficult to see thin objects such as hairlines. There is, however, an option to display guides "at the back" in the **Preferences** dialog box (File menu). In PageMaker 6 you can also set this from the Layout menu, Guides and Rulers submenu, and in PageMaker 6.5 directly from the View menu.

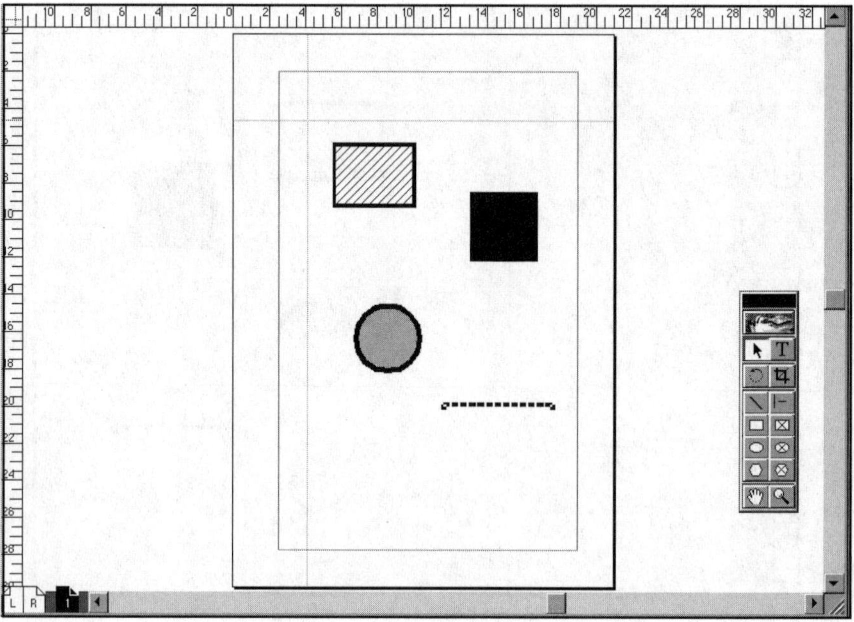

Using Guidelines

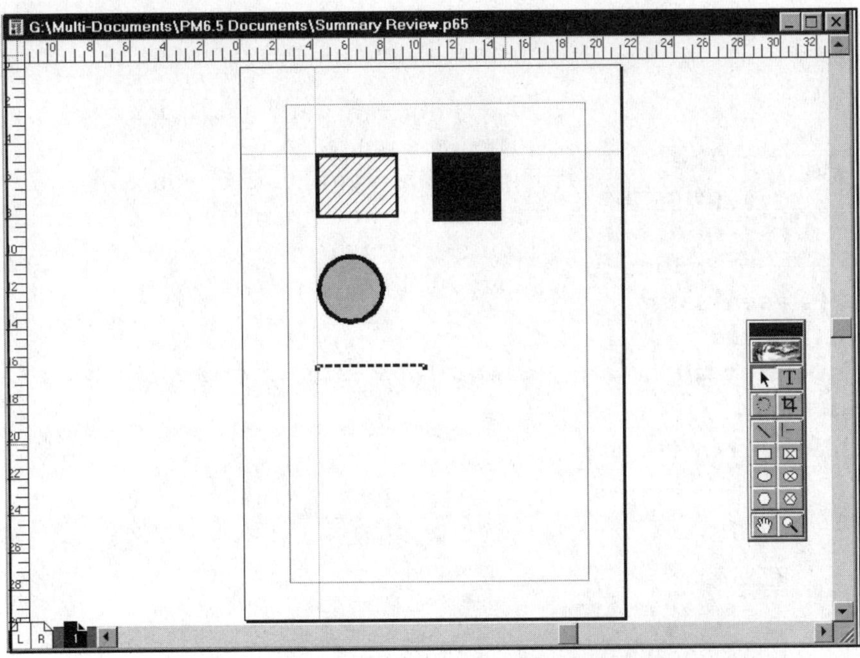

Provided the **Snap to Guides** feature is active (View menu), all guidelines will be magnetic. As you move or resize shapes using the Mouse, they will snap into place when close to a guideline. This helps you to control the structure of your page design.

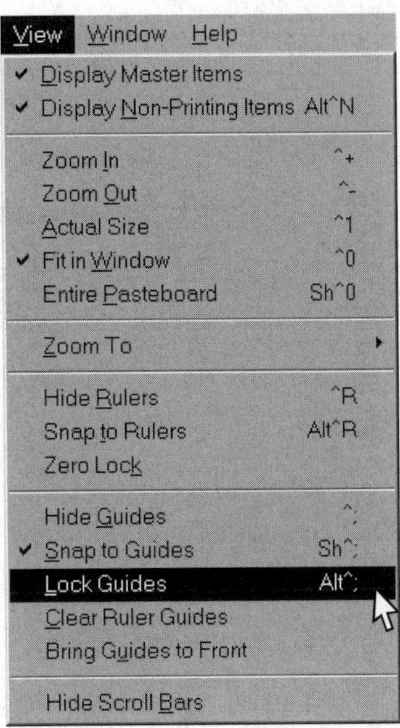

REMEMBER

You can lock your guides to prevent the possibility of accidentally moving them later on.

Defaults

Defaults determine the initial effects applied to newly created PageMaker elements.

REMEMBER

The principle of defaults applies to all PageMaker attributes, including fill, colour and type specifications.

For example, if the defaults have not been changed since PageMaker was installed, you will find that all new shapes have a default line style of one point, and a default fill of none.

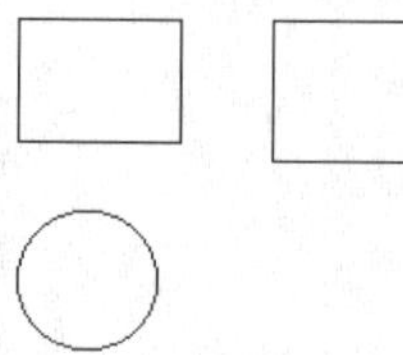

Changing a Document's Default Line Style

1. Deselect any elements by clicking on the pointer tool.
2. Choose the required default line style from the Element menu. Because nothing was selected the default line style will change.

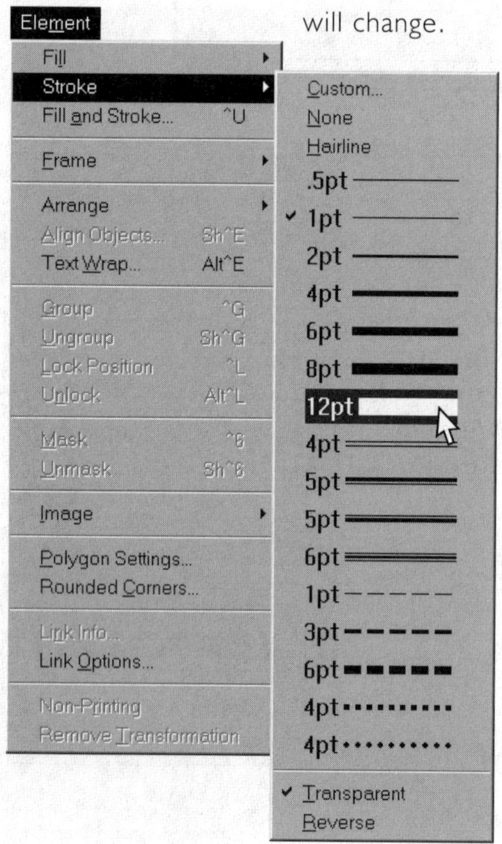

In this example all new shapes will now initially have a line style of 12 points.

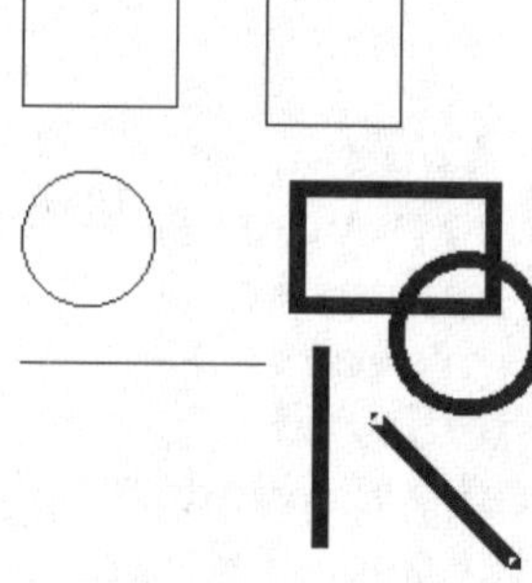

Changing PageMaker's Global Defaults

The previous example demonstrated altering defaults which apply to the working document only. This information is always saved as part of the document file.

It is also possible to change the global defaults, which will affect initial default values for all new PageMaker documents.

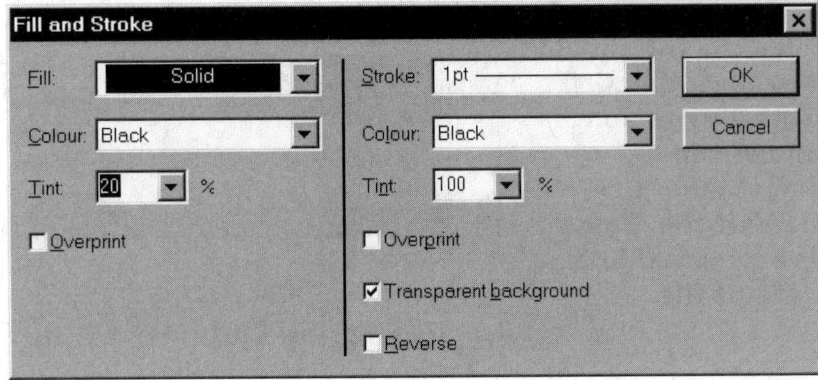

1. Close any open documents (**File** menu).
2. Any settings you make now will change PageMaker's general defaults. In this example, from now onwards all new PageMaker documents will use a 20% grey tint for boxes and circles.

Choosing Document Setup from the File menu at this time will let you specify default attributes for new documents.

The PMx.CNF File

This file contains PageMaker's global default information. You may wish to access this file for the following reasons:

The "x" here is used to denote the PageMaker version number, e.g. if you are using version 6 then the file should be called PM6.CNF. This illustration shows the PageMaker 6.5 default file. Below is a PageMaker 5 default file.

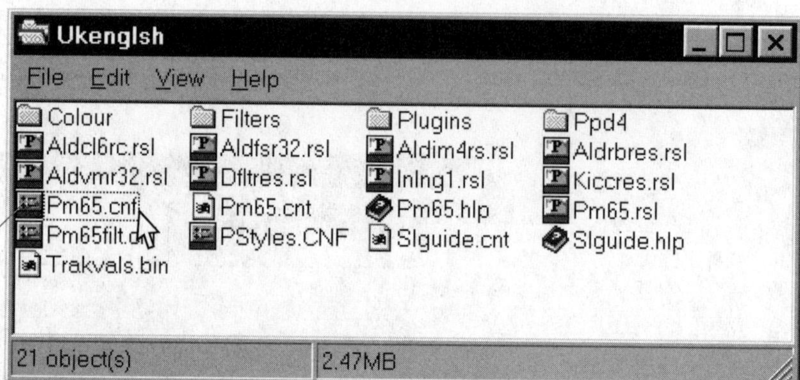

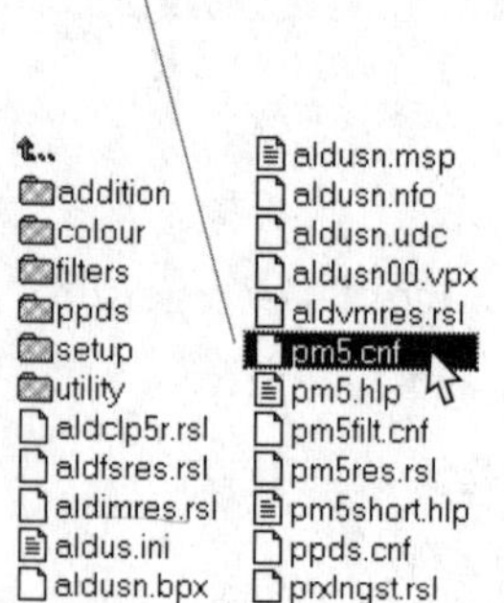

1. **Restoring Defaults to the Factory Settings**
   Simply delete the PMx.CNF file. A new one will be created the next time you launch PageMaker.

2. **Backing up Default Settings**
   If you back up PMx.CNF to floppy disk, you will be able to restore your default settings later on by copying the file back again. This is particularly useful if someone else has been using your machine and changing the settings from those which you prefer.

3. **Copying Defaults to Other Machines**
   Simply copy the PMx.CNF file to the same directory on other machines which have PageMaker installed. This allows you to develop company-wide standards for text and graphic defaults (including colour schemes and corporate fonts) on one PC which you may then copy across to others.

The Rotation Tool Version 5 and above

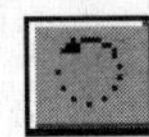

This allows you to freely rotate any PageMaker element directly on screen using the mouse.

1 Select the item to be rotated.

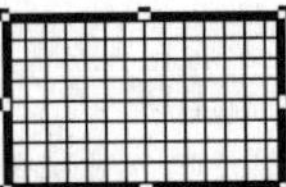

2 Choose the Rotation tool.

3 Move to the point where you wish the *pivot* for rotation to be. Hold down the Mouse button and drag several centimetres to the right. (Do not let go of the button yet.)

The further you initially drag from the pivot point, the better your control over the rotation angle.

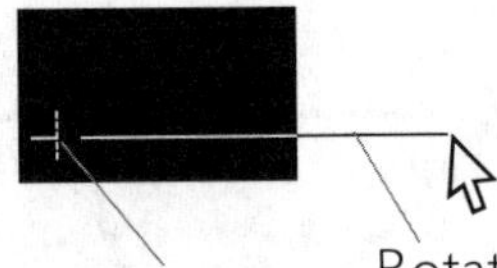

4 A line will appear which can be used as a rotation lever. By dragging in a circular motion around the pivot point you can rotate the element in either a clockwise or anticlockwise direction.

If the Control palette is active, then you will be able to read off the angle of rotation in degrees as you rotate.

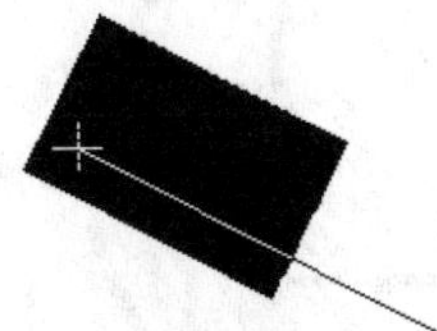

Dragging in a clockwise direction about the pivot point

5 When you have achieved the desired angle, release the Mouse button. The element has been rotated.

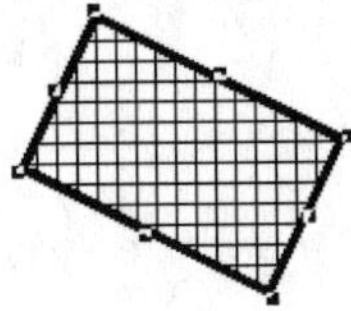

To rotate using the numeric Control palette, see Chapter 6, "Transformations".

Front and Back

Items created more recently tend to appear in front of those which are older. Before version 6 of PageMaker, moving an element had the side-effect of bringing it in front of all others. However, in version 6 and above the order of elements is preserved even when they are edited.

You can control the stacking order of elements using the Element menu, arrange submenu.

To Bring Elements to the Front of Others

1. Select the element(s).

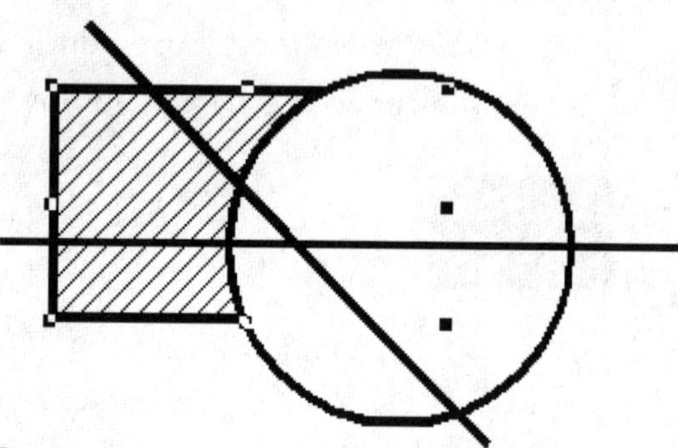

2. Choose Bring to Front from the Element menu, Arrange submenu.

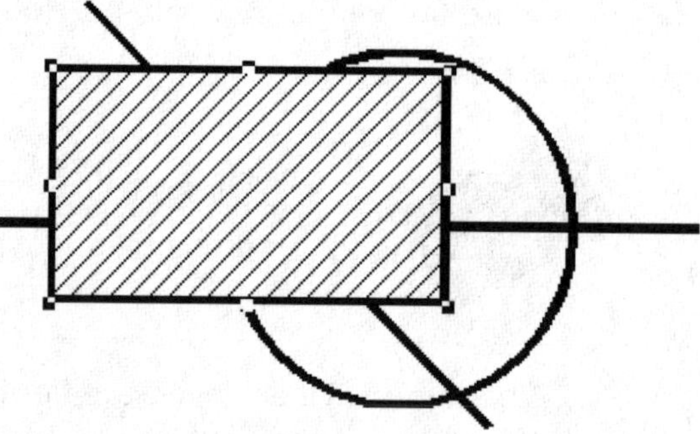

To Send Elements Behind Others

1. Select the element(s).
2. Choose Send to Back from the Arrange submenu.

In PageMaker 6 (and above) you can also move elements one "layer" at a time using the Bring Forward and Send Backward commands from the Arrange menu.

PageMaker 6.5 introduced a special Layers palette which lets you set up independently controlled layers within your publication. See chapter 16, "Layers".

Chapter Four

Importing Graphics

This chapter shows you how to import graphic elements from other application packages. Once inside your PageMaker document these can be treated in much the same way as internal elements. Additionally, they can be cropped, and TIFF files can be adjusted using Image Control.

Covers

The Place Command

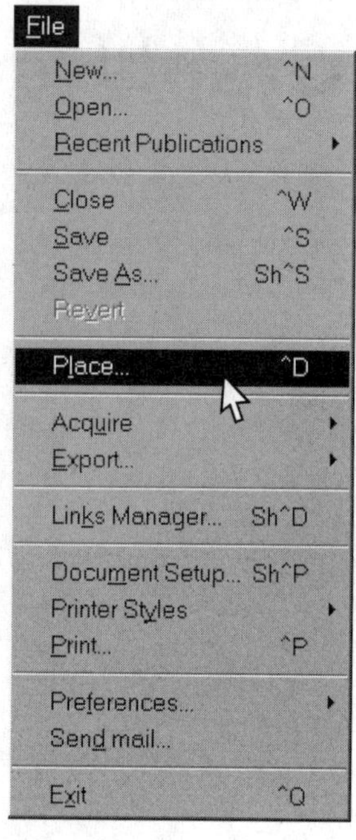

Graphics generated in other application packages can be brought into a PageMaker document by using the **Place** command.

1 Choose **Place** from the **File** menu. The Place dialog box will appear.

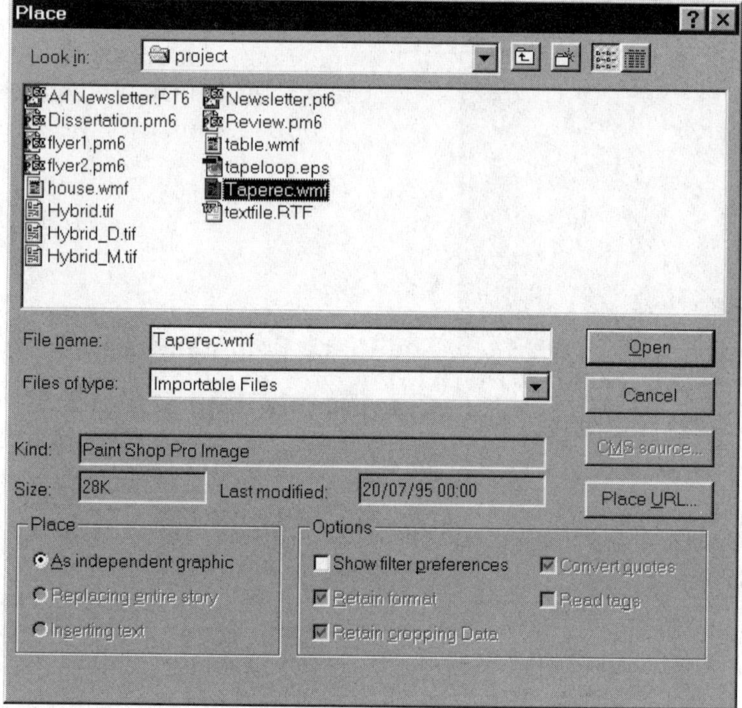

2 Use the directory list to find the location of the file to be imported, or type the path manually.

3 Either type the file name followed by **Return**, or double-click directly on a name displayed in the directory list.

4 Back on the page, your pointer will change into a loaded graphic icon. This gives you the opportunity to decide where the graphic will be positioned initially.

...cont'd

Loaded icons indicating type of graphic file about to be imported.

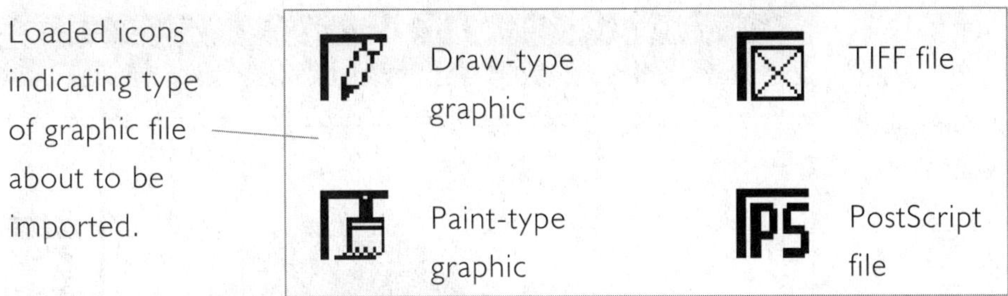

5 Position the loaded icon and click once.

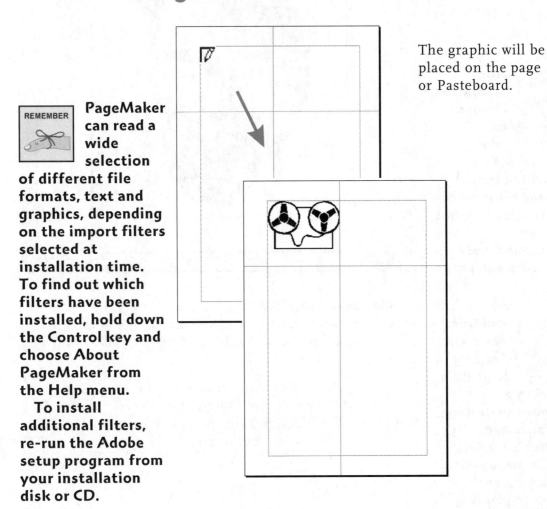

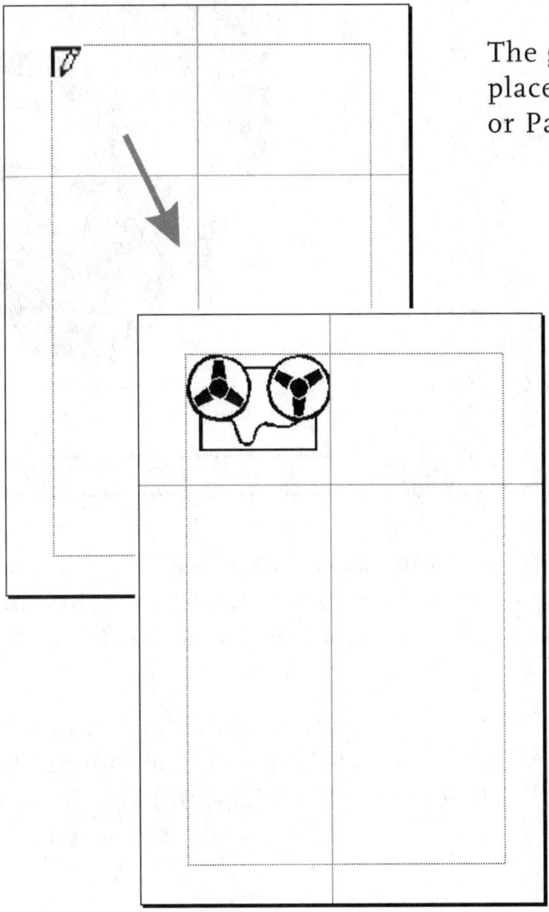

The graphic will be placed on the page or Pasteboard.

REMEMBER

PageMaker can read a wide selection of different file formats, text and graphics, depending on the import filters selected at installation time. To find out which filters have been installed, hold down the Control key and choose About PageMaker from the Help menu.

To install additional filters, re-run the Adobe setup program from your installation disk or CD.

Graphic File Formats

This picture started life as two images digitised using a video still camera. They were then enhanced and combined using an image editing application to produce a grey-level TIFF file composite.

High resolution images look clearer when printed out (provided the printer can match the resolution), but take up proportionately more storage space.

Holding down the Control key while resizing a bitmapped graphic will size it in "jumps", limiting you to sizes which work best with your selected printing device.

Bitmapped Graphics

TIFF files and Paint files are bitmapped. This means that they are represented as a series of dots (or blocks) which build up an image.

It is important to note the *resolution* of bitmapped graphics. If the resolution is high then the component dots will be small, which improves the quality of the image. Resolution is normally measured in dots per inch (dpi).

At 400% view size you can clearly see the blocks which make up the image...

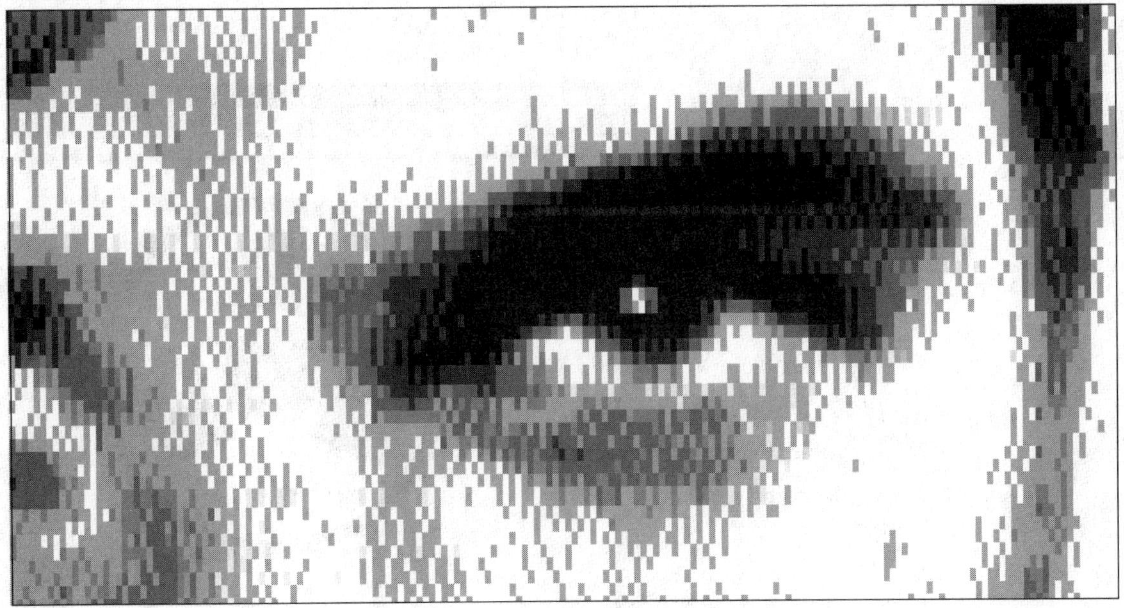

Resizing Imported Graphics

1. Click on the element with the pointer tool.
2. Resize in the normal way (as for native PageMaker elements) by dragging on the object handles.
3. Hold down the **Shift** key if you want the graphic to remain in its original proportions.

Remember that you can also move or resize any element using the Control palette. This will give you precise numeric control (see Chapter 3).

Moving Imported Graphics

1. Again, make sure the element has been selected with the pointer tool.
2. Move by dragging anywhere within the shape.

The Draw-type loaded graphic icon

Draw-type Graphics

These are stored not as images, but as objects. The graphic is created as a series of (sometimes complex) mathematical shapes, and is redrawn to any required resolution.

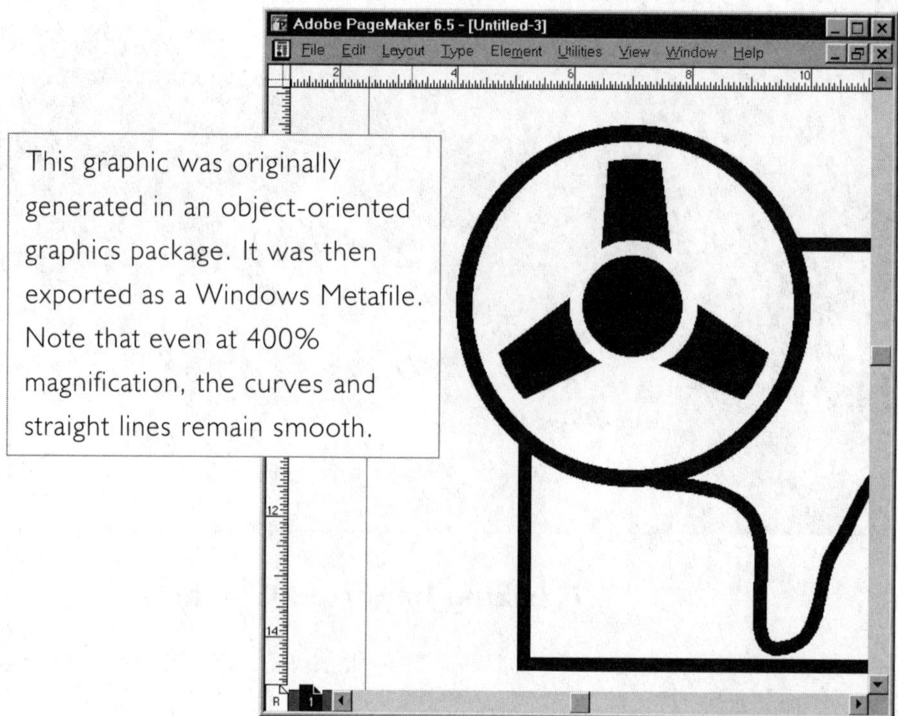

This graphic was originally generated in an object-oriented graphics package. It was then exported as a Windows Metafile. Note that even at 400% magnification, the curves and straight lines remain smooth.

You can freely resize these graphics without losing definition. The final resolution is determined by the output device.

EPS Files

EPS files are represented by this icon.

EPS stands for Encapsulated PostScript. This is a page description language, a widely used standard in professional printing. EPS files may contain a combination of bitmapped and Draw-type graphics as well as text.

Since PostScript is a printer language, your EPS file may not display on the screen. Some EPS files get around this by incorporating a TIFF preview image, which may still look "grainier" than the final printed version.

The Cropping Tool

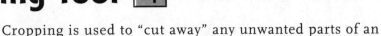

Cropping is used to "cut away" any unwanted parts of an imported graphic.

1. Select the cropping tool from the Toolbox.
2. Click once on the imported graphic to display its handles.
3. Line up the *centre* of the cropping tool with a handle.
4. Hold down the Mouse button (you may have to wait a few seconds while the image is prepared for cropping).
5. Drag towards the centre of the object. Part of the image will disappear.

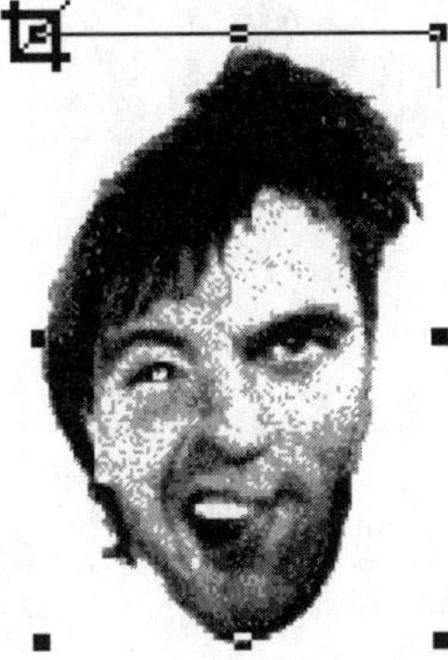

Dragging inwards with the cropping tool.

6. Repeat this process with other handles if necessary.

Dragging within the shape with the cropping tool.

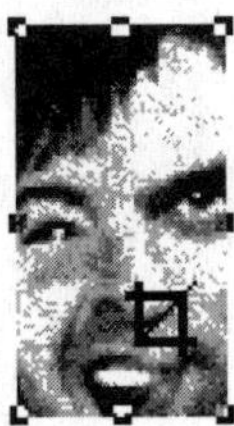

Cropping is non-destructive. This means that you can always restore the shape by pulling the handles back out again.

HANDY TIP

If you move within the shape and then hold down the Mouse button, the cropping icon will change into a grabber hand. You will then be able to reposition the whole shape within its cropped "window".

Image Control

Image Control can be used to help "balance" several images on the page, so they appear to have the same lightness and contrast.

1 Select an imported TIFF file with the pointer tool.

2 Choose **Image Control** from the Image submenu of the **Element** menu.

The following dialog box will appear:

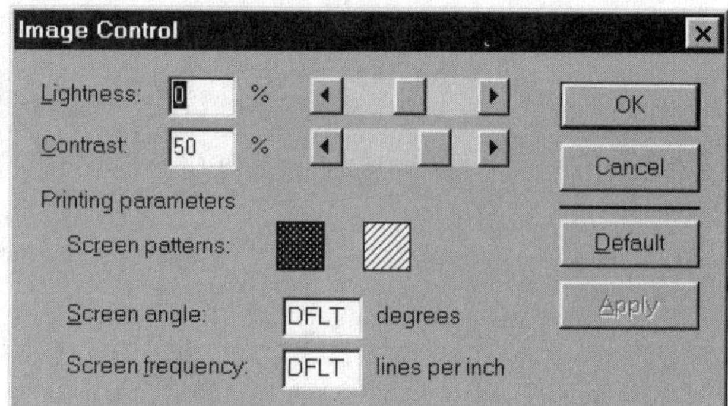

3 Make a change and click the **Apply** button to preview the effect on the image.

4 Click **OK** when satisfied, or **Cancel** to abort.

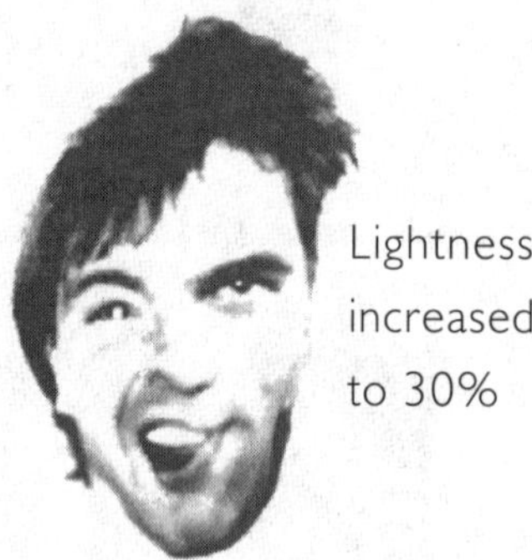

Lightness increased to 30%

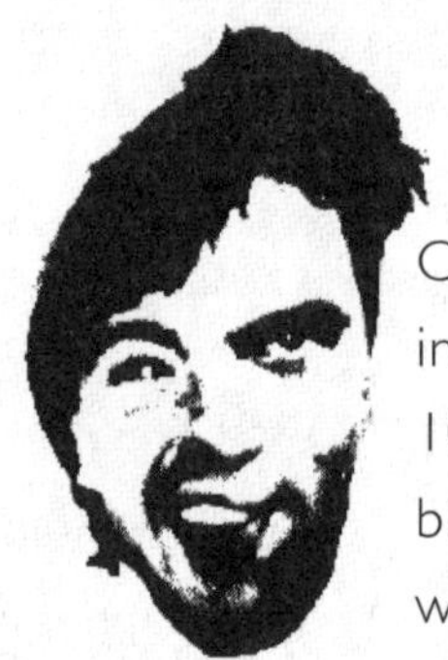

Contrast increased to 100% (pure black and white)

Contrast of minus 50% (inverted image)

Screening is the process where grey levels are simulated with solid black dots. This is done by printing a fine pattern of dots; the further apart the dots the lighter the overall grey effect.

This also applies to colour: for example, screened red dots will simulate a shade of pink.

Chapter Five

The Text Tool

PageMaker contains a wealth of text-editing features. In this chapter we'll look at how to enter and edit text, as well as the range of character and paragraph attributes which can be changed.

Covers

Adding Text

The Text tool

1 Select the Text tool.

2 Click anywhere on the page within the margin guides. An insertion point (text cursor) will appear at the left margin.

3 Type in the text.

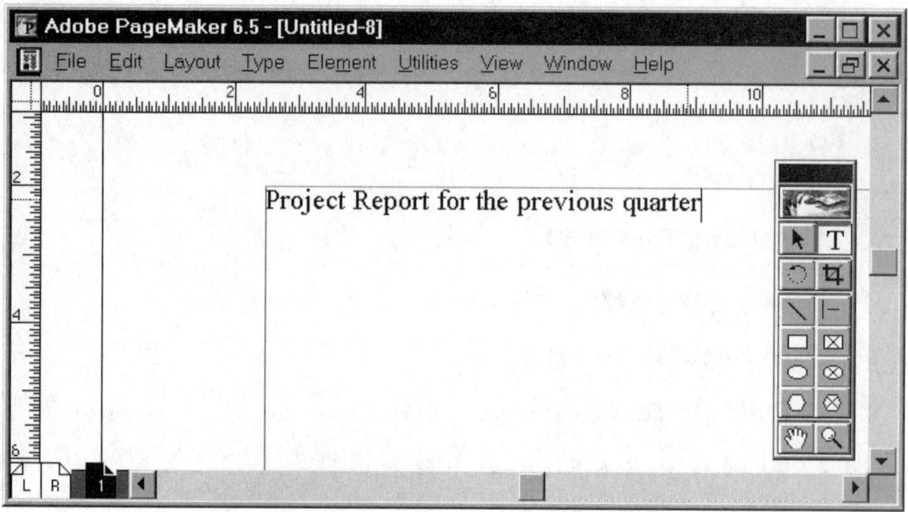

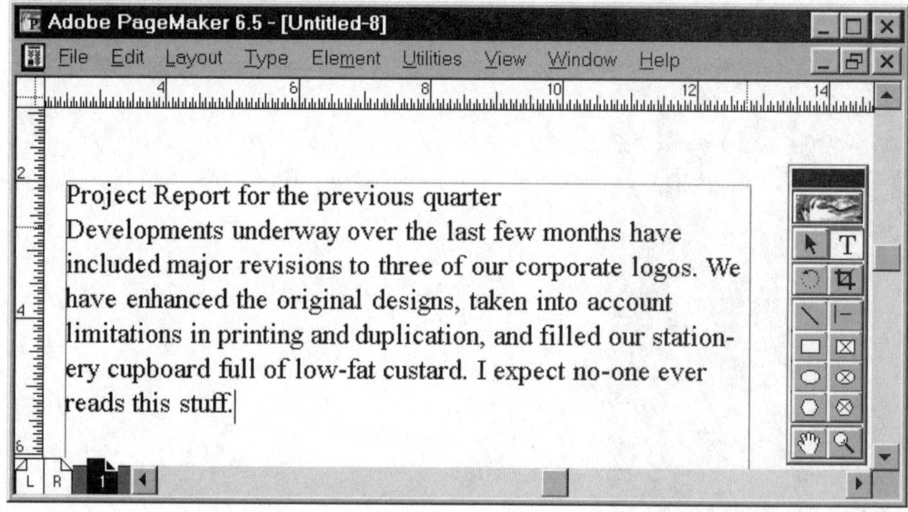

Changing Text

1 With the Text tool, drag across the text you wish to select.

2 You now have the opportunity to make changes to this text.

REMEMBER

You can activate or de-activate the Control palette from the Window menu.

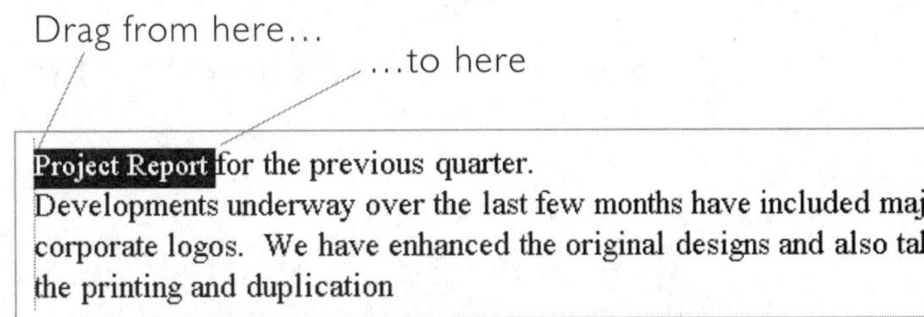
Drag from here...
...to here
Project Report for the previous quarter.
Developments underway over the last few months have included maj
corporate logos. We have enhanced the original designs and also tal
the printing and duplication

3 You can use the Control palette to alter any of the text attributes. Note that changes only affect the selected text.

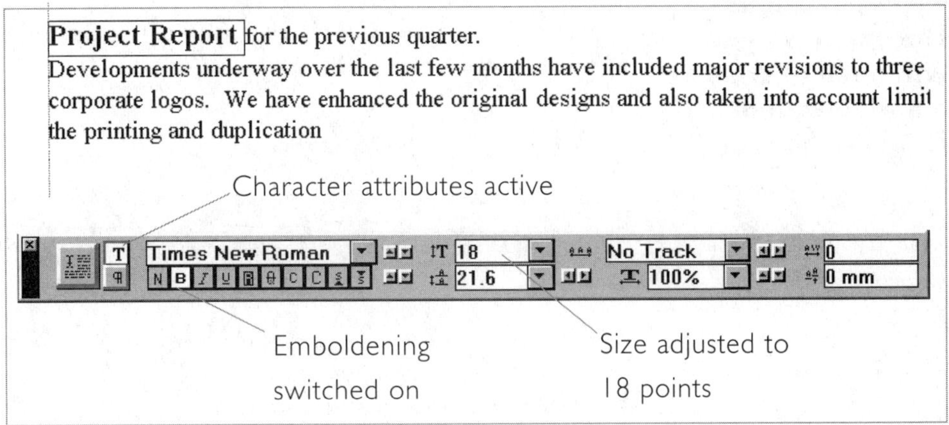
Project Report for the previous quarter.
Developments underway over the last few months have included major revisions to three
corporate logos. We have enhanced the original designs and also taken into account limit
the printing and duplication
Character attributes active
Times New Roman
18
21.6
No Track
100%
0
0 mm
Emboldening switched on
Size adjusted to 18 points

Other Ways to Select Text

Double-click:	selects a word
Triple-click:	selects the surrounding paragraph
Select All:	(from the Edit menu) selects all text in a story
Shift-click:	selects from previous insertion point to Mouse location

Manipulating Text

Selected text can be copied, cut and pasted (from the Edit menu) in the same manner as graphics (see Chapter 3).

Changing text attributes is achieved most easily with the Control palette. This operates in two modes, character and paragraph level.

Character-level Attributes

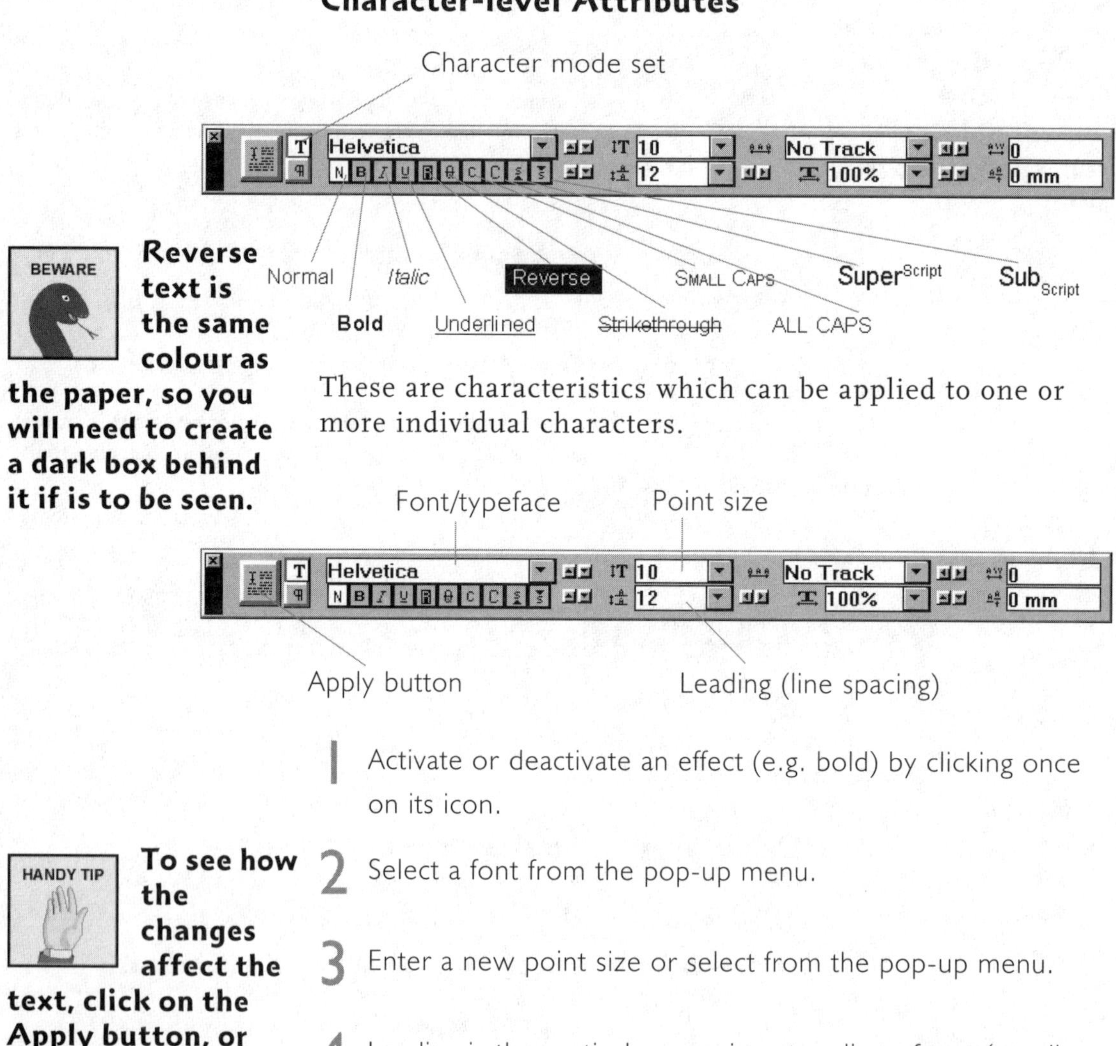

BEWARE **Reverse text is the same colour as the paper, so you will need to create a dark box behind it if is to be seen.**

These are characteristics which can be applied to one or more individual characters.

1. Activate or deactivate an effect (e.g. bold) by clicking once on its icon.

2. Select a font from the pop-up menu.

3. Enter a new point size or select from the pop-up menu.

4. Leading is the vertical space given to a line of text (usually measured in points). An automatic setting is available from the pop-up menu.

HANDY TIP **To see how the changes affect the text, click on the Apply button, or press Escape to abort the new setting.**

Paragraph-level Attributes

These are characteristics which affect entire paragraphs of text.

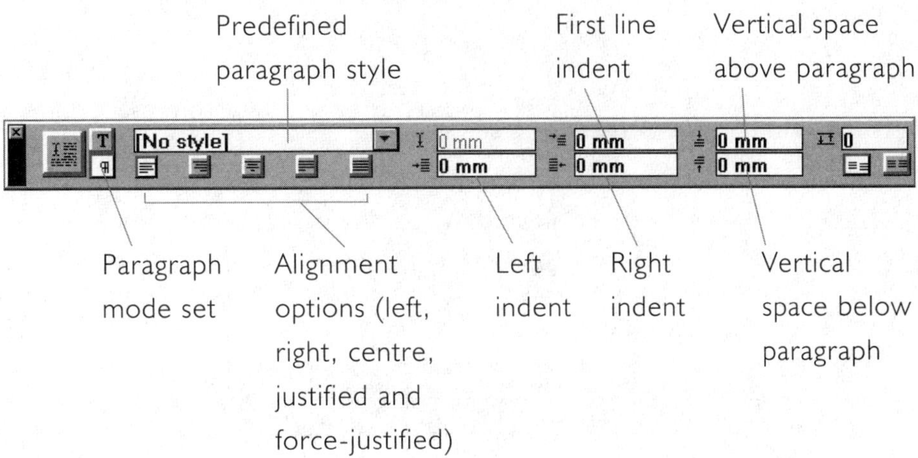

Examples of Paragraph Settings

This text has a space below paragraph of 5mm. It is left aligned with a first line indent of 10mm. This paragraph uses centre alignment.	This text is justified. This means that space is adjusted between words/letters so that each line begins and ends at the same place, apart from this final line. Force justification affects all lines in the paragraph.

Menu Options

Individual settings may also be made using the Type menu. Note that some of these options have keyboard shortcuts listed.

For more information about predefined paragraph styles, see Chapter 11, "Style Sheets".

Default Text Settings

Setting Document Defaults

1. Make sure that no text is selected, and no insertion point active. The best way to do this is to click on the pointer tool.

2. Make the required settings from the Control palette or Type menu.

3. From now on all new text created in the current document will initially have these new attributes.

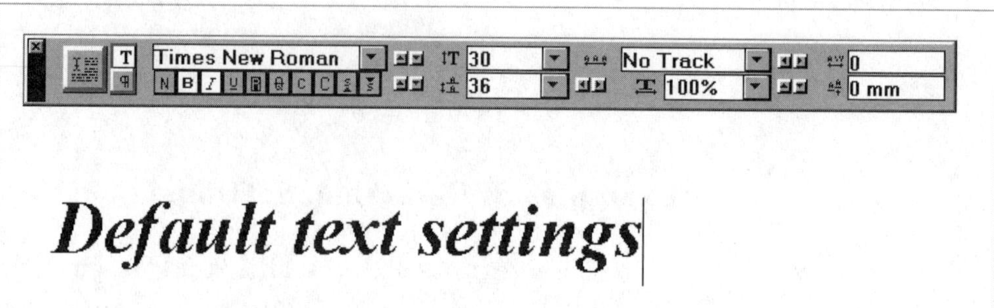

Setting PageMaker Global Text Defaults

1. Close all documents.

2. Make the required text settings. These are automatically saved in the PageMaker CNF file (see the topic “Defaults” in Chapter 3).

Working with Blocks of Text

If you click on your text with the pointer tool, it will be treated as a single PageMaker element: a text block. This can be moved or resized without altering the attributes of the text within.

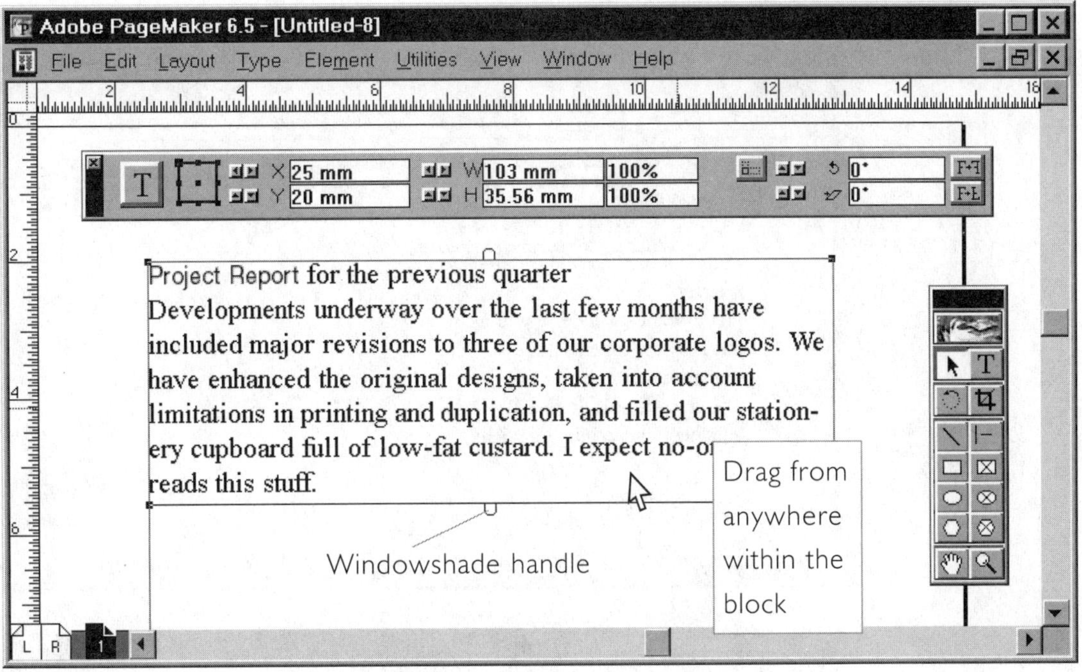

Moving a Text Block

1. Select with the pointer tool.
2. Drag from anywhere within the block (avoid the handles).

Text blocks have two extra handles known as windowshades. These are normally blank but are sometimes used to indicate text which is continued to or from another block.

You cannot alter the text attributes with the pointer, only the text tool. Making text attribute changes with the pointer tool active will instead alter the document defaults.

Resizing Text Blocks

This can be done either by dragging on the object's handles or via the Control palette:

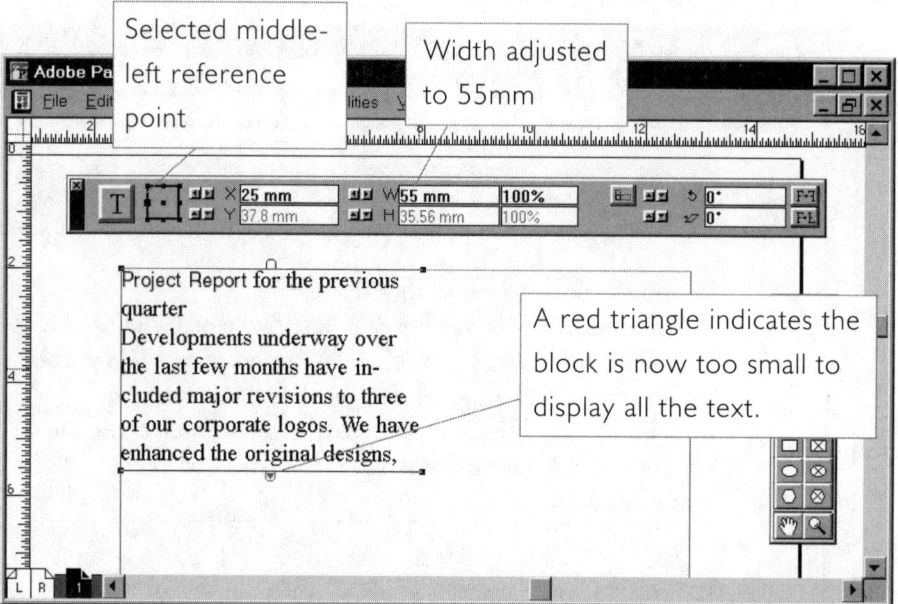
Selected middle-left reference point
Width adjusted to 55mm
A red triangle indicates the block is now too small to display all the text.
Adobe Pa
File Edit
X 25 mm
Y 37.8 mm
W 55 mm
H 35.56 mm
100%
100%
0°
0°
Project Report for the previous quarter
Developments underway over the last few months have included major revisions to three of our corporate logos. We have enhanced the original designs,

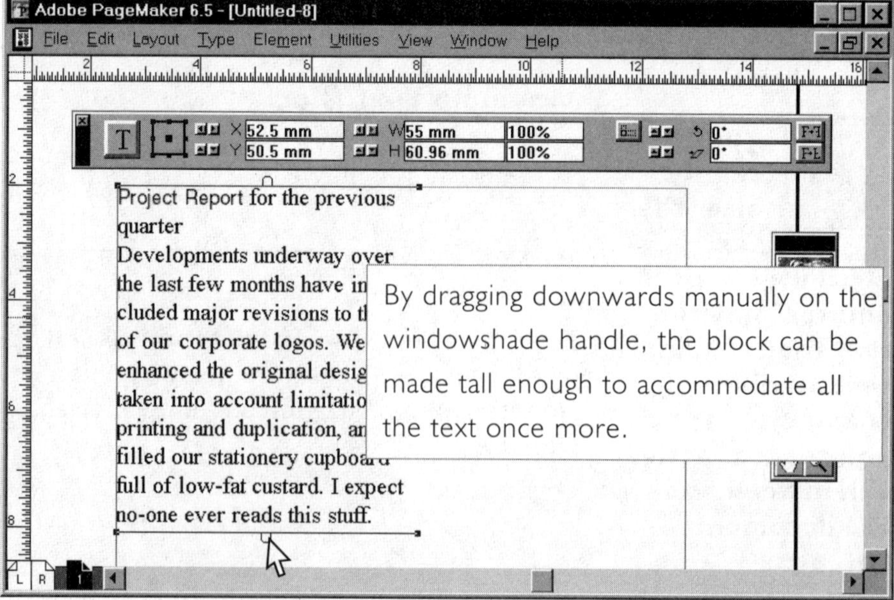
Adobe PageMaker 6.5 - [Untitled-8]
File Edit Layout Type Element Utilities View Window Help
X 52.5 mm
Y 50.5 mm
W 55 mm
H 60.96 mm
100%
100%
0°
0°
Project Report for the previous quarter
Developments underway over the last few months have in cluded major revisions to t of our corporate logos. We enhanced the original desig taken into account limitatio printing and duplication, an filled our stationery cupboard full of low-fat custard. I expect no-one ever reads this stuff.
By dragging downwards manually on the windowshade handle, the block can be made tall enough to accommodate all the text once more.

More Advanced Text Effects v4 and above

Kerning

If all characters are evenly spaced out, some combinations of letters give the illusion of too much horizontal space:

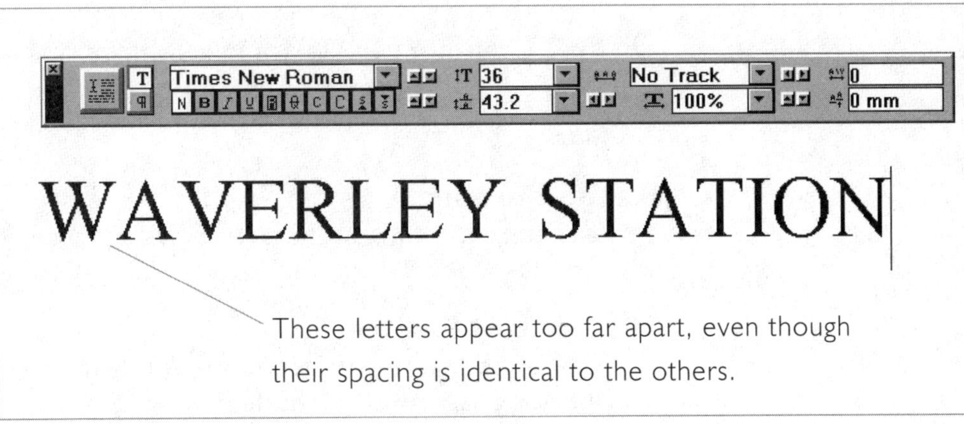

PageMaker recognises these pairs of characters automatically, and will adjust accordingly. This is known as automatic pair kerning (accessed by selecting Paragraph, Spacing from the Type menu).

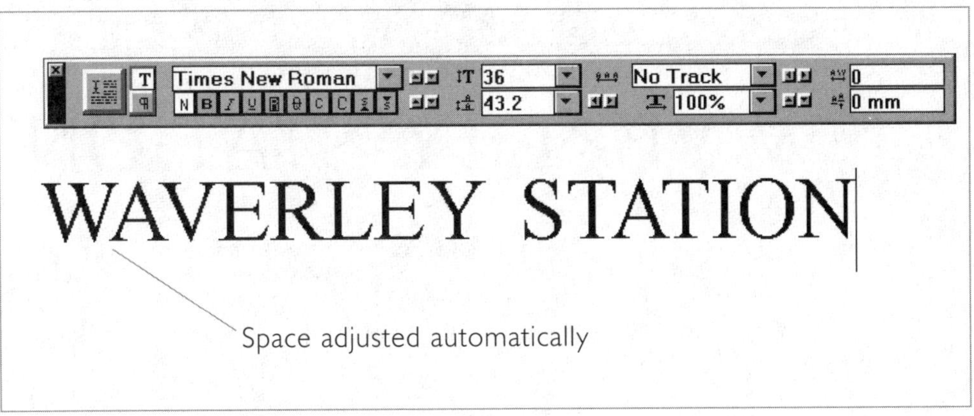

Kerning can also be carried out manually:

1. Click an insertion point (using the text tool) between the characters to be kerned.

2. Type **Control** and **Backspace** to kern the characters together. **Control**, **Shift** and **Backspace** will move them further apart.

Range Kerning

You can kern a range of characters by firstly selecting them with the text tool.

The Control Palette

You can use the Control palette for full numeric control over kerning, as in the example below:

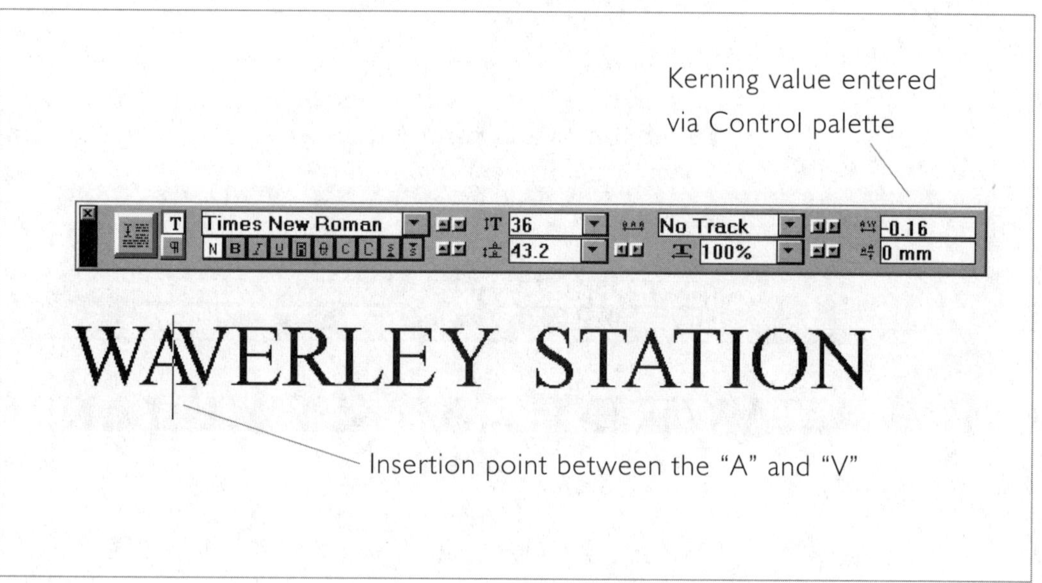

Tracking v4 and above

This is similar to kerning in that it deals with the horizontal space between letters.

Tracking is a paragraph-level attribute which takes note of the font and the size of the text to which it applies. PageMaker has five intelligent tracking algorithms, ranging from **Very Tight** through **Normal** to **Very Loose**.

Tracking can be applied either from the Type menu or the Control palette:

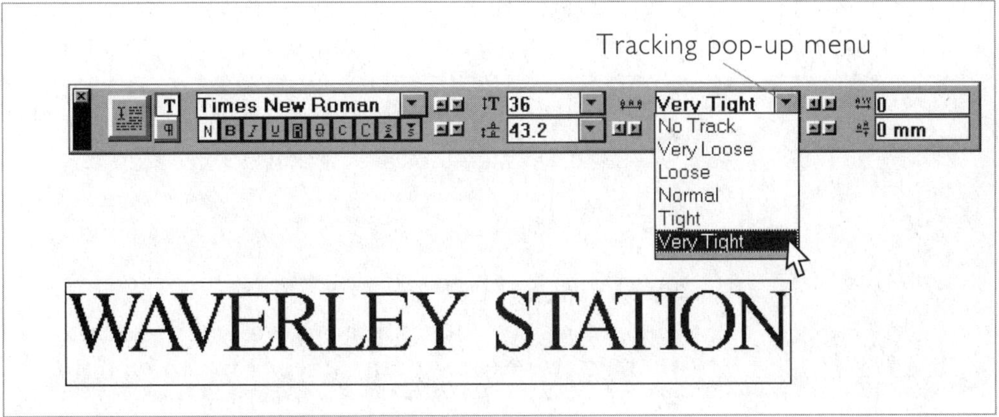

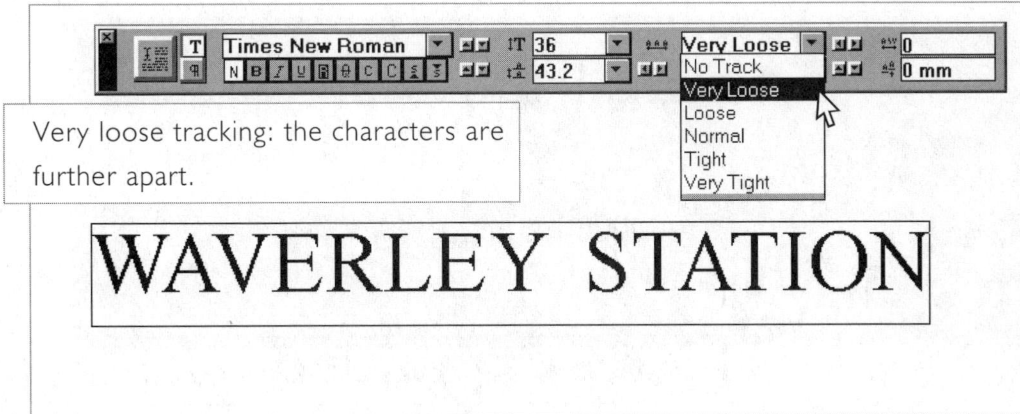

Very loose tracking: the characters are further apart.

In general, tracking keeps big characters closer together – since spacing is much more noticeable at large point sizes.

Shift Baseline v5 and above

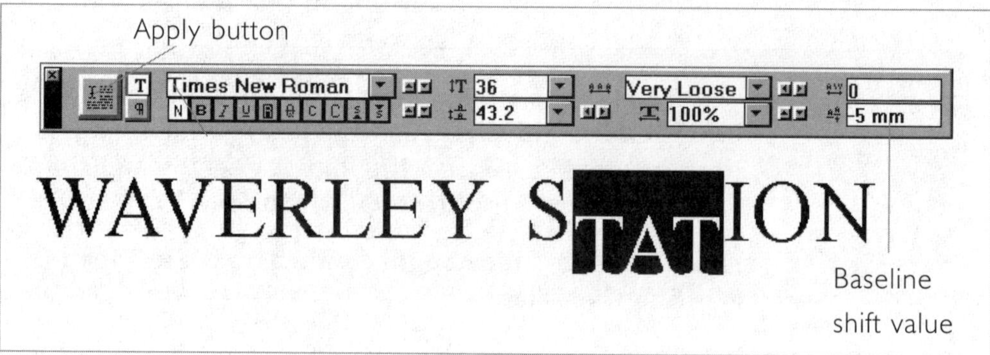

1. Select the required characters with the text tool.
2. Enter the baseline shift value into the Control palette. A negative value indicates a shift downwards.
3. Click the **Apply** button.

Set Width v5 and above

This scales text horizontally by a given percentage, without altering its vertical point size. This can be done either from the Type menu or by the Control palette as a character-level attribute:

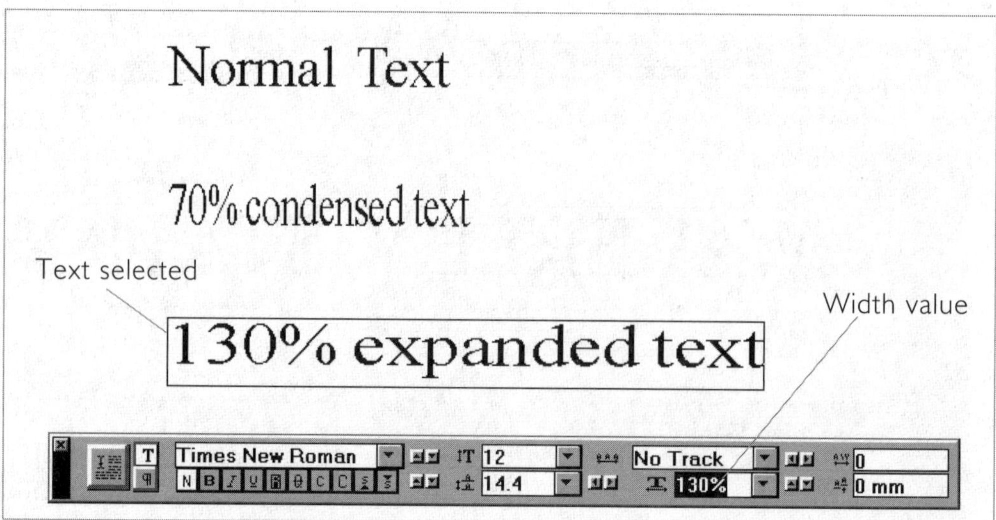

Chapter Six

Transformations

This chapter takes you through different transformations which can be applied to graphic and text elements. Some, like cropping, only apply to imported graphic items.

Covers

Skewing v5 and above

Text and graphic objects can be skewed about a reference point to give them a twisted effect:

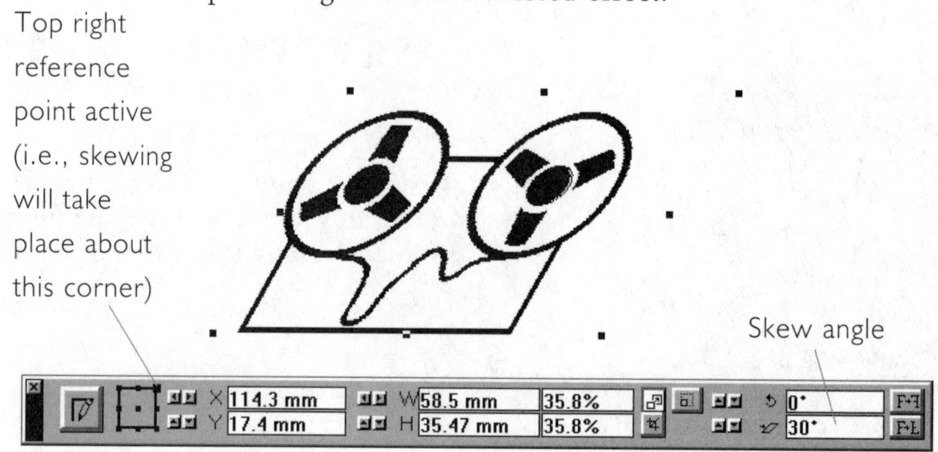

1. Select the object and reference point.
2. Enter the skew angle and click the **Apply** button.

Reflecting v5 and above

You can return any element to its original state by choosing Remove Transformation from the Element menu (Arrange in V6).

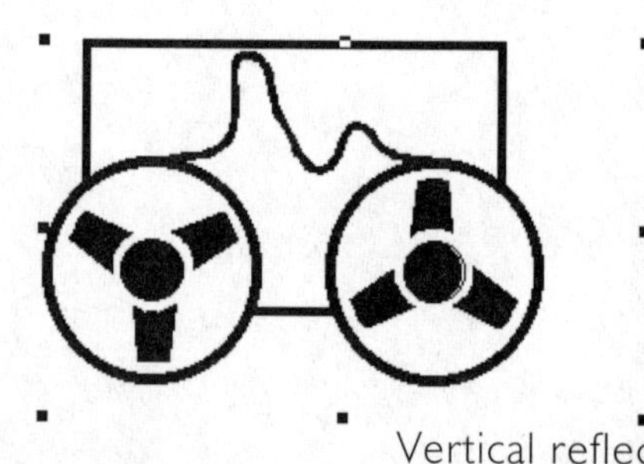

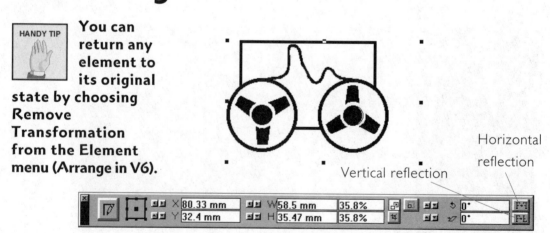

Horizontal reflection

Vertical reflection

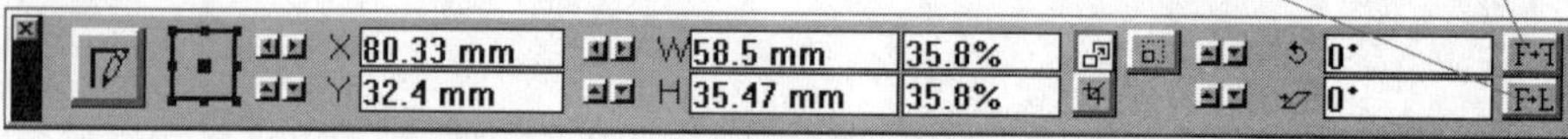

1. Select the object and reference point.
2. Click on either the horizontal or vertical reflection icon.

Cropping and Resizing with the Control Palette

Graphic images can be cropped and resized very precisely using the Control palette, as follows:

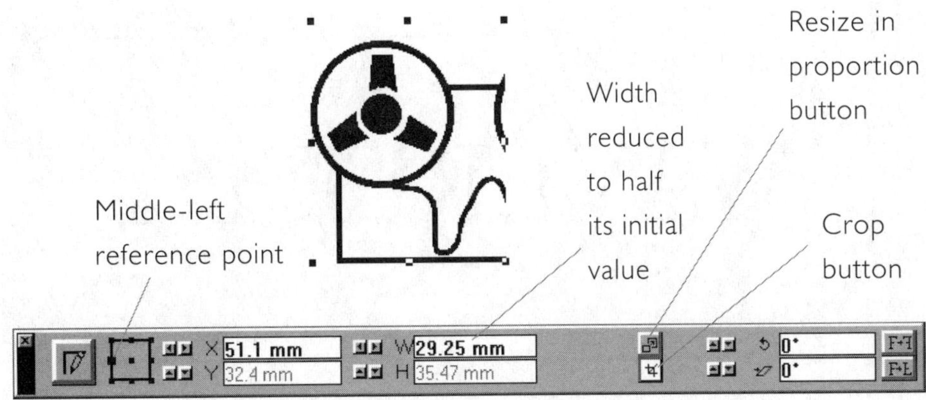

1 Select the element and choose a reference point. In this example we are using the middle-left object handle.

2 Select the crop or resize button. You can now either adjust the reference point's coordinates, or edit the overall width/height of the object. The element will be cropped or resized to accommodate the changes. In this case we have cropped the image, adjusting the width to exactly half its previous value.

You can type arithmetic expressions into the Control palette, e.g. 58.5/2 will evaluate to 29.25 when you press the Enter key or click on Apply.

Combining Effects

The transformations discussed on the previous pages can be combined to produce different effects, as shown below:

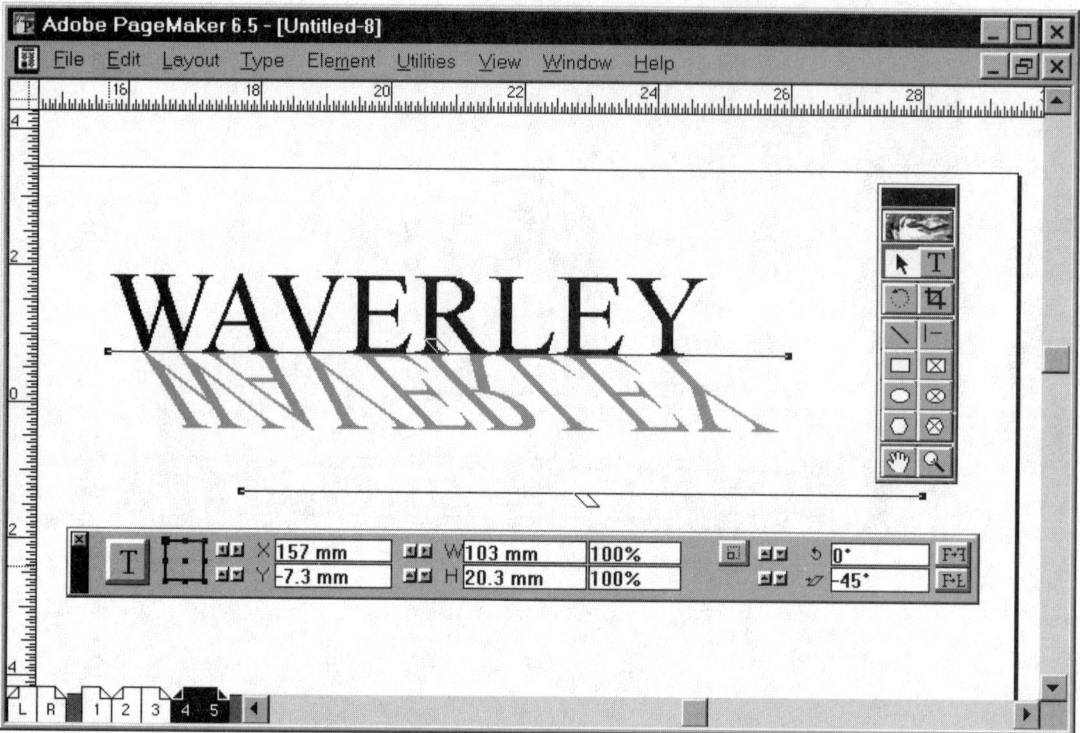

In the above example the following steps were taken:

1. The text block was selected, then **Copy** and **Paste** (from the Edit menu) were chosen.
2. The copy was vertically reflected using the icon in the Control palette.
3. It was then skewed minus 45 degrees about its top left corner.
4. A 30% grey colour was applied using the Colour palette (see Chapter 12).
5. The transformed element was positioned accordingly.

Rotating with the Control Palette

Rotation only applies to PageMaker versions 6 and higher. In previous versions it is possible to rotate in 90 degree increments.

1 Make sure the Control palette is active (**Window** menu).

2 Select the element for rotation.

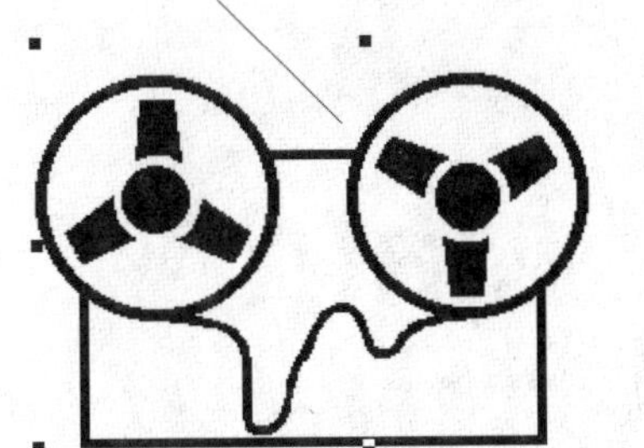

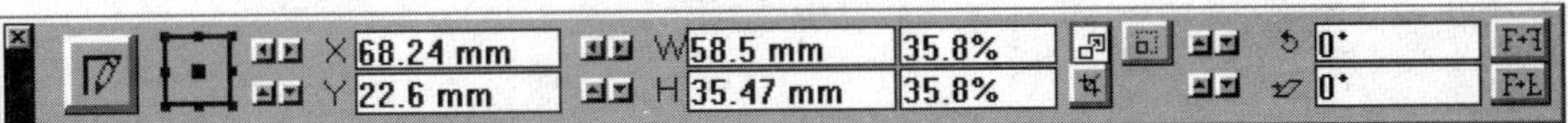

3 Choose the reference point (in this example we shall rotate the object about its centre).

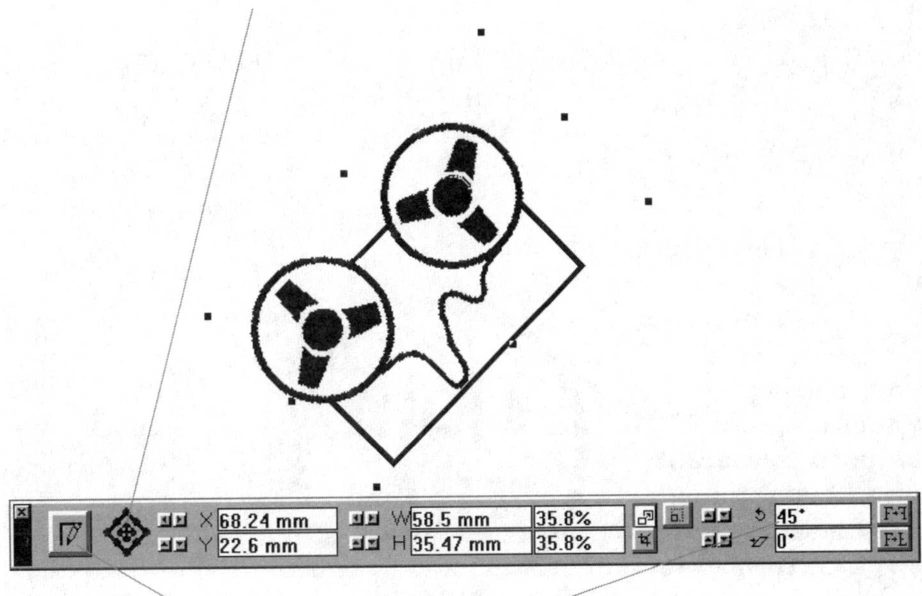

4 Enter the angle of rotation and then click the **Apply** button.

Locking Elements v6 and above

If you have PageMaker version 6 or above then you can use the Lock Position feature to fix elements in a certain position on the page.

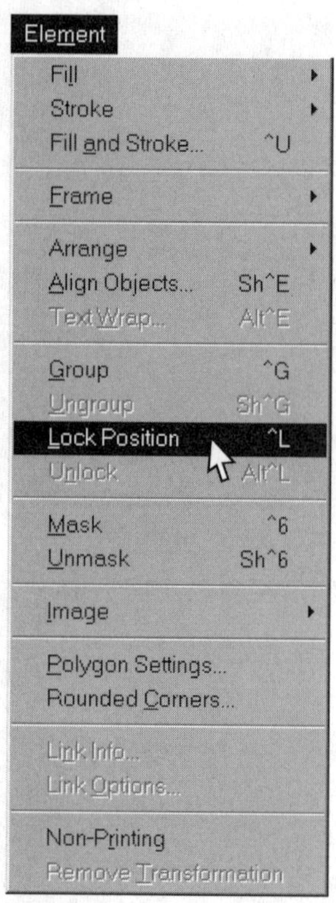

1. Select the elements to be locked.
2. Choose **Lock Position** from the **Element** menu (**Arrange** menu in V6).

The elements are now immovable. If you want to change their position or size, or if you want to delete them, then you must firstly select them, then choose **Unlock** from the Element menu (Arrange menu in V6).

The best way to protect an element if you're using PageMaker 5 or below is to place it on a Master page, or use PS-Group (from the Utilities/Aldus Additions menu) to attach it to something else.

If you try to move a locked shape your Mouse pointer turns into a padlock icon (PageMaker 6.5). In PageMaker 6 the object's handles are grey rather than black.

Chapter Seven

Importing Text

This chapter shows you how to import text files prepared in another package such as a word-processor. Once it has been brought in, the text behaves exactly as if it was created with PageMaker.

Covers

Placing Text

This is exactly the same as importing graphics:

1 Choose **Place** from the **File** menu. The Place dialog box will appear.

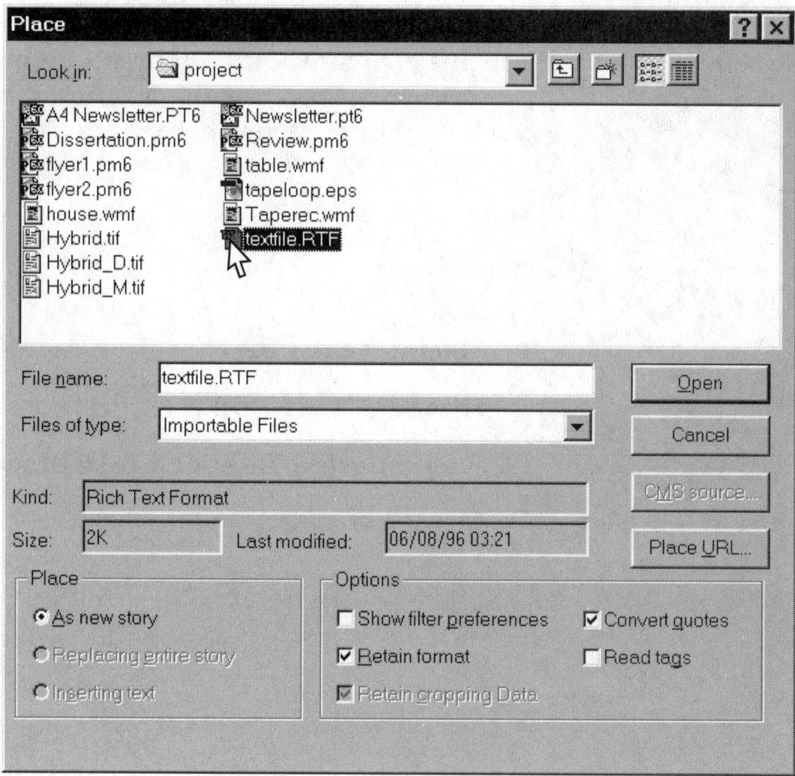

2 Locate the file to be placed by using the directory box or by typing the path in the File name box.

3 Either enter the file name or select the required file from the directory box and click **Open**.

4 PageMaker will return to layout view – your pointer will be a loaded text icon. Click somewhere inside the page margins (or where you wish the top-left corner of the text block to be). The text will flow onto the page.

Text Place symbol (loaded icon)

When importing text, PageMaker only ever works with its own private copy of the original file. This allows you to freely edit the placed text without disturbing the source document.

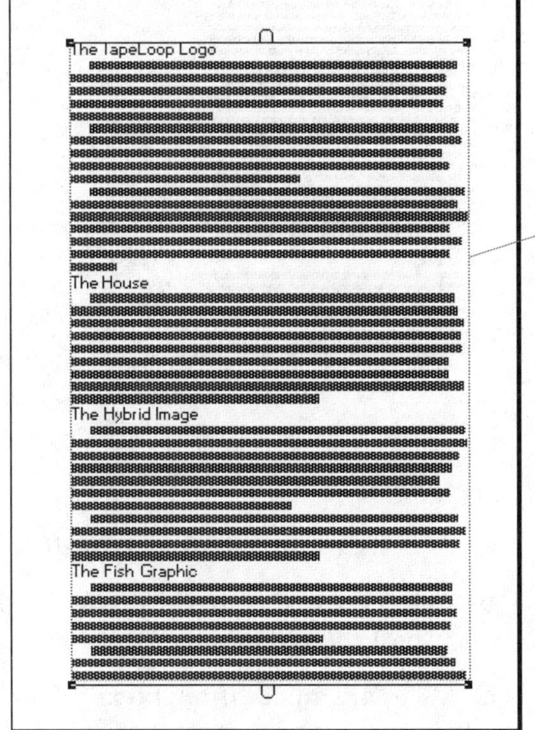

The text will normally flow within the page margins.

If you click and drag with the loaded text icon you can pre-draw the text box into which the story will be placed.

Threaded Text

A small red triangle in the lower windowshade handle indicates that there is more text than can be currently displayed in the text box.

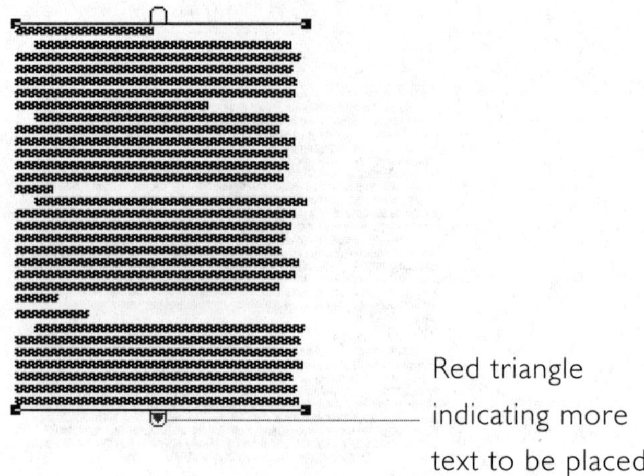

To remedy this you can:

a) Increase the block size by dragging on a handle.

b) Decrease the size of the text using the Control palette or Type menu.

c) Create an additional text box (or boxes) into which the story may be continued (the next section explains how to do this).

To Thread Text Into Another Block

1. Click once directly on the red triangle using the pointer tool. The pointer will turn into the loaded text icon once more, giving you the opportunity to place a second text block.

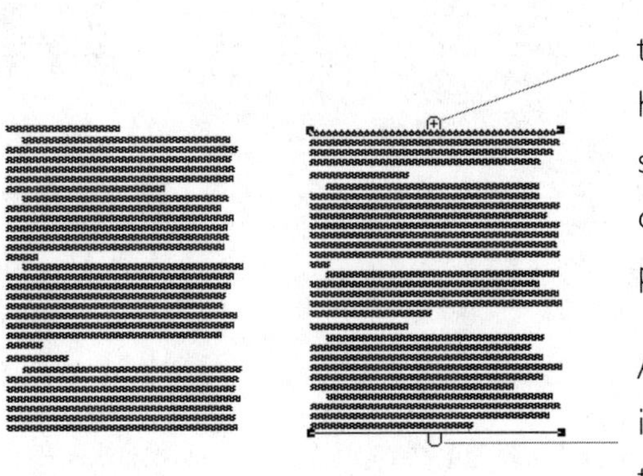

The small + symbol in the top windowshade handle indicates that the story has been continued from a previous block of text

An empty handle indicates the end of the story

2. Click to place the second block. There is still only one story, but it is now threaded through two text blocks.

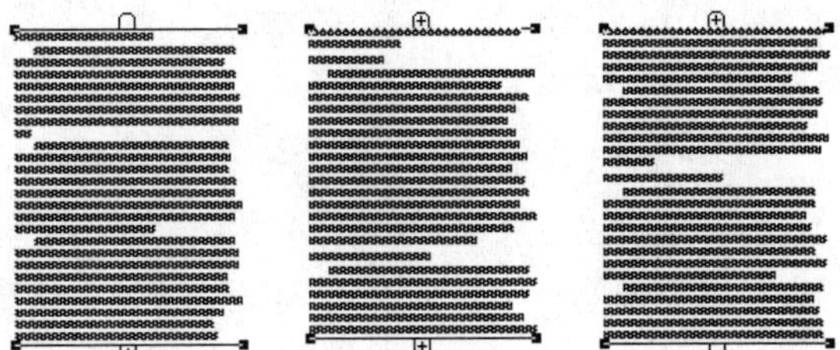

You can use this technique to thread a story through three or more text blocks. The + symbols in the windowshade handles remind you that the blocks are linked.

Selecting with the Text Tool

1. Click anywhere inside a block with the text tool.

2. Choose **Select All** from the **Edit** menu. The text in all of the threaded blocks will be selected.

Manipulating Threaded Text Blocks

To change the proportion of text held by any of a number of threaded text blocks, drag up or down on the windowshade handles.

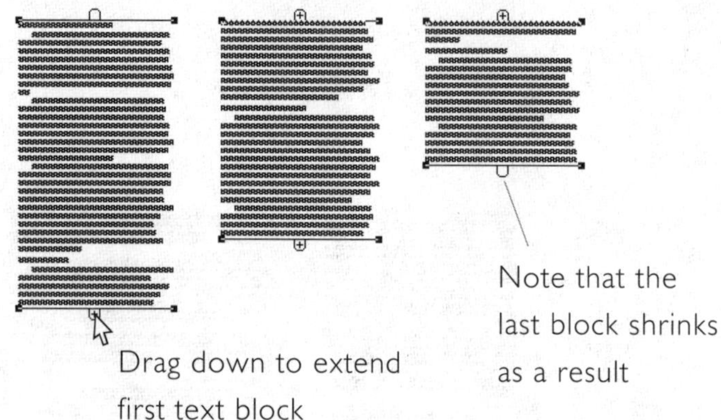

Note that the last block shrinks as a result

As long as these blocks are linked by threaded text, changing one will affect the others.

Closing a Text Block

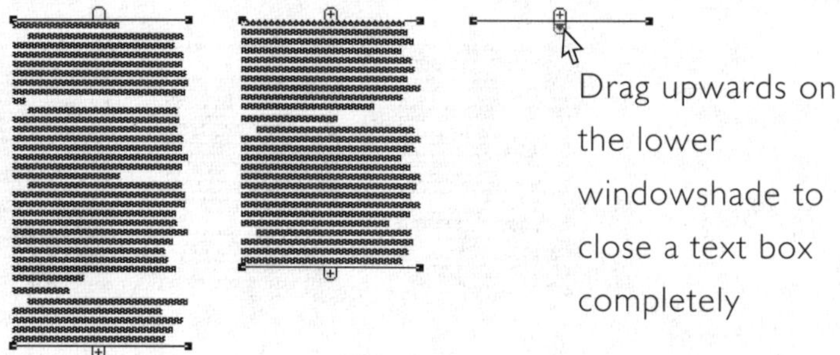

Drag upwards on the lower windowshade to close a text box completely

If you completely close a threaded text block (by dragging on a handle with the pointer tool), the text itself will not be destroyed – instead it will flow into the next block.

If the closed block was the last in the story, the previous block will contain a red triangle in its lower windowshade handle, giving you the chance to re-place the text.

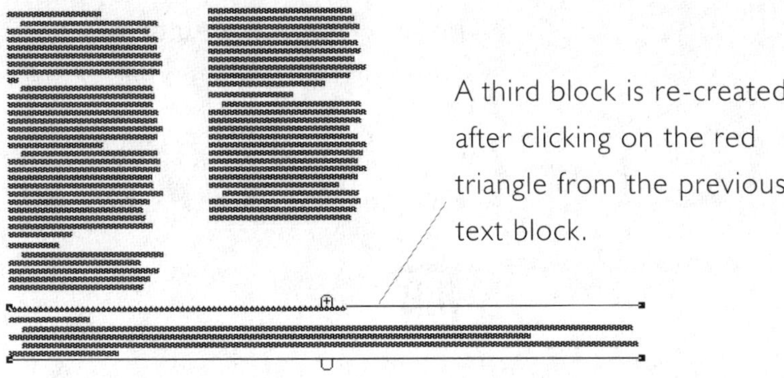

A third block is re-created after clicking on the red triangle from the previous text block.

Text is often threaded through blocks on consecutive pages.

You can reflow text at any point:

1. Click on a + sign on one of the existing blocks. The loaded text icon will appear, which gives you the opportunity to place the text from that point onwards in the story (note this will affect later text blocks which currently form part of the story).

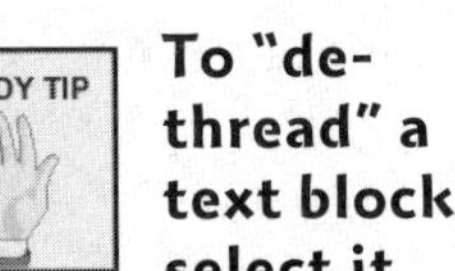

To "de-thread" a text block, select it with the pointer tool, choose Cut (Edit menu), then Paste. The block will return as an independent text element.

2. Click or click-drag to place the remaining text. You can abort this action by clicking on the pointer tool.

Summary

A complete *story* may be imported using the Place command, and may occupy several threaded text blocks.

A text block has *windowshade* handles, which give an indication as to how the text is threaded.

An empty windowshade handle denotes the end of a story.

A red triangle reminds you that there is more text still to be placed.

A plus sign (+) indicates that the story is continued to/from another existing text block.

Autoflow

1. Make sure that the **Autoflow** option is active (there should be a tick next to its entry on the **Layout** menu).
2. Go to the **File** menu, and place a text file in the normal way. This time your loaded text icon will look like this:

3. Locate the position for the first text block and click once. PageMaker will place this block and then automatically generate all the additional text blocks according to the margins and column guides which are present. New pages will be created if required.

Keyboard Shortcuts

Normal manual textflow (default setting).

Autoflow: hold down the **Control** key.

Semi-automatic flow: hold down **Control** and **Shift** together. With this option you still need to click to position each text block, but it is not necessary to click each red triangle.

Chapter Eight

Master Pages

Master pages offer you a very effective way of setting up and controlling the overall design of your documents. This chapter shows you how they work, and also how to set up regular or irregular text column guides.

Covers

Master Pages

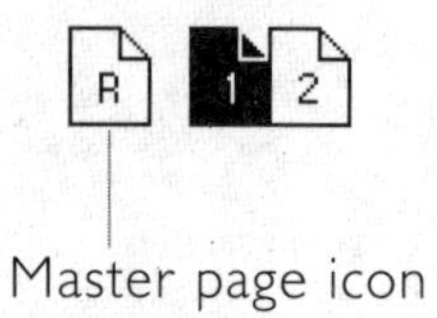

Master page icon

In a single-sided document, the page icon labelled **R** represents the document's Master page. In a double-sided document there are two Master pages labelled **L** and **R** (representing Left and Right pages).

Any elements placed on a Master page will normally appear on all the other pages as a fixed background.

This helps to set up a consistent design for your document.

1. Click on the **R** Master page icon.
2. Add some text or graphic elements to the page.

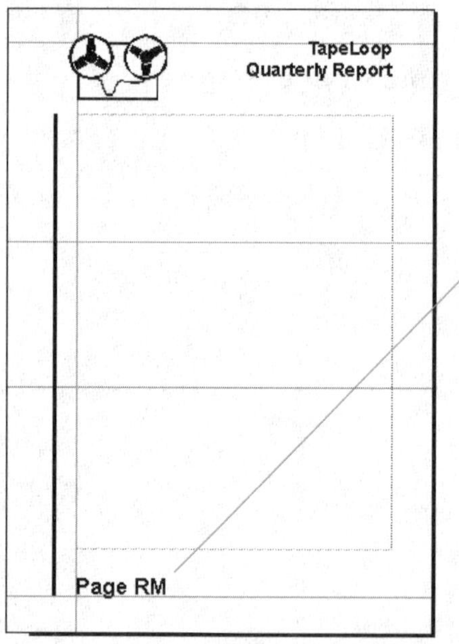

A special page-number character is created by typing Control-Alt-P (or Control-Shift-3 for PageMaker 6 and earlier).
This appears as LM or RM on a Master page, but is replaced by the page number itself on others.

Move to the numbered pages in your document. If your document is single-sided, then all pages will use the Master design as their background. If the document is double-sided, then left and right pages will take their design from the **L** and **R** Master pages respectively.

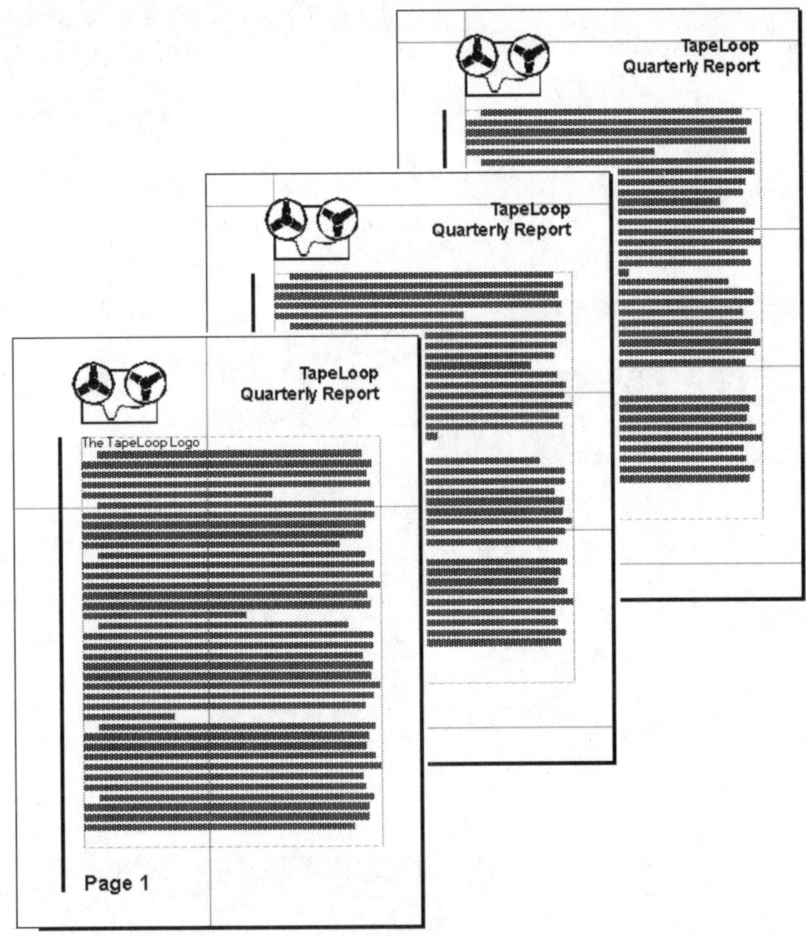

On individual document pages, you can switch off the Master items by clicking on **Display Master Items** in the Layout menu (View menu in V6.5) to remove the tick.

Although Master elements are fixed (non-editable) on other pages, you can edit guidelines from a Master page. If you change them, however, you can reset them to their original state with **Copy Master Guides** (from the Layout menu).

Multiple Master Pages V6 and above

PageMaker version 6 (and above) allows you to work with more than one design for Master pages.

1. Make sure the Master Pages palette is active (**Window** menu).
2. Click here to view the Master Page pop-up menu.

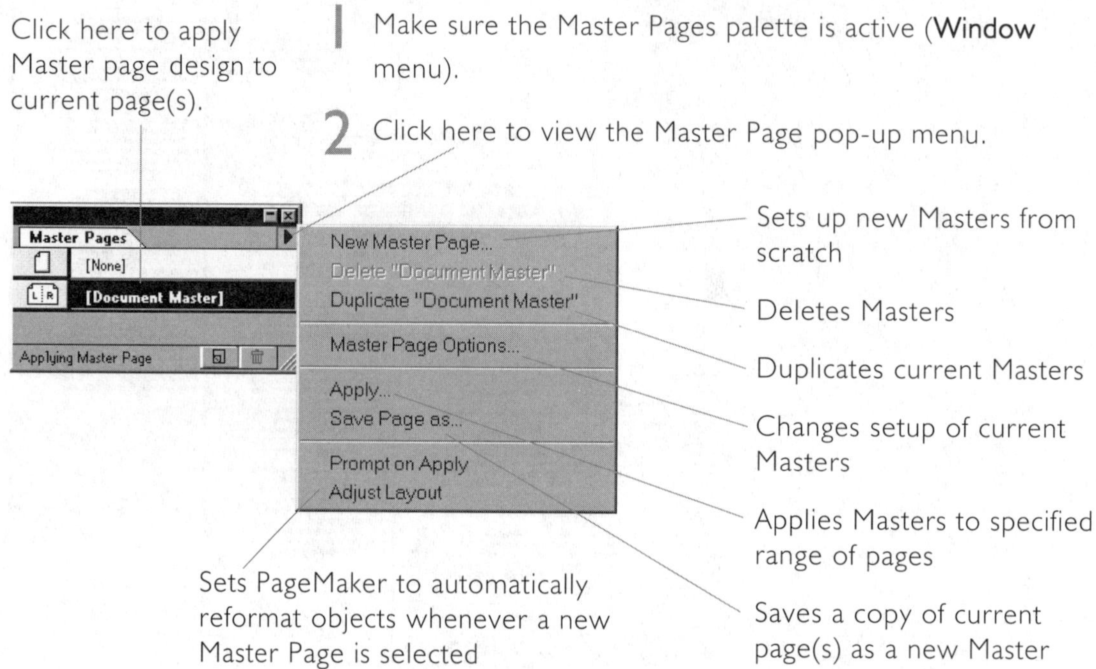

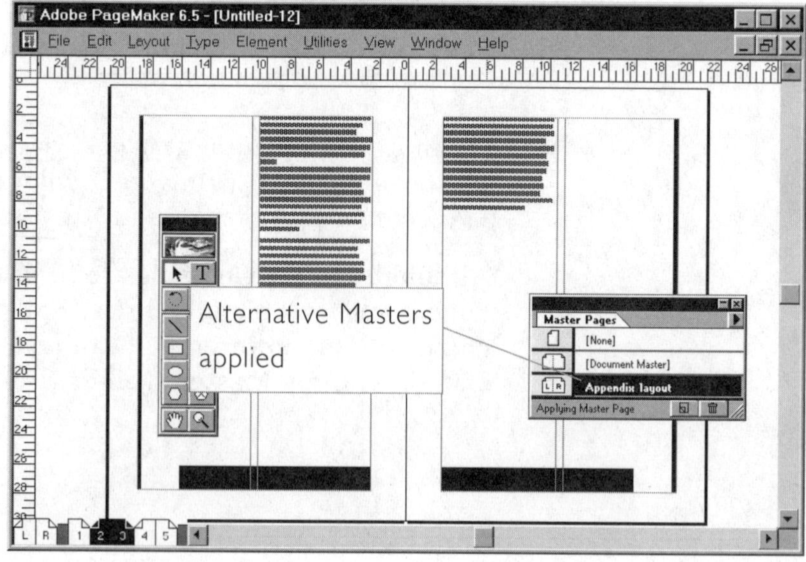

Column Guides

You can instruct PageMaker to automatically format pages with multiple columns of text.

1 Choose **Column Guides...** from the **Layout** menu. The following dialog box will appear:

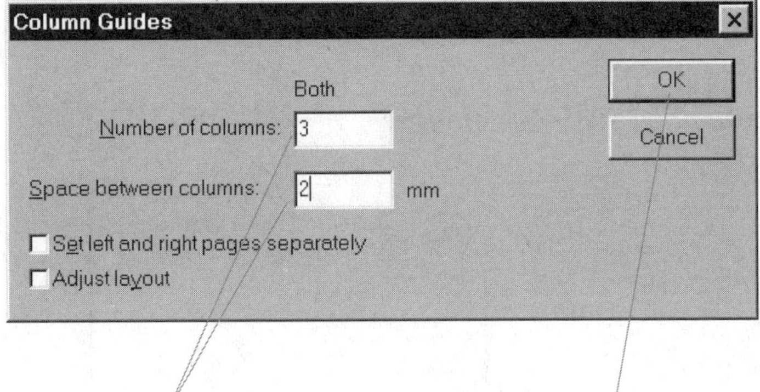

2 Enter the number of columns required and the space between them.

3 Click **OK**.

When you return to the page these dark blue guides will appear. They are magnetic (like other guides). Furthermore, when placing text you will find that it flows into a column rather than completely over the page.

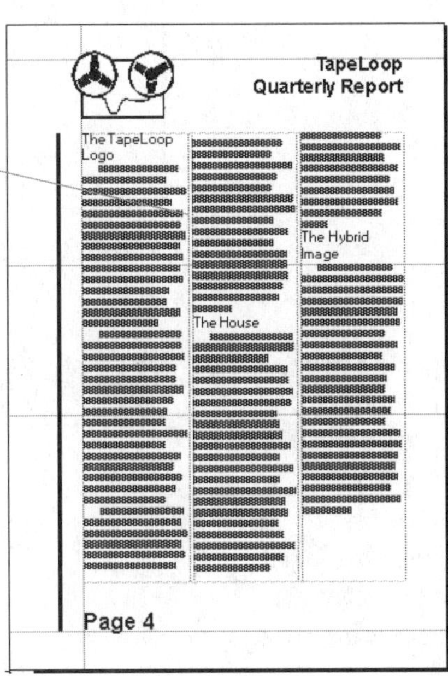

Irregular Columns

1. Create the required number of columns using the previous method. They will initially be of equal width.

2. Manually drag the blue column boundaries left or right using the pointer tool. It may help to have the Control palette active, as you will be able to read off the Y coordinate as you move.

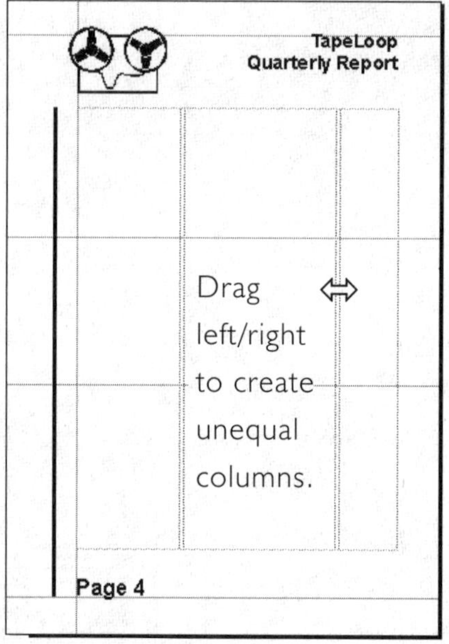

You would normally create the guides and columns on the Master page(s). This lets you set up a consistent layout all the way through the document.

For more help on controlling page layout, see the section on the Grid Manager at the end of the next chapter.

Chapter Nine

Working with Large Amounts of Text

This chapter takes you through a range of PageMaker features designed to make working with large amounts of text much easier. In particular we'll look at controls which save you from too much manual resizing and repositioning of text blocks as you try to shuffle headings and main stories into their correct places.

Covers

Character Specifications

Virtually all the text effects found in the Control palette are also accessible from the Type menu:

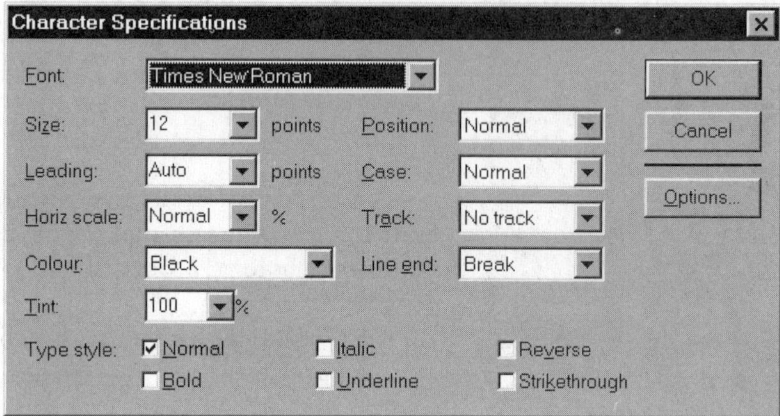

1. Select the text you want to change.
2. Choose **Character** from the **Type** menu. Virtually all the character-level text attributes are present.
3. The **Options** button allows you to customise the SMALL CAPS size as well as Super/Subscript.

Paragraph Specifications

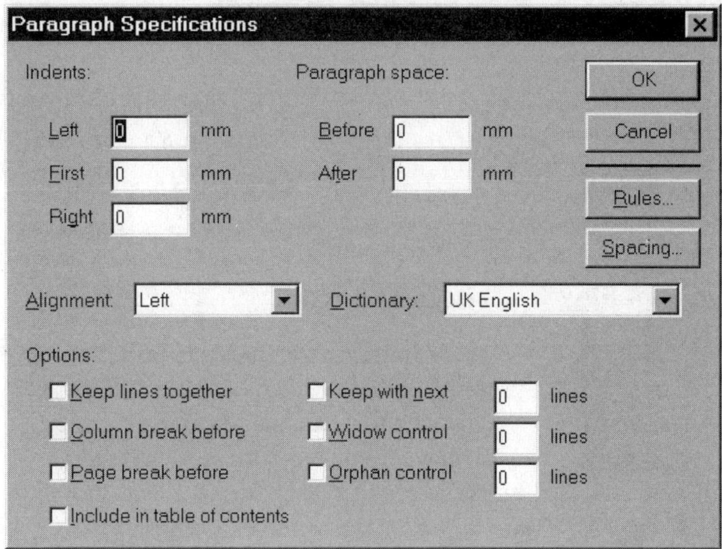

1. Either click an insertion point within the paragraph you want to change, or select multiple paragraphs with the text tool.
2. Choose **Paragraph...** from the **Type** menu.
3. All the paragraph-level attributes can be accessed from this dialog box, e.g. space above/below, indents, alignment. The other attributes will be discussed later in this chapter.

Dictionary

Your PageMaker installation will include UK dictionaries, but you can also use additional dictionary files. These are used for the purpose of spell-checking and hyphenation. From this dialog box you can specify the dictionary to be used for each paragraph.

Widows and Orphans V4 and above

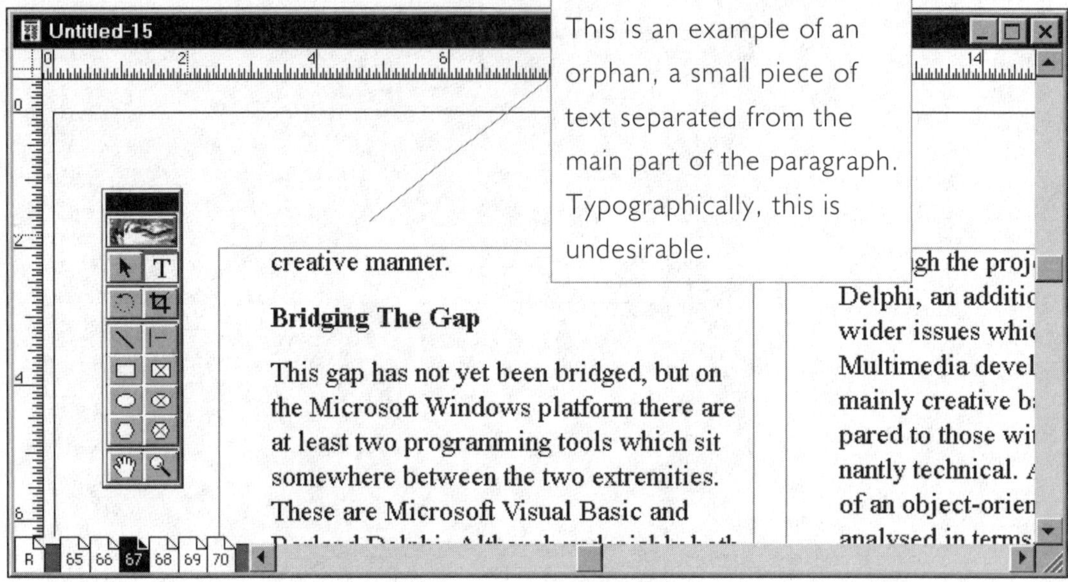

In the example below, we are using the Paragraph Specifications dialog box (select **Paragraph...** from the Type menu) to set orphan size automatically to a minimum of 3 lines:

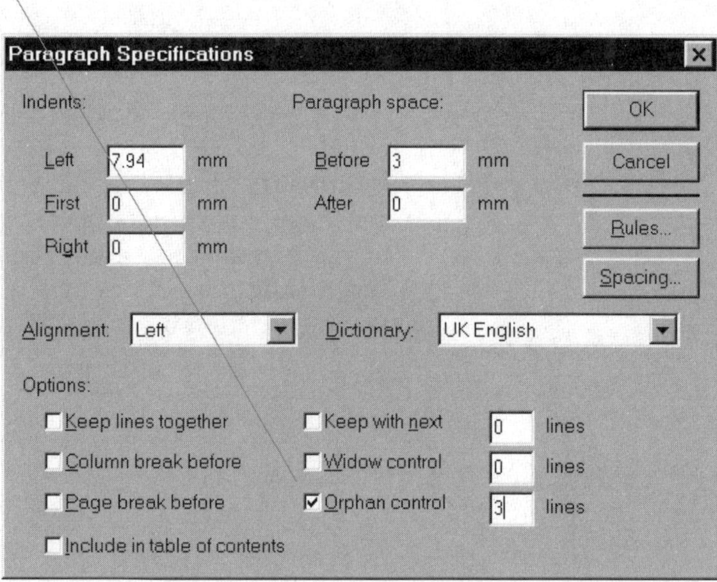

PageMaker will now automatically readjust text blocks so that no orphans of less than 3 lines appear:

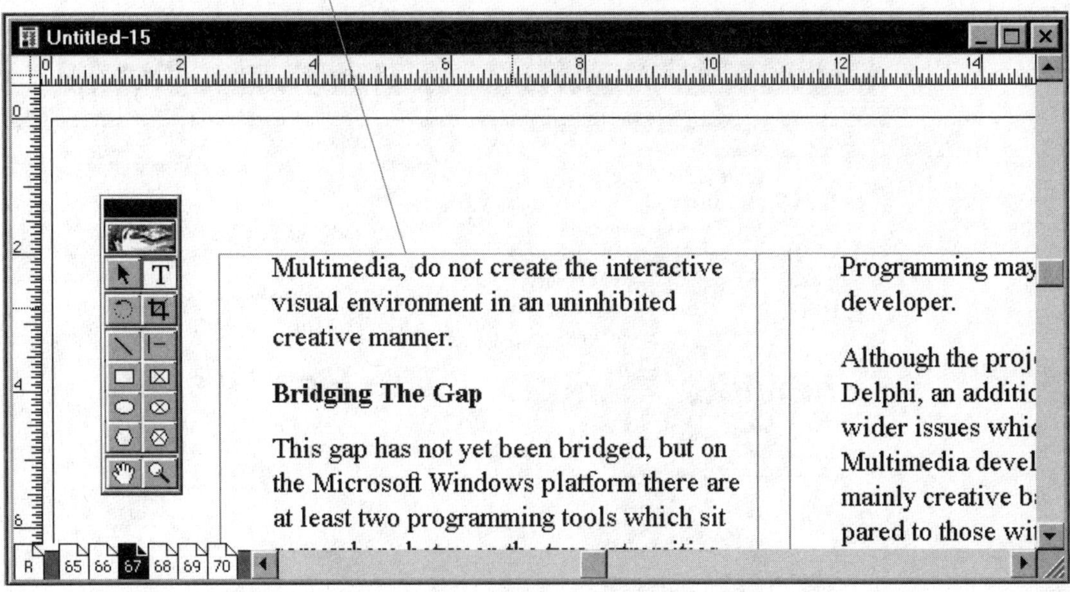

This is an example of a widow, a similar problem where a small piece of text at the beginning of a paragraph is separated from the main text.

Widow control is also available from the Paragraph Specifications dialog box.

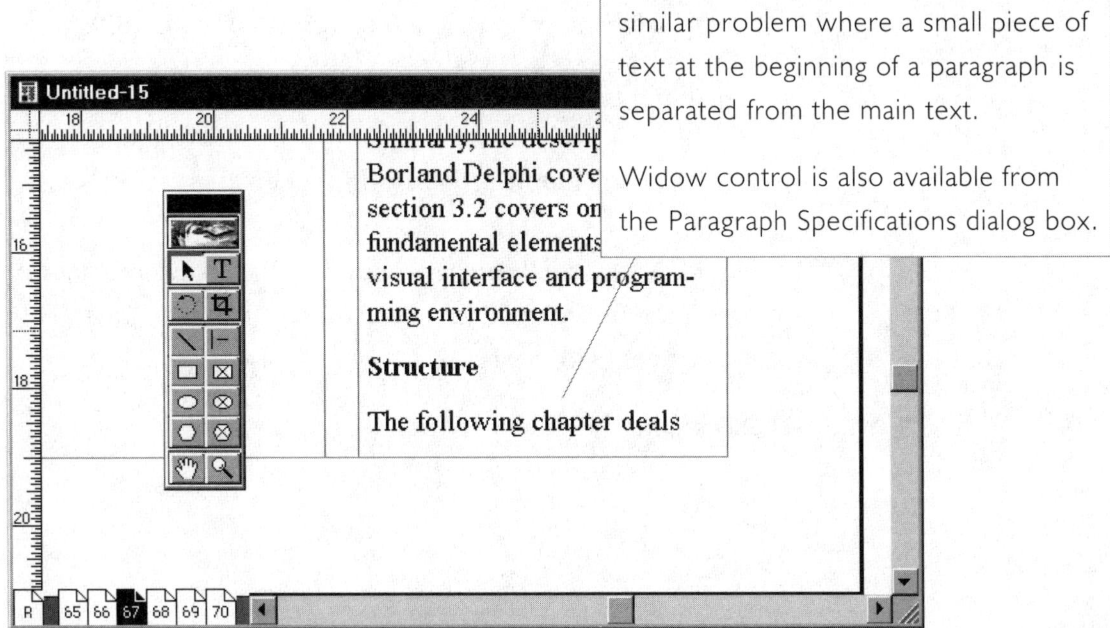

Keep With Next Command V4 and above

Sometimes we want to make sure that a paragraph such as a heading is kept with the next few lines, to avoid the following problem:

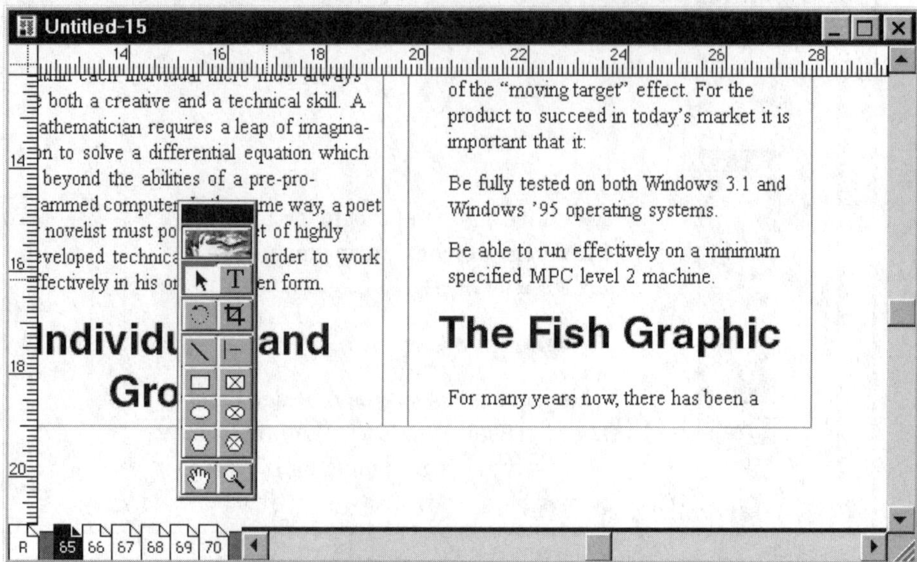

The **Keep with next** feature is used to do this, as follows:

1. Select the heading paragraph.
2. Choose **Paragraph...** from the **Type** menu.
3. To make sure the heading is kept with the next three lines of text (i.e. not broken over two columns or pages), enter "3" in the **Keep with next** box.
4. Click **OK**.

Column and Page Breaks V4 and above

Sometimes we wish to ensure that there is always a column or page break before certain text paragraphs. In the example below we have set all three headings to include a column break, so each starts at the top of its own block:

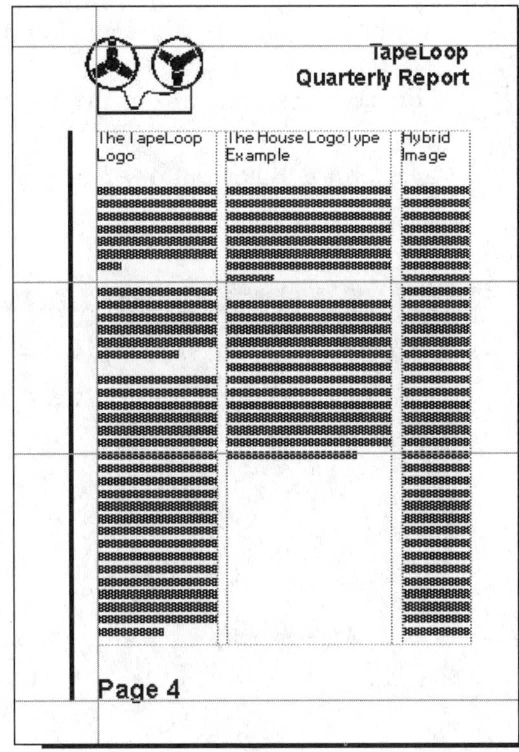

See Chapter 11, "Style Sheets", for a more automatic way of setting these attributes to multiple headings.

1. Select the heading paragraph.
2. Choose **Paragraph...** from the **Type** menu.
3. Set **Column break before**.
4. Click **OK**.
5. Repeat for the other headings. From now on, no matter how you move or edit the text, PageMaker will always adjust the blocks so that each heading appears at the top of a column.

Paragraph Rules V4 and above

Paragraph rules are lines directly above or below a paragraph. Unlike normal horizontal lines, they are attached to the text itself.

Creating

1 Select the required paragraph with the text tool.

2 Choose **Paragraph...** from the **Type** menu.

3 Click on the **Rules** button. Enter the required details in the dialog box which appears:

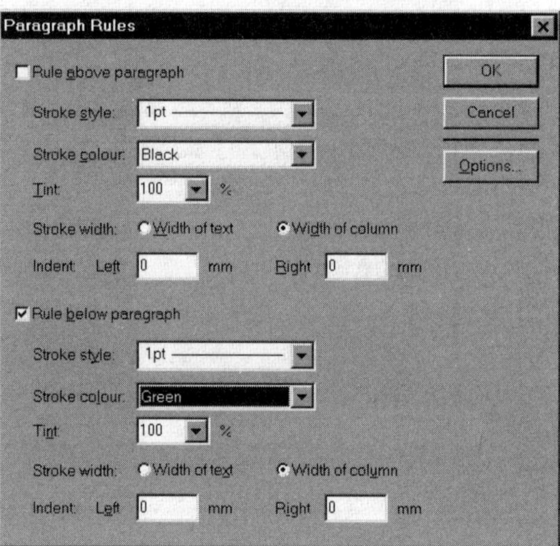

Here we are setting a 1-point green line to appear below the selected paragraph.

Although the measurement system is currently millimetres, you can enter other units into most dialog boxes. Points and picas are specified as in the following example: 3p6 represents 3 picas and 6 points (note 1 pica = 12 points).

4 Clicking on the **Options** button will allow you to specify how far above/below the baseline the rule should appear:

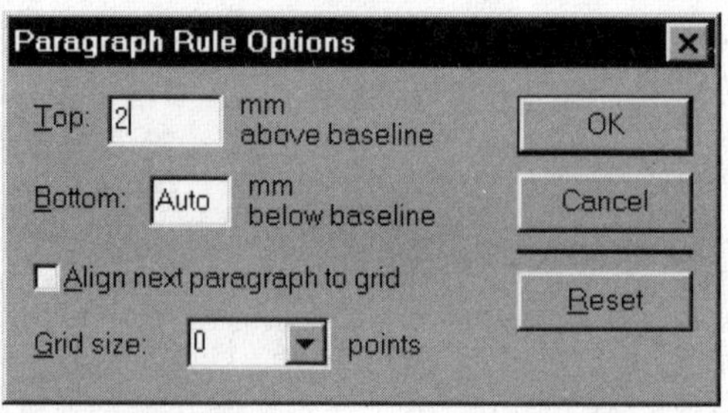

5 Click **OK** in each of the open dialog boxes to set the rules.

In the following example, these paragraph settings have been applied to the three centred headings:

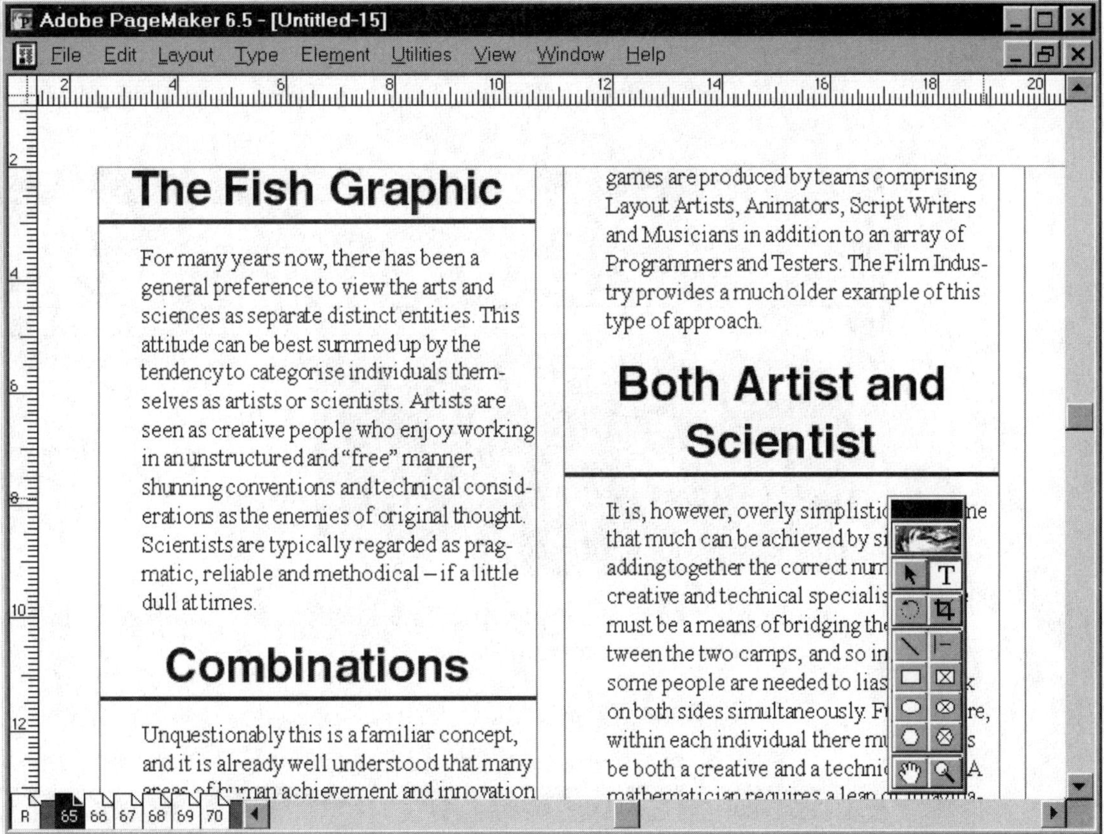

If this text is moved or edited, the paragraph rules will move too, so that they are always in the correct position.

Usually, paragraph rules are used as part of a style definition. See Chapter 11, "Style Sheets", for more information.

Indents/Tabs

When entering text, the **Tab** key will move the insertion point to the next specified horizontal tab position. It is useful to be able to specify your own tabulation:

1. Select some text in which the Tab key has been used.

2. Choose **Indents/Tabs...** from the **Type** menu. The following ruler will appear in position above the text:

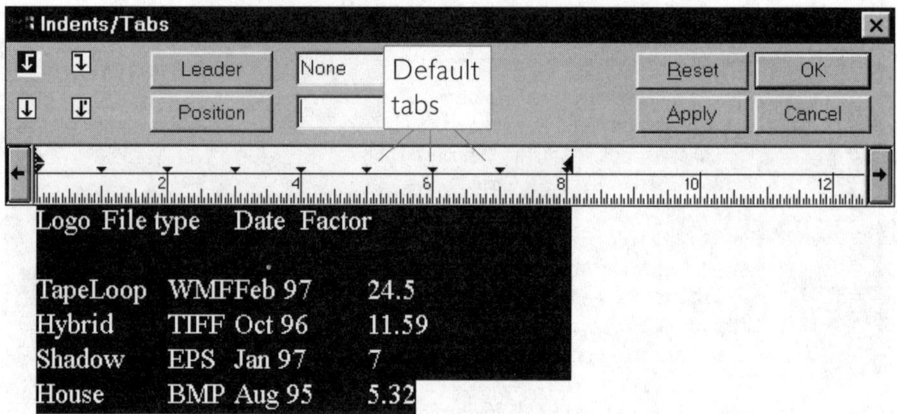

In the above example, the **Tab** key had been pressed once in between each item.

3. Click once above the ruler to create your own tab marker. You can then select the type of tab from the four tab icons.

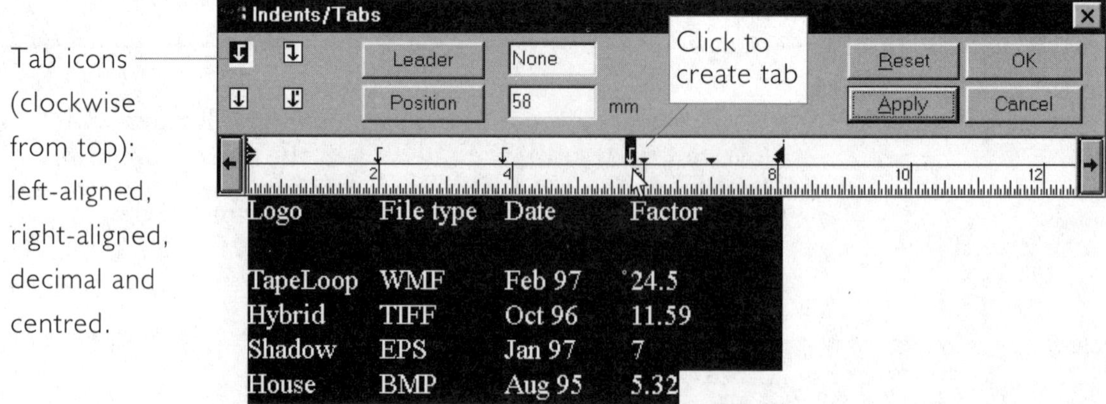

4. To see changes in the text without quitting the dialog box, click the **Apply** button.

...cont'd

In the previous example we created three left-aligned tabs at 4 cm intervals. To move a tab, simply drag its icon left or right. To delete a tab drag it back down into the ruler (it will disappear).

Setting Leaders

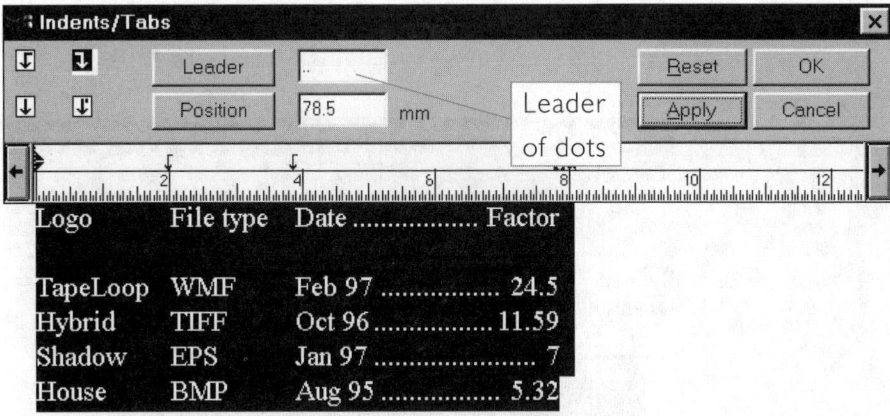

1. Select a tab by clicking directly on it.
2. Choose a suitable symbol from the **Leader** pop-up menu.
3. Click **Apply**.

In the above example, we have set a leader of dots which fill the space leading up to the third tab position.

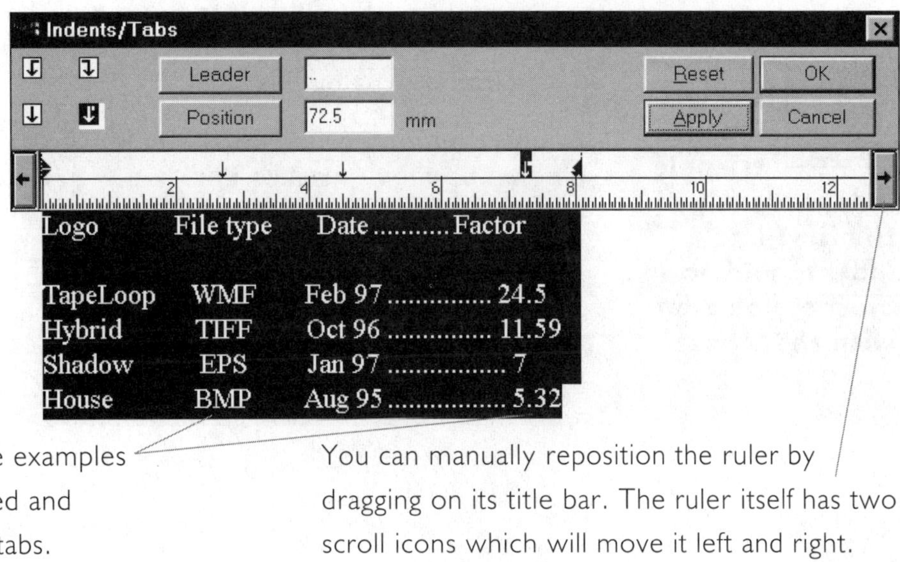

Here are examples of centred and decimal tabs.

You can manually reposition the ruler by dragging on its title bar. The ruler itself has two scroll icons which will move it left and right.

Setting Indents

The larger triangles at the sides of the ruler represent the left and right indents. (The left indent is split into first and subsequent paragraph lines.) Although these are normally controlled numerically in the Paragraph Specifications dialog box, you can move them here manually by dragging.

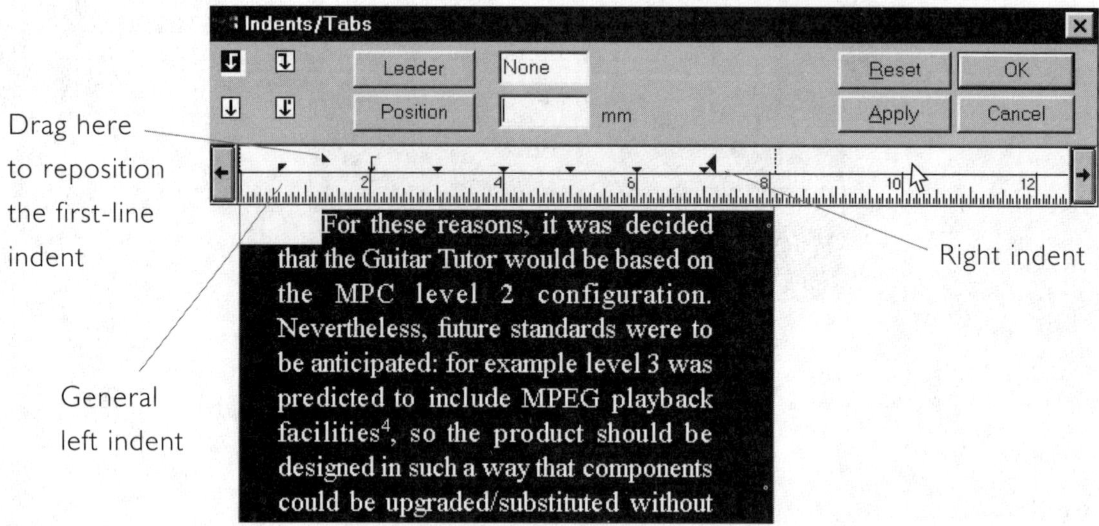
Indents/Tabs
Leader
None
Reset
OK
Position
mm
Apply
Cancel
Drag here to reposition the first-line indent
Right indent
General left indent
For these reasons, it was decided that the Guitar Tutor would be based on the MPC level 2 configuration. Nevertheless, future standards were to be anticipated: for example level 3 was predicted to include MPEG playback facilities4, so the product should be designed in such a way that components could be upgraded/substituted without

In this example we have set the general left indent to 13mm, the first-line indent to 6mm and the right indent to 73mm. These changes will be reflected in the Paragraph Specifications dialog box.

By entering measurements in the box provided, and using the pop-up menu marked **Position**, you can add, delete and move tabs numerically rather than manually.

HANDY TIP

To move the left-indent triangle independently of the first-line indent, hold down Shift as you drag with the Mouse.

Hyphenation

Manual hyphenation involves the user typing a special code (Control-hyphen) when entering text. This sets a possible hyphen position within a word.

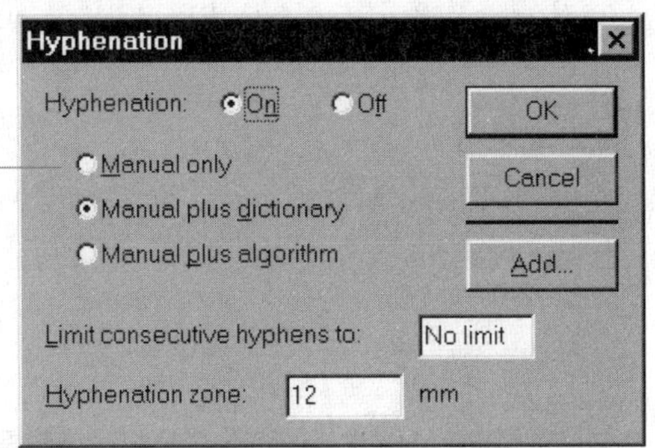

1 Select the text you wish to change with the text tool.

2 Choose **Hyphenation** from the **Type** menu.

As well as switching hyphenation on and off, you can control the degree of hyphenation:

Limit consecutive hyphens to: will allow you to set a limit to the number of consecutive lines which can end with hyphens.

Hyphenation zone: is the width of text at the end of a line which PageMaker will consider for hyphenation.

PageMaker uses a hyphenation dictionary which contains markers within words at places where it is allowable to create a break.

Adding to the Dictionary

1 Select the word.

2 Choose **Hyphenation** from the Type menu and click **Add**.

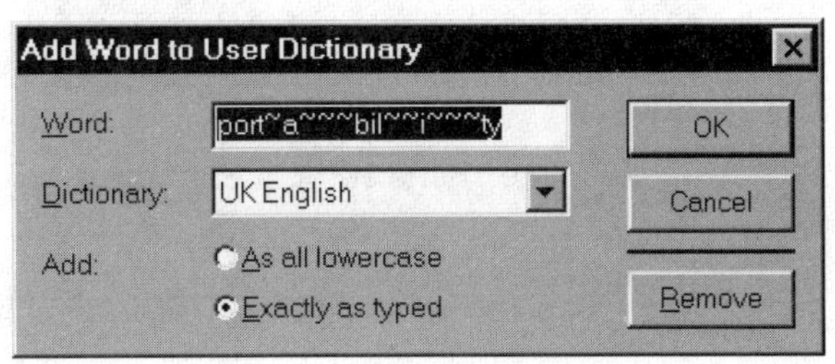

3 Type the word using the tilde (~) to indicate possible hyphens. One tilde represents the most preferential break, two is less preferential and so on.

REMEMBER

If a word is not present in the hyphenation dictionary, PageMaker will use an intelligent algorithm to "guess" suitable positions for hyphens.

Inline Graphics V4 and above

These are graphic elements which (like paragraph rules) are treated as part of a text block.

HANDY TIP

This is a very useful technique if you want an illustration to be kept with a certain piece of text even after radical editing at later stages.

Placing

1. With the text tool, place an insertion point where you want the graphic to appear.
2. Choose **Place** from the **File** menu.

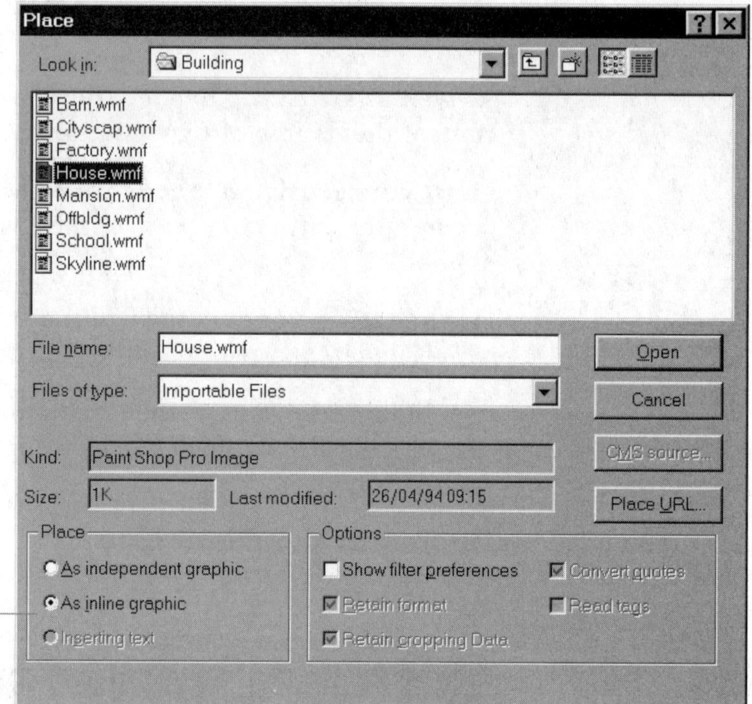

Note the option to place as an inline graphic

3. Choose the graphic file, making sure the option to place as an inline graphic is active. If it is greyed out there is no insertion point active in your document, so repeat steps 1-2.
4. Click **Open**. The graphic will appear as part of the text. It can still be resized with the pointer tool, but otherwise it's treated as a large text character.

Inline Graphic Example

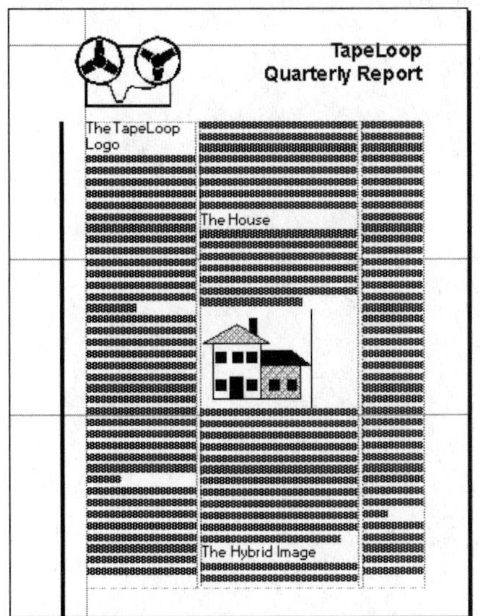

Note the example on the left. A paragraph at the top of the first column was deleted to produce the example on the right. Note how the inline graphic moves with the text...

Note that text effects such as centre alignment are also available for inline graphics.

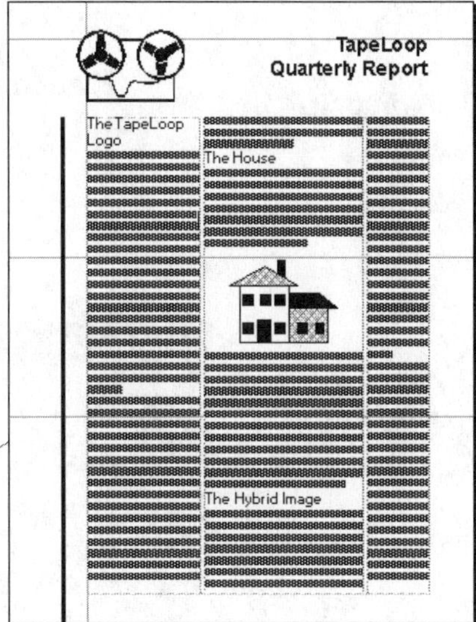

Changing an Inline Graphic to a Normal Graphic

1. Select the element with the Pointer tool.
2. From the **Edit** menu, choose **Cut**, then **Paste**.

The graphic will return as a normal element, free from the text block.

Changing a Normal Graphic to an Inline Graphic

1. Select the element with the Pointer tool.
2. Choose **Cut** from the **Edit** menu.
3. Select the Text tool and create an insertion point at the desired location within a text block.
4. Choose **Paste**.

The graphic will appear as part of the text block.

Text Wrap

This graphic has no wrap selected.

This is used to prevent graphics and text from overlapping each other. It is applied to a graphic element to create a text-exclusion boundary.

Regular Wrap

1. Select the graphic.
2. Choose **Text Wrap...** from the **Element** menu. The following dialog box will appear:

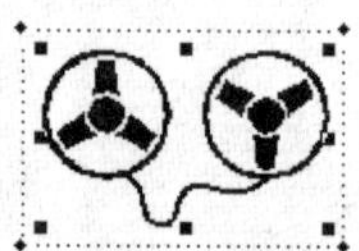

This graphic has a text-wrap boundary (represented by the dotted line).

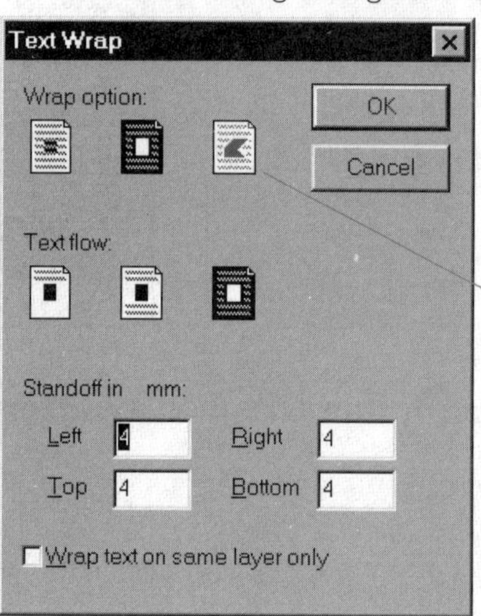

The three wrap options (from left to right) are:

- No wrap (normal)
- Regular wrap
- Irregular wrap

You can also choose whether you want text to flow above, above and below, or all around the graphic element.

3. Currently, **No wrap** is selected. Click on the second option, which allows text to wrap around a regular object.
4. Select the type of text flow required, usually the third option (text flowing all around the graphic).
5. Enter the standoff distance for each side. Click **OK**.

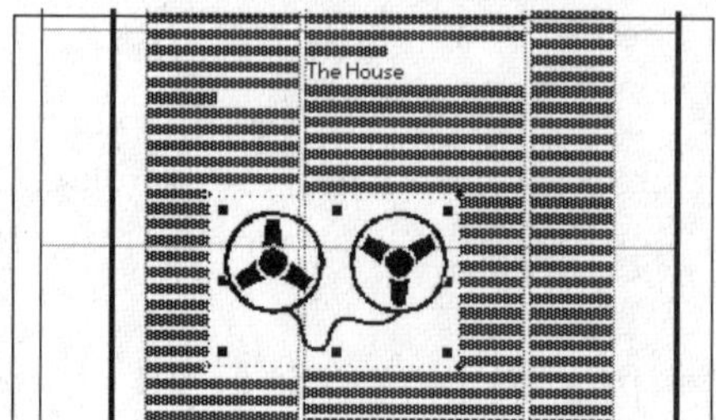

If you now move the graphic over some text, the text will reflow around it at the specified distance.

Irregular Wrap

You can create an irregular text wrap by manually editing the exclusion zone around a regularly wrapped graphic.

1. As before, create a regular wrap around the graphic.

2. Zoom in so that you can see the dotted line clearly. The line joins small diamond-shaped handles, which can be manually dragged about with the pointer tool.

To create a new "handle", click on a vacant part of the dotted line.

To edit the boundary into an irregular shape, drag one of the handles.

To delete a handle, simply drag it into its neighbour.

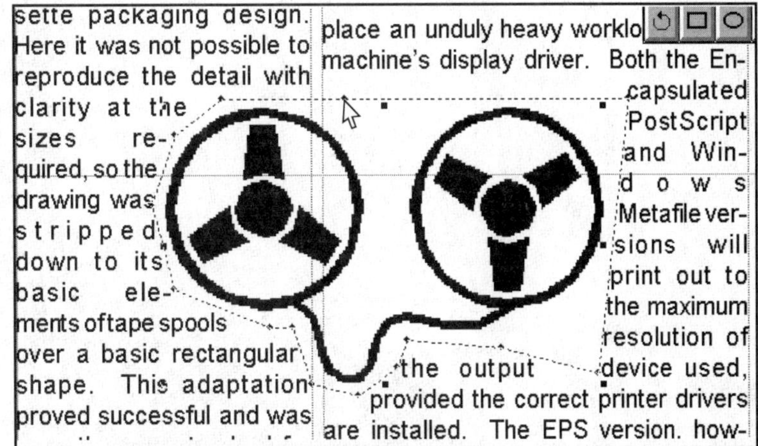

If screen redraw is slow during editing of the boundary, hold down the spacebar. The text will not reflow until you release.

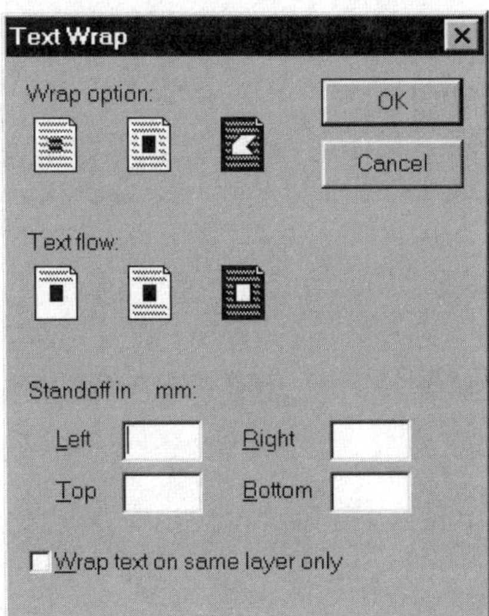

If you now return to the Text Wrap dialog box, you will see that the irregular wrap option (previously greyed out), is now active.

The Grid Manager V6.5

The Grid Manager is one of the most useful Plug-ins to ship with PageMaker version 6.5. It helps you to set up and easily access regular systems of guidlines from any document.

1 Choose **Grid Manager** from the **Utilities** menu, **Plug-ins** submenu...

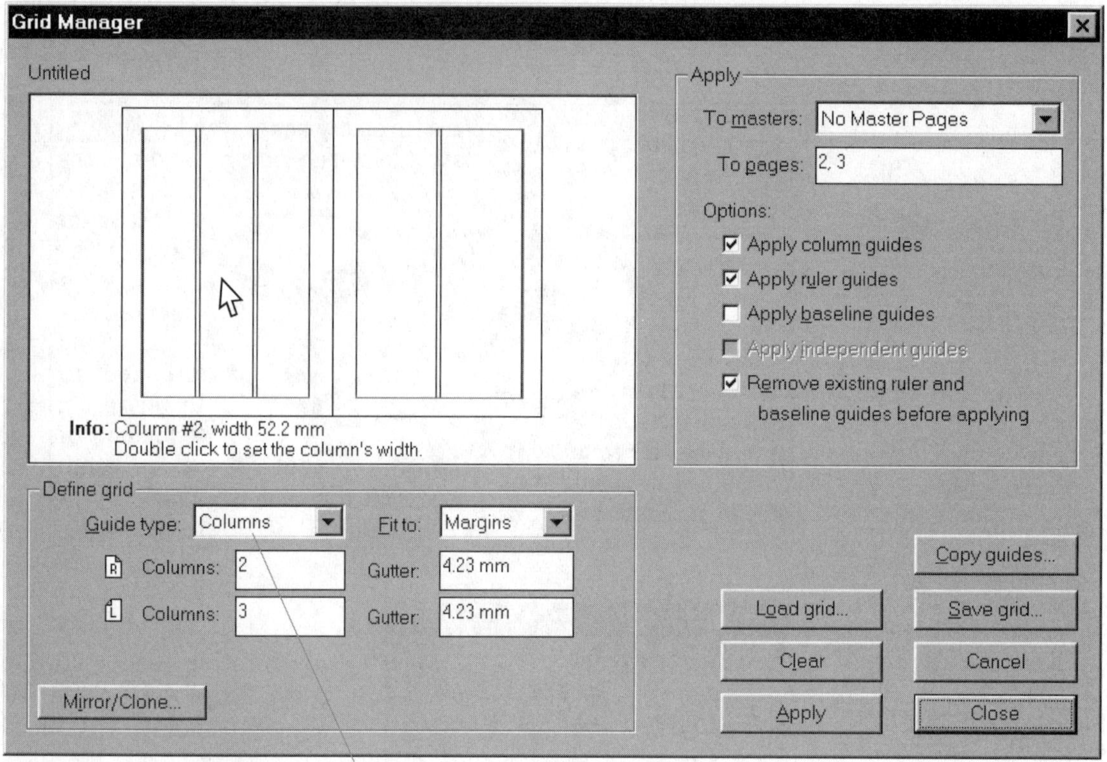

Grid Manager

Untitled

Info: Column #2, width 52.2 mm
Double click to set the column's width.

Apply
To masters: No Master Pages
To pages: 2, 3
Options:
Apply column guides
Apply ruler guides
Apply baseline guides
Apply independent guides
Remove existing ruler and baseline guides before applying

Define grid
Guide type: Columns
Fit to: Margins
R Columns: 2 Gutter: 4.23 mm
L Columns: 3 Gutter: 4.23 mm
Mirror/Clone...

Copy guides...
Load grid... Save grid...
Clear Cancel
Apply Close

Although PageMaker version 6 doesn't have a Grid Manager, it does contain a similar Plug-in called the Guide Manager.

2 Choose the Guide type. You can divide your page into Columns, set up Vertical and Horizontal rules, or a Baseline grid. A Baseline grid sets horizontal guides at regular intervals, matching the baseline of your body text.

3 Enter the appropriate settings, then use either the **Apply** button, or Save to save your settings to a Guides file.

Chapter Ten

The Story Editor V4 and above

The Story Editor offers you a different view of the text contained in your document. It provides a quick way of editing and navigating around large stories, as well as word-processing features such as a Spelling Checker and Search/Replace facilities.

Covers

Using the Story Editor

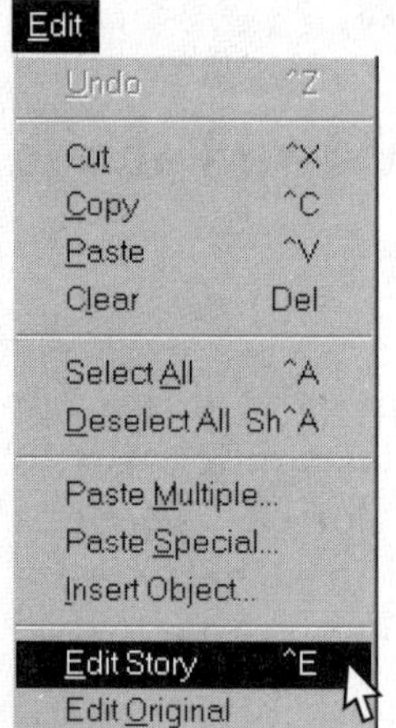

The Story Editor provides you with a simplified view of text, with an entire story in one window (even if it is split into many text blocks in normal layout view).

Starting Up

1. Select the text to be edited.
2. Choose **Edit Story** from the **Edit** menu.

For convenience and fast editing purposes, the story is displayed in one font and one size. The subtler text effects are not shown.

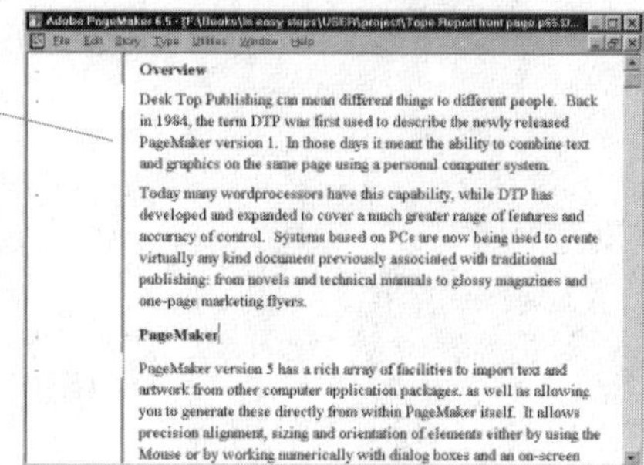

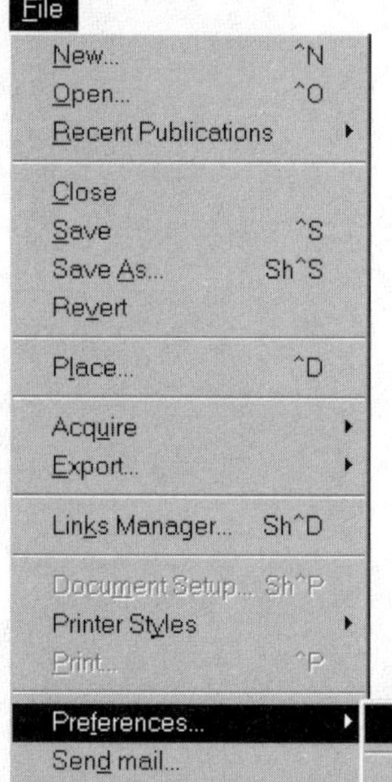

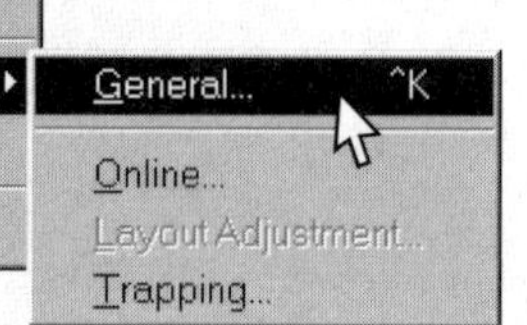

If you choose Preferences from the File menu, and click on the More button, you will be able to change the Story Editor font and point size.

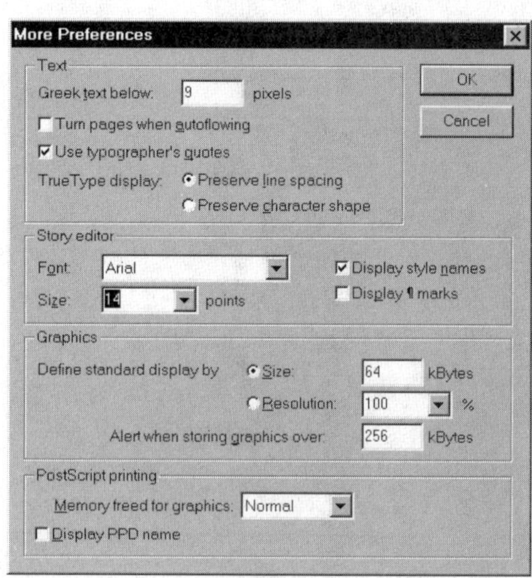

You can also call up the Preferences dialog by double-clicking directly on the pointer tool.

The Spelling Checker

PageMaker allows you to take some of the pain out of proof-reading your text by providing a Spelling Checker which will query any word it finds that does not match an entry in its extensive dictionary. To use this feature, open the Story Editor as described opposite, then do the following:

REMEMBER **The dictionary PageMaker uses will depend on the setting made in the Paragraph Specifications dialog box (select Paragraph... from the Type menu).**

1 Choose **Spelling...** from the **Utilities** menu. The following dialog box will appear:

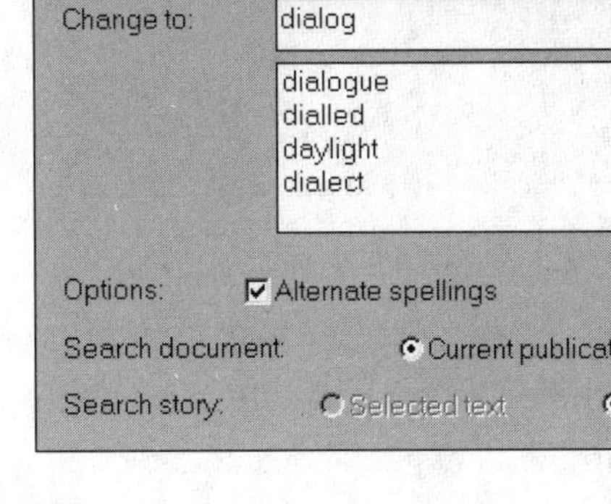

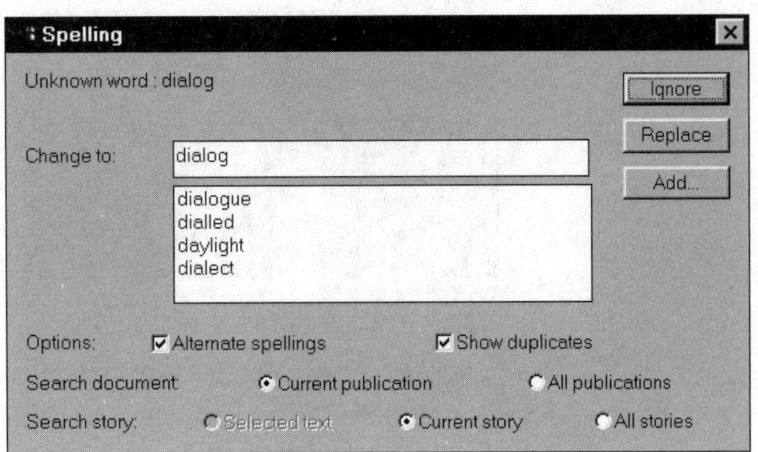

HANDY TIP **Another way to call up the Story Editor is to triple-click on a text block with the pointer tool.**

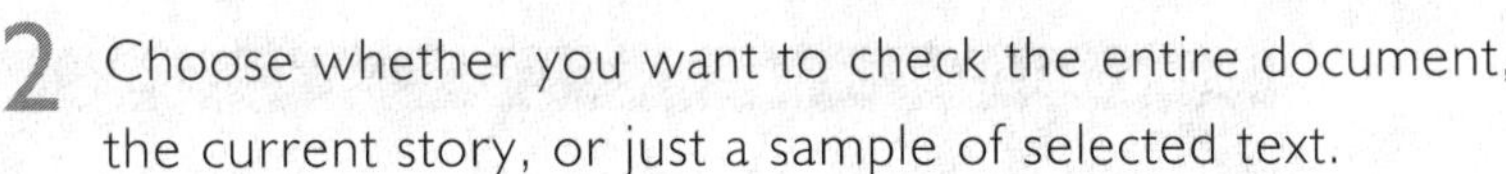

2 Choose whether you want to check the entire document, the current story, or just a sample of selected text.

3 Click the **Start** button.

PageMaker will warn you of any words it cannot locate in its dictionary. If the word is indeed incorrect then you have the choice to re-enter it or choose from a selection of closest matches in the dictionary. If the word is correct (e.g. a proper noun) then you can instruct PageMaker either to ignore this occurrence or to add it to the user section of the dictionary.

REMEMBER **PageMaker will also warn you about duplicate words and possible capitalisation errors.**

4 When the spell check is complete, close the Spelling window to return to the main part of the Story Editor.

Find and Change

These are both options in the Utilities menu. You can search a story for specific text or attributes, and automatically replace any instances with different words or effects. From the Story Editor, do the following:

1. Choose **Change...** from the **Utilities** menu.

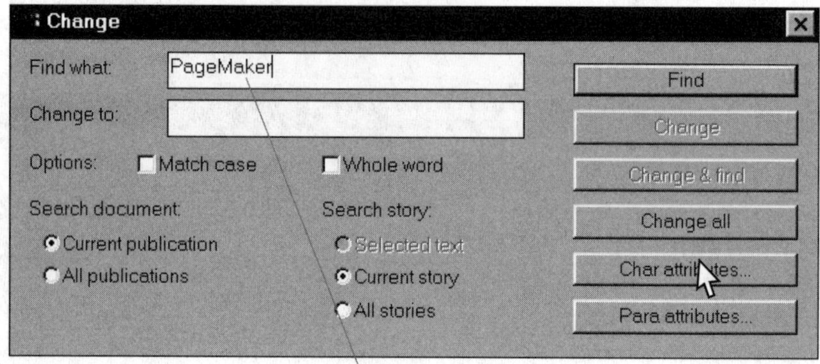

2. You can now enter the search text, and text which will replace this. You can also search/replace on the basis of attributes by clicking one of the Attributes buttons. This example changes all instances of "PageMaker" to bold.

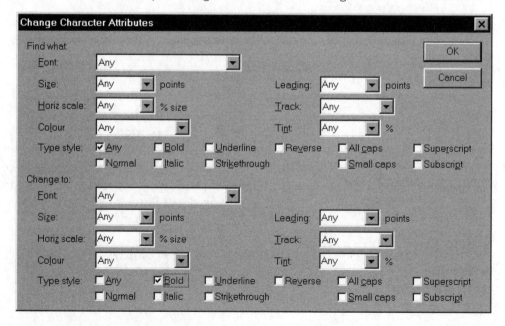

3 You can manually step through the search (using the **Find next** and **Change** buttons) or click on **Change all** to instruct PageMaker to carry out the task automatically.

4 When finished, close the Change window to return to the main Story view. The result can be seen below:

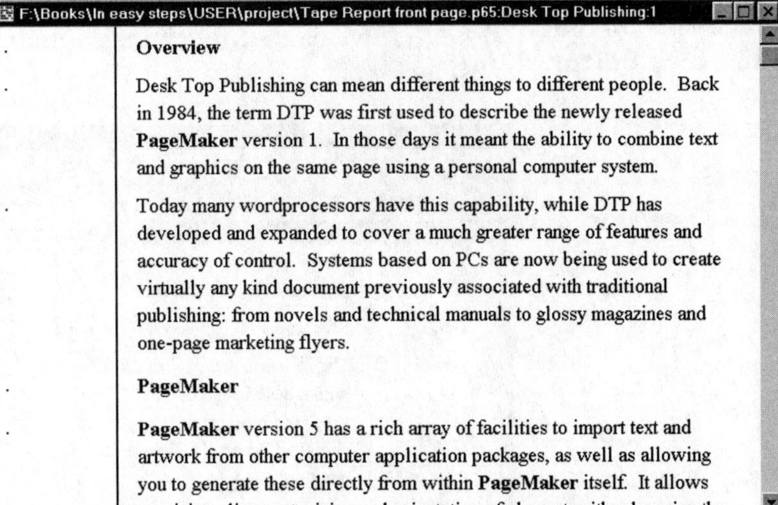
F:\Books\In easy steps\USER\project\Tape Report front page.p65:Desk Top Publishing:1

Overview

Desk Top Publishing can mean different things to different people. Back in 1984, the term DTP was first used to describe the newly released **PageMaker** version 1. In those days it meant the ability to combine text and graphics on the same page using a personal computer system.

Today many wordprocessors have this capability, while DTP has developed and expanded to cover a much greater range of features and accuracy of control. Systems based on PCs are now being used to create virtually any kind document previously associated with traditional publishing: from novels and technical manuals to glossy magazines and one-page marketing flyers.

PageMaker

PageMaker version 5 has a rich array of facilities to import text and artwork from other computer application packages, as well as allowing you to generate these directly from within **PageMaker** itself. It allows precision alignment, sizing and orientation of elements either by using the

HANDY TIP

To find out how to access special characters, go to the Help menu and choose Shortcuts. At the bottom of the window which appears, click on the Special Char button. You can then either view the character shortcuts on screen or print by choosing Print Topic from the Help window's File Menu.

The **Find** function works in exactly the same way. It is also possible to search/replace using metacharacters:

Wildcard character	^?	Registermark symbol	Alt R
Carriage return	^p	Caret	^ ^
Line break	^n	White space	^w
Tab	^t	Thin space	^<
Discretionary (soft) hyphen	^Sh -	Non-breaking space	^ Alt Space
Non-breaking hyphen	^Alt -	En space	^>
Computer-inserted hyphen	^c	Em space	^m
In-line graphic marker	^g	En dash	Alt -
Index marker	^;	Em dash	Alt Sh -
Page # marker	^ Alt P	Non-breaking slash	^Alt /
Bullet	Alt-8	Single open quote	Alt [
Copyright symbol	Alt-G	Single close quote	Alt]
Section marker	Alt 6	Double open quote	Alt Sh {
Paragraph marker	Alt 7	Double close quote	Alt Sh }

(^ means press the Control key, Sh means Shift)

Story and Layout Views

Invoking the Story Editor with no text selected will open up a new story. You will be asked to place this on leaving the Story Editor.

You can return to Layout view (pages and Pasteboard) from the Edit menu, or by closing down the Story window.

In PageMaker you can operate many story windows which can be arranged, minimised, maximised or resized in the normal way.

In the example below we have several documents open simultaneously: their layout windows have been minimised so that we can easily choose which document or story to select.

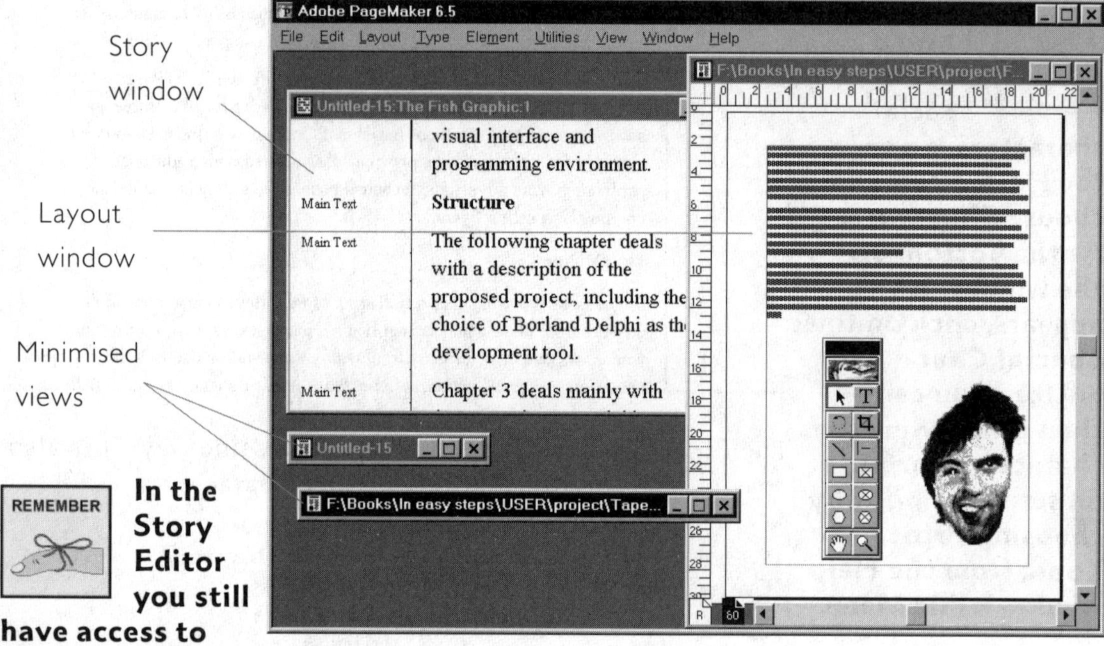

In the Story Editor you still have access to the Type menu, and with it the full range of PageMaker text effects. Remember however that you will not see many of the changes until you return to Layout view.

Display Invisible Characters

1. From Story view open the **Story** menu.

Note the option to display normally invisible characters in the Story Editor. It is often useful to be able to distinguish visually between spaces, tabs and return characters. (You can also set this from **File/Preferences.../More...**)

Chapter Eleven

Style Sheets V3 and above

Although many people find it possible to avoid the use of styles altogether, they provide an extremely effective way of controlling the design and formatting of headings and main text. As well as allowing you to make drastic changes to a document at any stage in the design process, styles can help you to ensure that the overall look and feel of your publications remain consistent.

Covers

Paragraph Styles

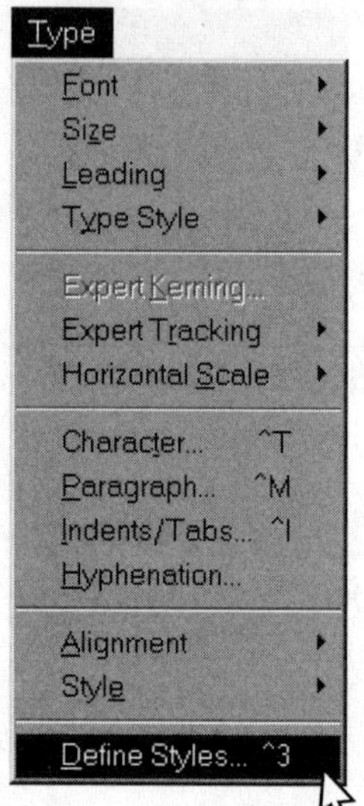

Styles allow you to save a complete set of text attributes under a single name, which you can then use quickly and easily throughout your documents.

Defining a Style

1 Choose **Define Styles** from the **Type** menu. The following dialog box will appear:

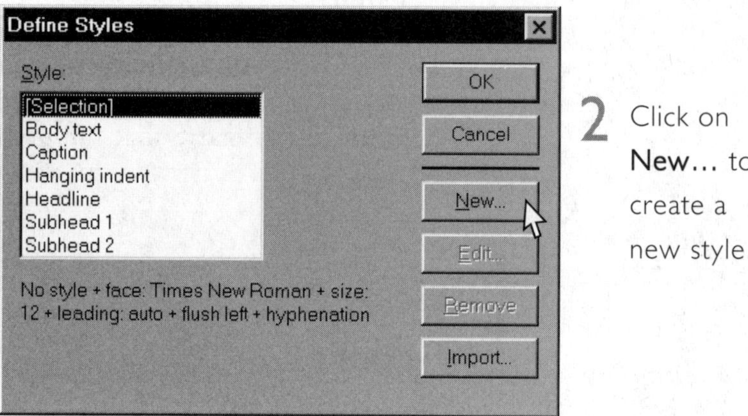

2 Click on **New...** to create a new style.

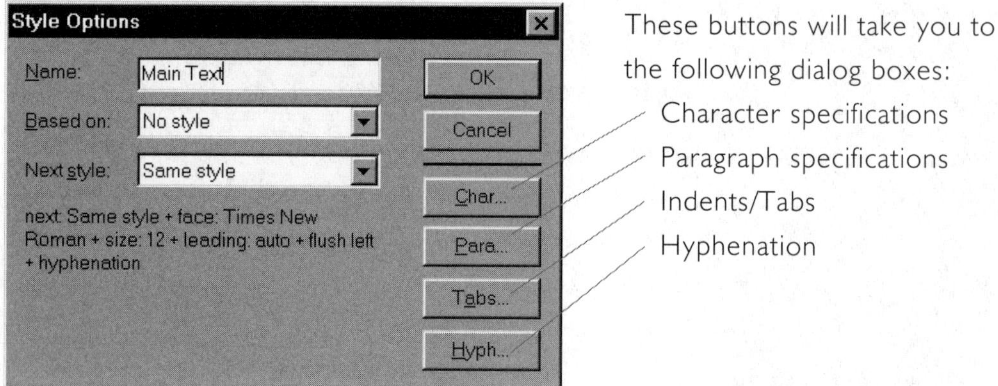

These buttons will take you to the following dialog boxes:

- Character specifications
- Paragraph specifications
- Indents/Tabs
- Hyphenation

3 Enter a name for the style, then use the **Char...**, **Para...**, **Tabs...** and **Hyph...** buttons to set the text attributes.

4 Click **OK** when you have finished.

Using Styles

1. Make sure the Styles palette is active (**Window** menu).
2. With the Text tool, select or click inside the paragraph you want to change.
3. Click on the appropriate style in the palette. The style, along with all its attributes, will be applied to the text. In this example, the style Subhead1 has been applied to all subheadings on the page:

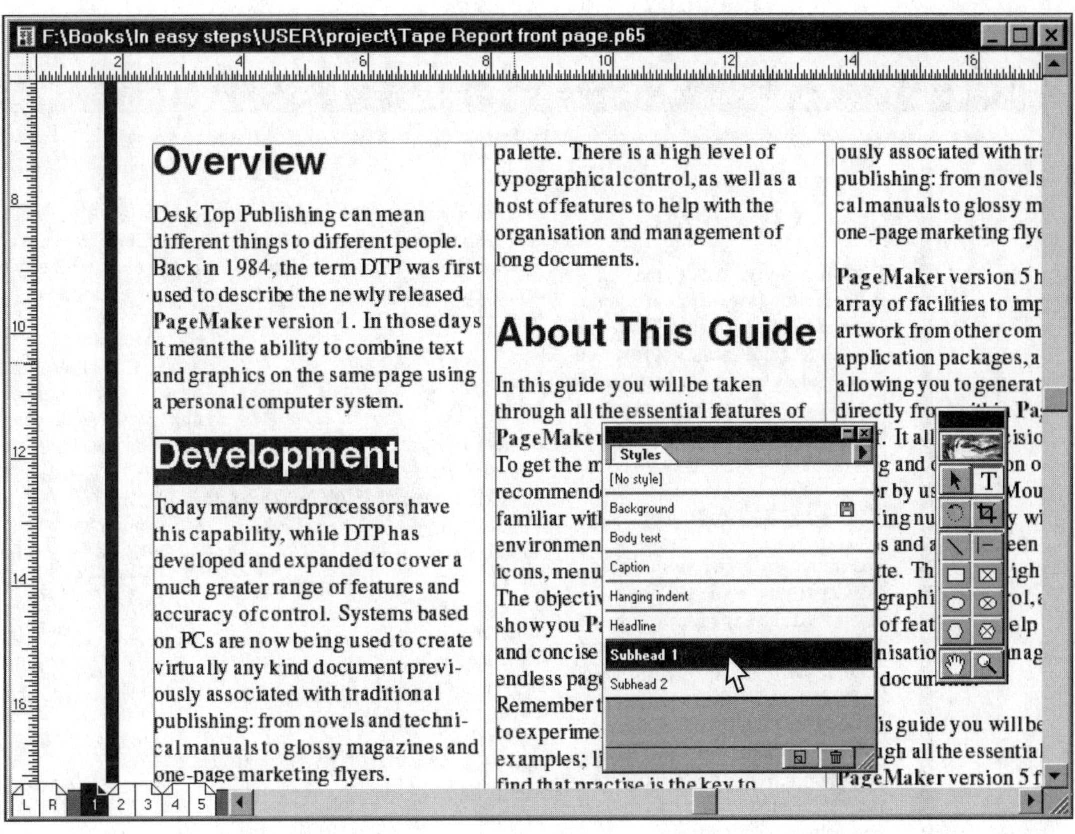

Changing a Style

A shortcut to the Edit Style dialog box is to hold down the Control key and click directly on the style name within the palette.

1. Choose **Define Styles...** from the **Type** menu.
2. Click on the style you wish to change, then on the **Edit...** button.
3. Make the changes to the attributes. If you hold down Shift when clicking **OK**, PageMaker will exit from all dialog boxes (even if you are several levels inside).

PageMaker remembers the style applied to each paragraph, so in this example all the Subhead1 paragraphs change instantly.

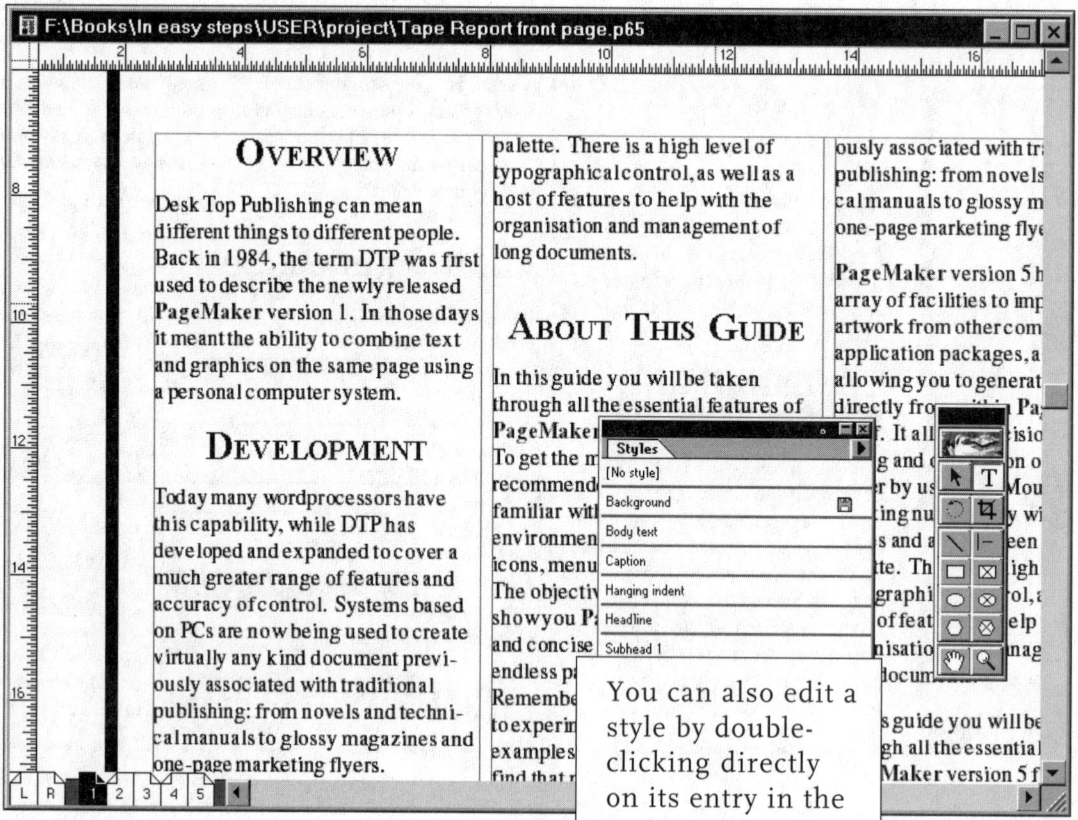

You can also edit a style by double-clicking directly on its entry in the Styles palette

Style by Example

Sometimes it is useful to be able to experiment with text effects directly on the page, so that you can test out ideas before deciding on the exact attributes for your styles. Once you have done this, you can sample the text to automatically create a style definition.

Let us assume that you have a specimen piece of text which already has all the attributes you would like to build into a style.

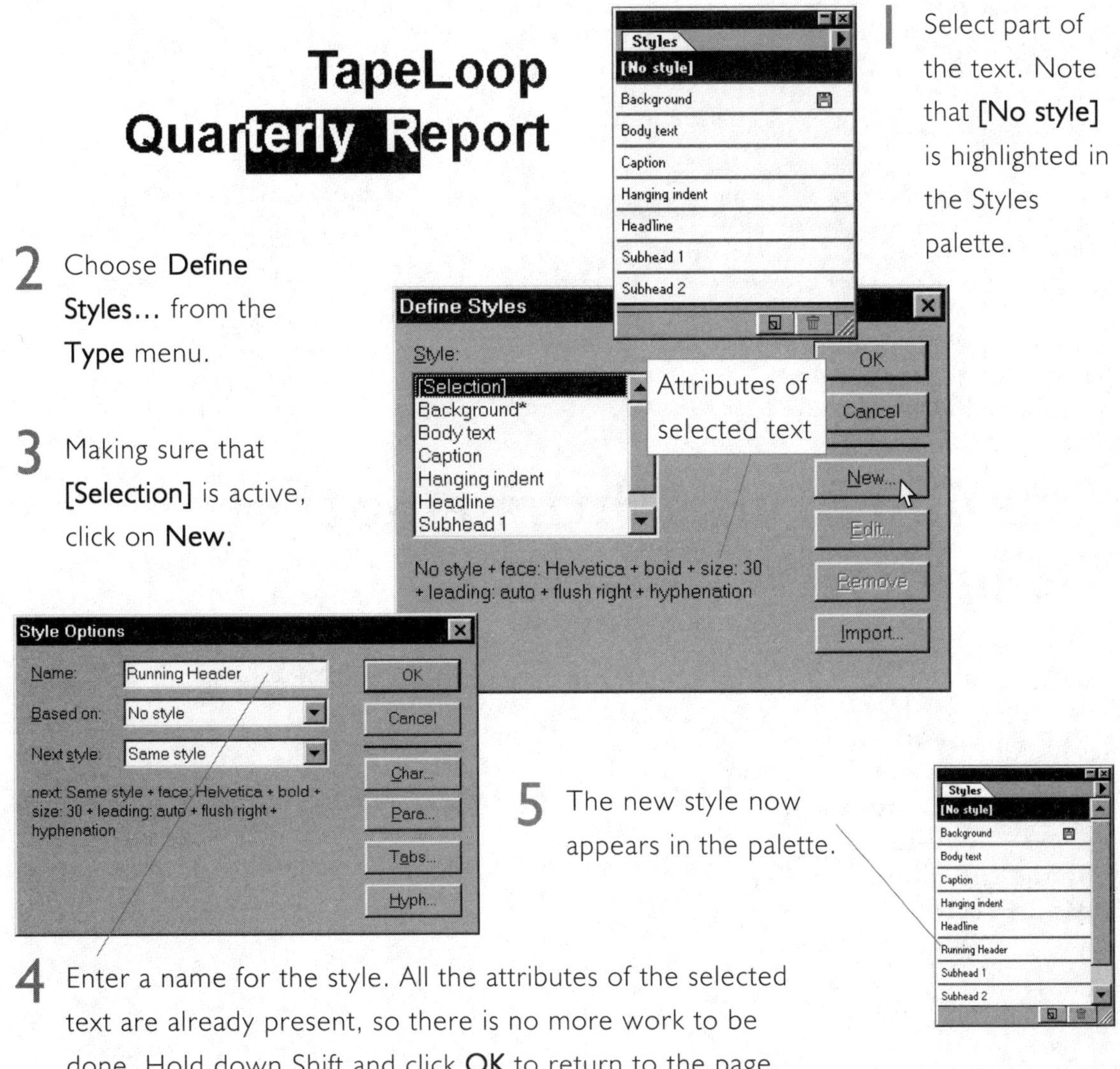

Styles in the Story Editor

You can also use the Style palette in the Story Editor. Because many text effects do not show up in a Story window, style names appear in the margin to help you keep track of current settings.

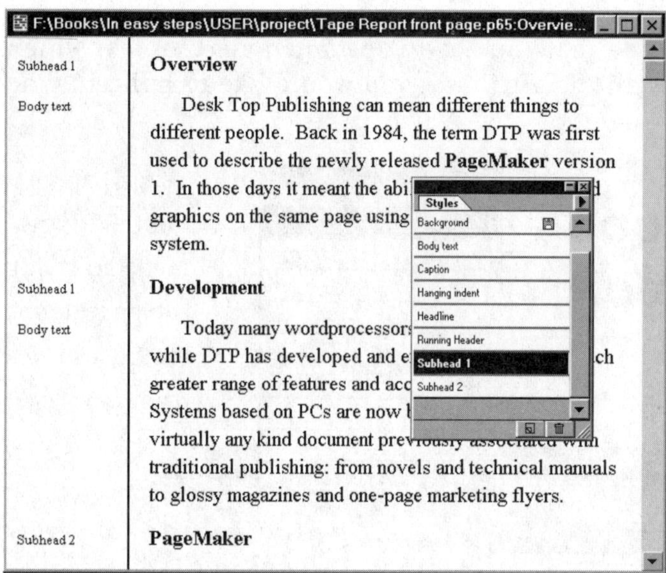

The facility to display style names in the margin of a Story window can be turned on and off from the More Preferences dialog box.

To reach this choose **Preferences** and **General** from the File menu, then click **More**.

Copying Styles From Another Document

If you close all documents you can change the global default styles.

1 Choose **Define Styles...** from the **Type** menu and click on the **Import** button.

2 Locate the document and click **OK**.

Chapter Twelve

Long Document Features

This chapter shows you how to set up an automatic Table of Contents and Index for your document. It also explains how to group together a series of PageMaker files as a "Book" publication. Additionally, the Colour palette and Print Dialog are covered.

Covers

The Book Command V4 and above

When working with a long publication, it is common practice to divide it amongst several PageMaker documents. You can still treat these as a single publication using the Book command.

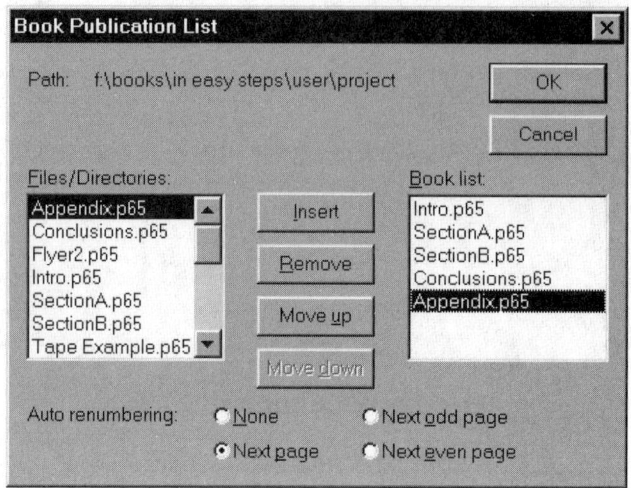

Choosing auto renumbering will cause PageMaker to open all other chapter files and modify their page numbers.

1. Choose **Book...** from the **Utilities** menu.
2. Locate each component file, using the **Insert** button to add them to the Book list.
3. Use the **Move up** and **Move down** buttons to assemble the "chapters" in the correct order.
4. Select the appropriate type of page numbering. Click **OK**.

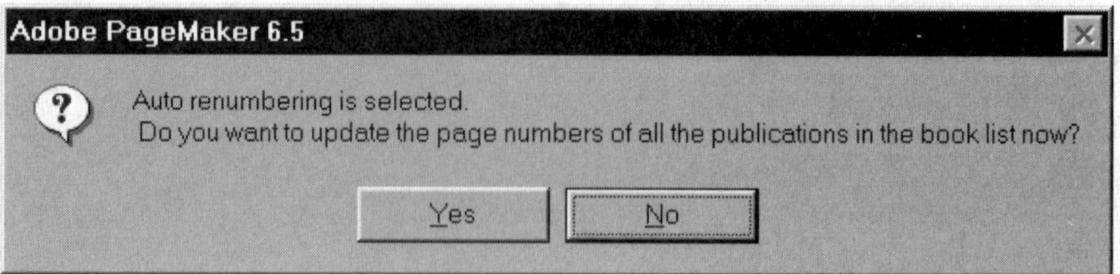

Although the individual files are still separate, there are features (such as printing, table of contents generation, and indexing) which can operate over the entire book.

Table of Contents V4 and above

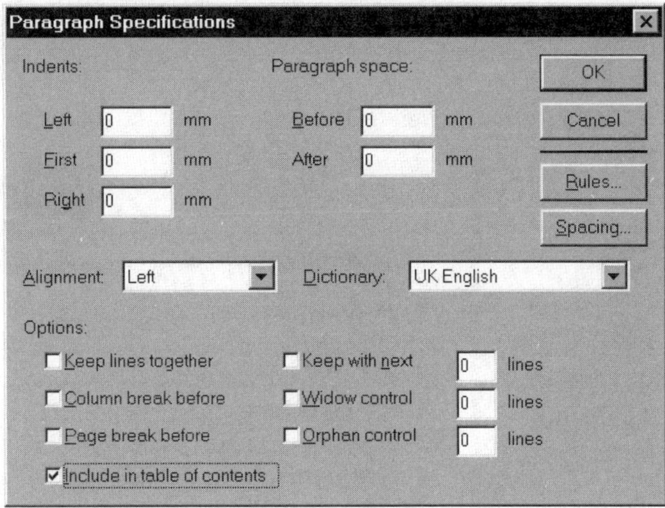

At the bottom left corner of the Paragraph Specifications dialog box (select **Paragraph...** from the Type menu), there is an option **Include in table of contents**.

Normally this option is set as part of the definition of heading or subheading styles of text (see Chapter 11 "Style Sheets").

Creating a Table of Contents

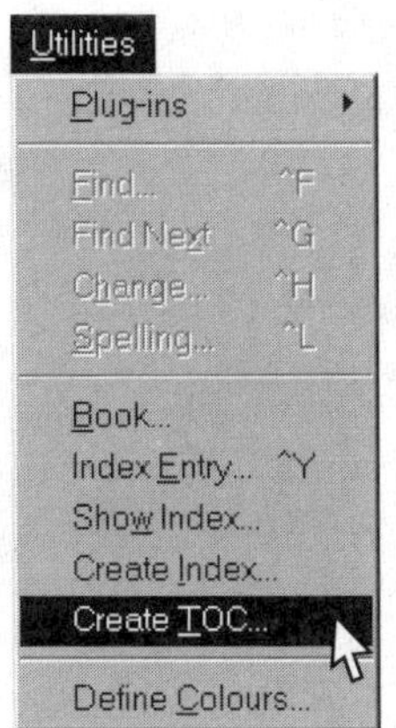

1. Set the **Include in table of contents** attribute for your heading styles, and also for individual paragraphs if necessary.
2. Choose **Create TOC...** from the **Utilities** menu.

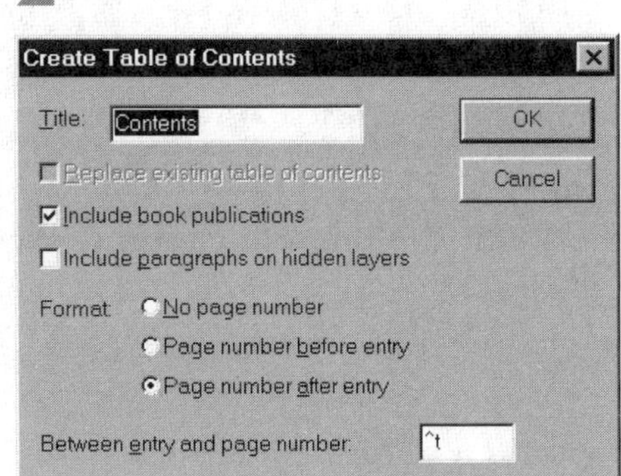

From this dialog box you can specify the TOC Title, as well as the format for the page references. Note that a TOC can be compiled for a complete book list.

When PageMaker is ready, it will display a text place symbol, allowing you to place the TOC on a suitable page:

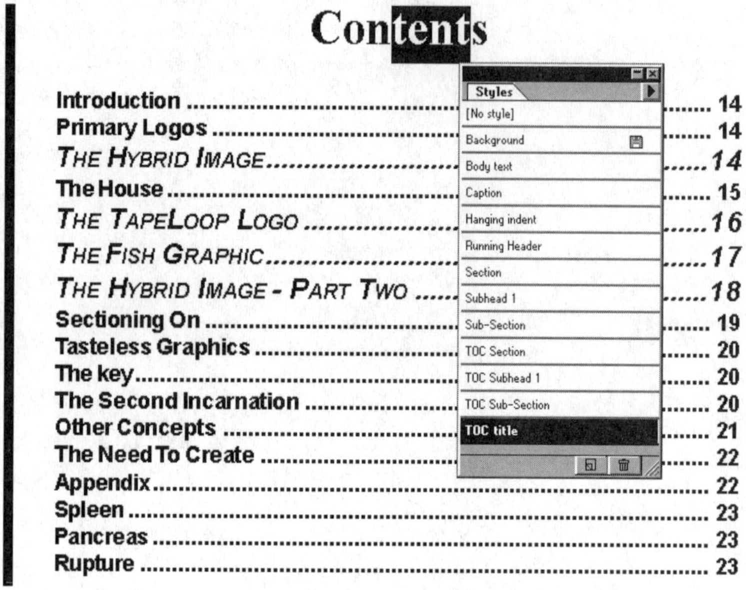

Contents

Introduction 14
Primary Logos 14
THE HYBRID IMAGE *14*
The House 15
THE TAPELOOP LOGO *16*
THE FISH GRAPHIC *17*
THE HYBRID IMAGE - PART TWO *18*
Sectioning On 19
Tasteless Graphics 20
The key 20
The Second Incarnation 20
Other Concepts 21
The Need To Create 22
Appendix 22
Spleen 23
Pancreas 23
Rupture 23

Styles
[No style]
Background
Body text
Caption
Hanging indent
Running Header
Section
Subhead 1
Sub-Section
TOC Section
TOC Subhead 1
TOC Sub-Section
TOC title

If you look in the Styles palette, you will see that new styles are created for each type of TOC entry. For example, the word "Contents" at the top of the table uses the style TOC title.

In the above example, three PageMaker styles had the **Include in table of contents** attribute set. PageMaker located all instances of these and included them in the Contents page. It also created three new styles corresponding to these, plus TOC title.

You are obviously free to edit and format this new table in any way you wish, but if you make the changes by editing these new styles, then it will be easy to rebuild the TOC.

You will need to rebuild the TOC should you add any new entries, edit the main document text, or change the page numbering.

Rebuilding the Table of Contents

By altering the TOC styles you can radically reformat the Contents page:

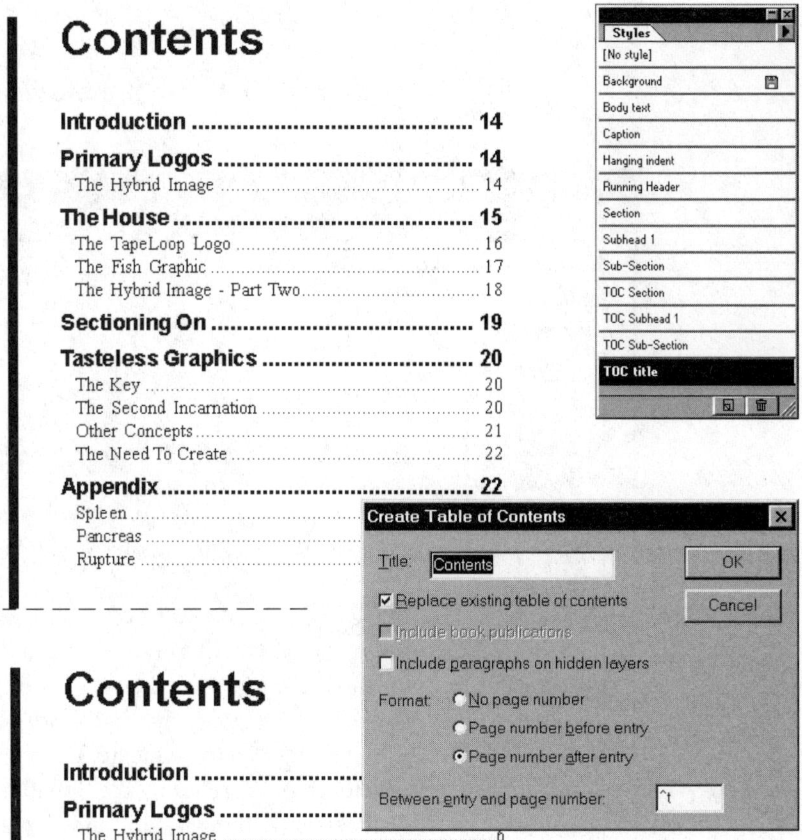

Styles
[No style]
Background
Body text
Caption
Hanging indent
Running Header
Section
Subhead 1
Sub-Section
TOC Section
TOC Subhead 1
TOC Sub-Section
TOC title

Contents

Introduction **14**
Primary Logos **14**
The Hybrid Image 14
The House **15**
The TapeLoop Logo 16
The Fish Graphic 17
The Hybrid Image - Part Two 18
Sectioning On **19**
Tasteless Graphics **20**
The Key 20
The Second Incarnation 20
Other Concepts 21
The Need To Create 22
Appendix **22**
Spleen ....
Pancreas ....
Rupture ....

In this example, we renumbered the pages in our document, so needed to recreate the TOC...

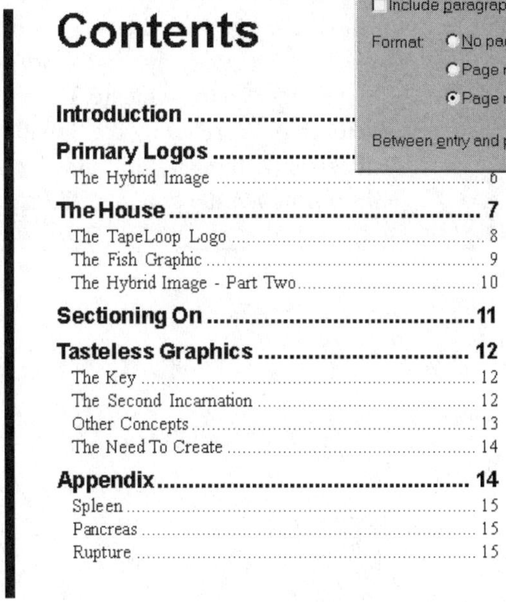

Create Table of Contents
Title: Contents
OK
Cancel
Replace existing table of contents
Include book publications
Include paragraphs on hidden layers
Format: No page number
Page number before entry
Page number after entry
Between entry and page number: ^t

Contents

Introduction ....
Primary Logos ....
The Hybrid Image 6
The House **7**
The TapeLoop Logo 8
The Fish Graphic 9
The Hybrid Image - Part Two 10
Sectioning On **11**
Tasteless Graphics **12**
The Key 12
The Second Incarnation 12
Other Concepts 13
The Need To Create 14
Appendix **14**
Spleen 15
Pancreas 15
Rupture 15

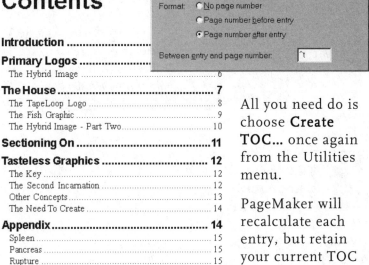

All you need do is choose **Create TOC...** once again from the Utilities menu.

PageMaker will recalculate each entry, but retain your current TOC style definitions.

Making Index Entries V4 and above

To create an index entry, do the following using either Layout or Story view:

1. Select the relevant word or phrase with the text tool.
2. Choose **Index Entry** from the **Utilities** menu.

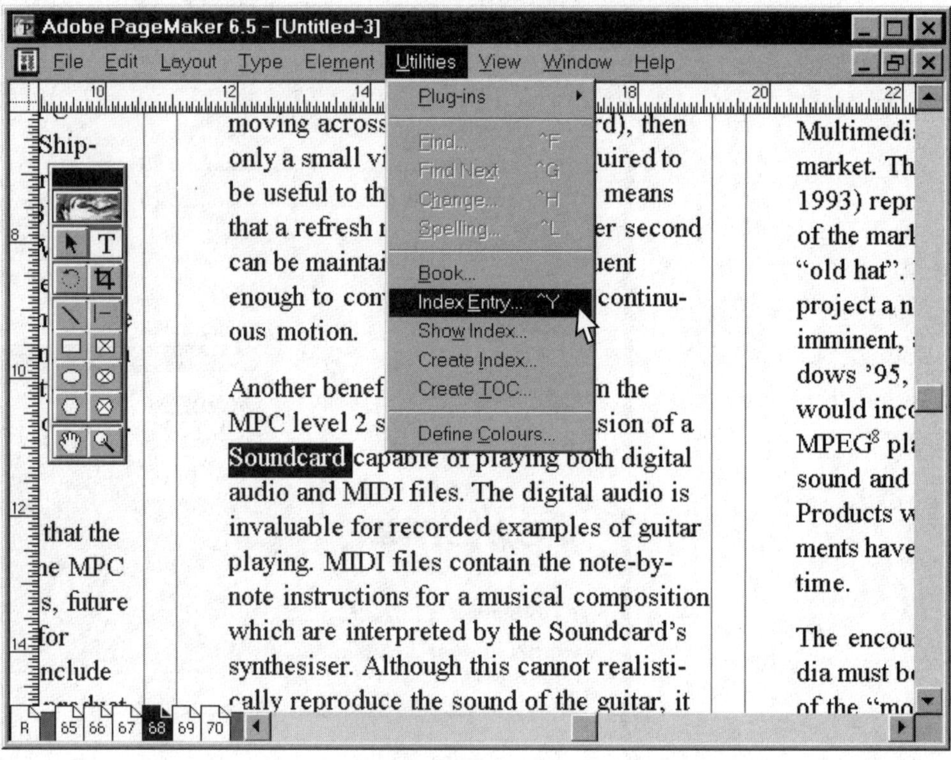

The Index Entry keyboard shortcut is ^Y (or ^; for PageMaker 6.0 and below).

The Add Index Entry dialog appears, as below:

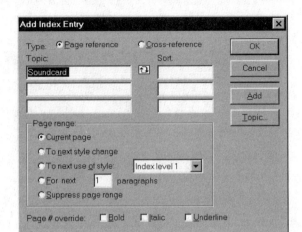

To see how these entries finally appear, look over the example index on page 135.

3 For a simple index entry accepting the default settings, simply click **OK**. PageMaker will set up an index entry which keeps track of the selected text.

More Complex Entries

Sorting Entries Manually

Use the **Sort** box to override the sort preferences:

In this example, the "Digital audio" entry will appear in the index under A rather than D.

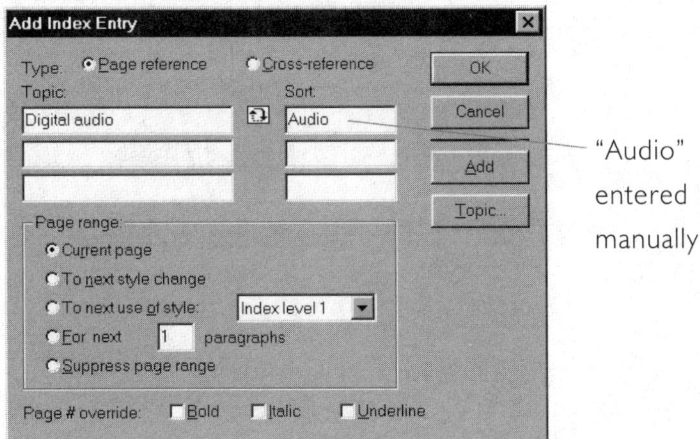

"Audio" entered manually

Subtopics

You can make an entry part of a more major index topic, or subdivide it into subtopics (to a maximum of three levels):

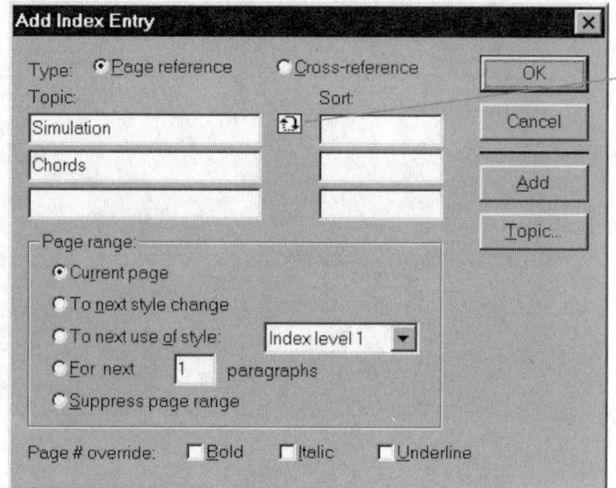

This button moves the text in the topic boxes down one level. The text in the lowest box moves back to the top.

Creating a Cross-reference

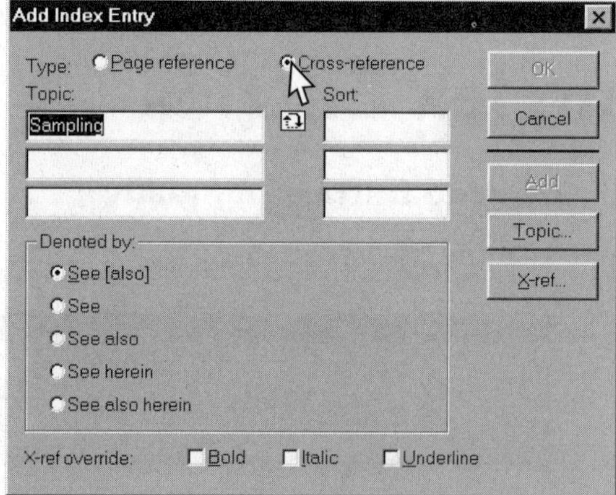

1. Click on the **Cross-reference** radio button at the top of the dialog box.

2. Choose the appropriate option: e.g., "See [also]" will add "also" if the entry has a page reference.

3 Click on the **X-ref** button.

The following dialog box will appear:

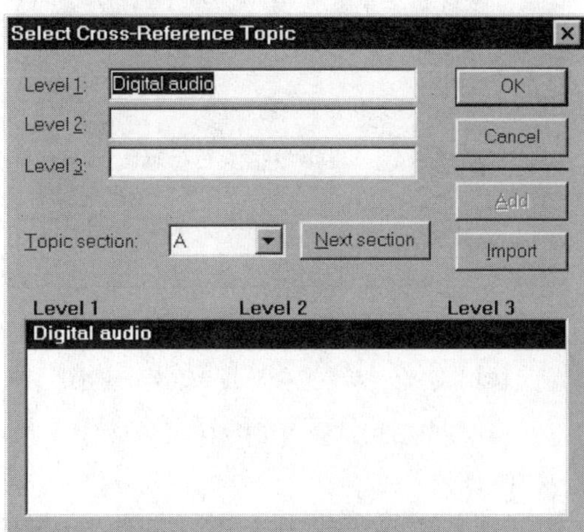

4 Select the initial letter of the required topic using the **Topic section** pop-up menu, or click on the **Next section** button. A list of the existing entries will be displayed.

5 Locate and select the topic to which you wish to cross-reference, then click **OK**.

Specifying a Range of Pages

Sometimes it is desirable to include a range of pages, rather than a single page reference next to an entry:

Here PageMaker will track a range of pages starting at the index entry, and ending at the next occurrence of text in the style "Main Text".

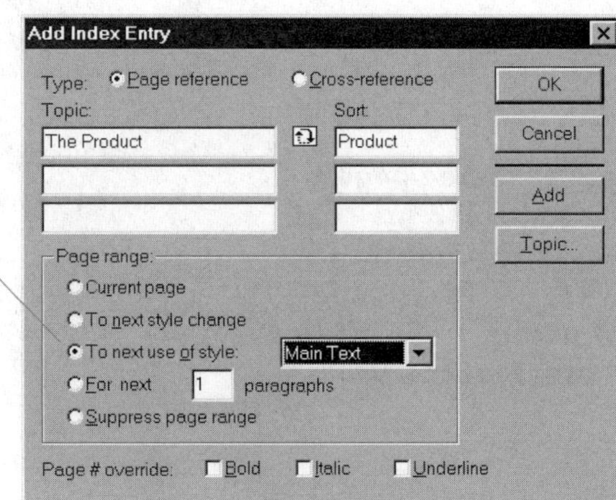

Creating the Index

An index is normally compiled across a book list. If you haven't already assigned a book list to the file that is to hold your index, follow the procedure outlined on page 126.

To create an index, open the file that you want to contain it (or create a new blank file), then do the following:

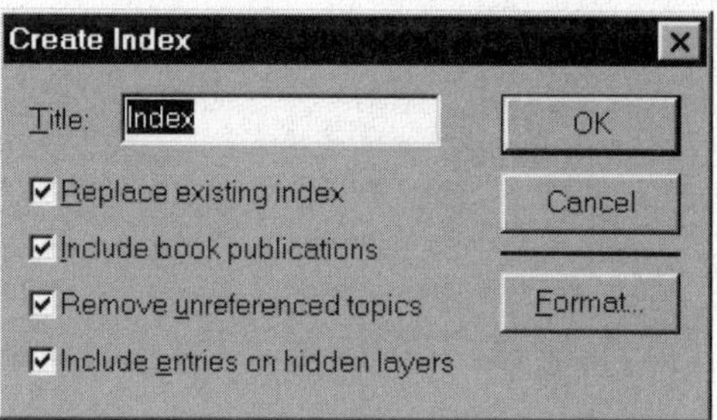

1 Choose **Create Index...** from the **Utilities** menu.

2 Edit the index title if necessary. Click on **Format...** to customise the appearance of the index.

Metacharacters are used in these format boxes. For example, the "Between page #s" box contains a comma and the metacharacter representing an en space (a space the width of the letter "n").

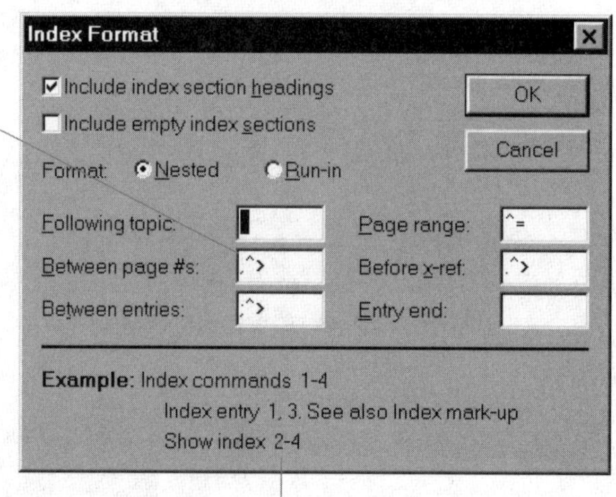

The example index text automatically changes to reflect any changes you make to the format.

HANDY TIP

See page 117 in Chapter 10 for a table of useful metacharacters.

3 Click **OK**. PageMaker will look through all book publications for index entries. When it is ready, you will be presented with a loaded text icon.

4 Find a suitable place for the index and click. The new index story will flow onto the page.

Example Index

Here is a short sample of an index generated by PageMaker, using some of the entries made on the preceding pages.

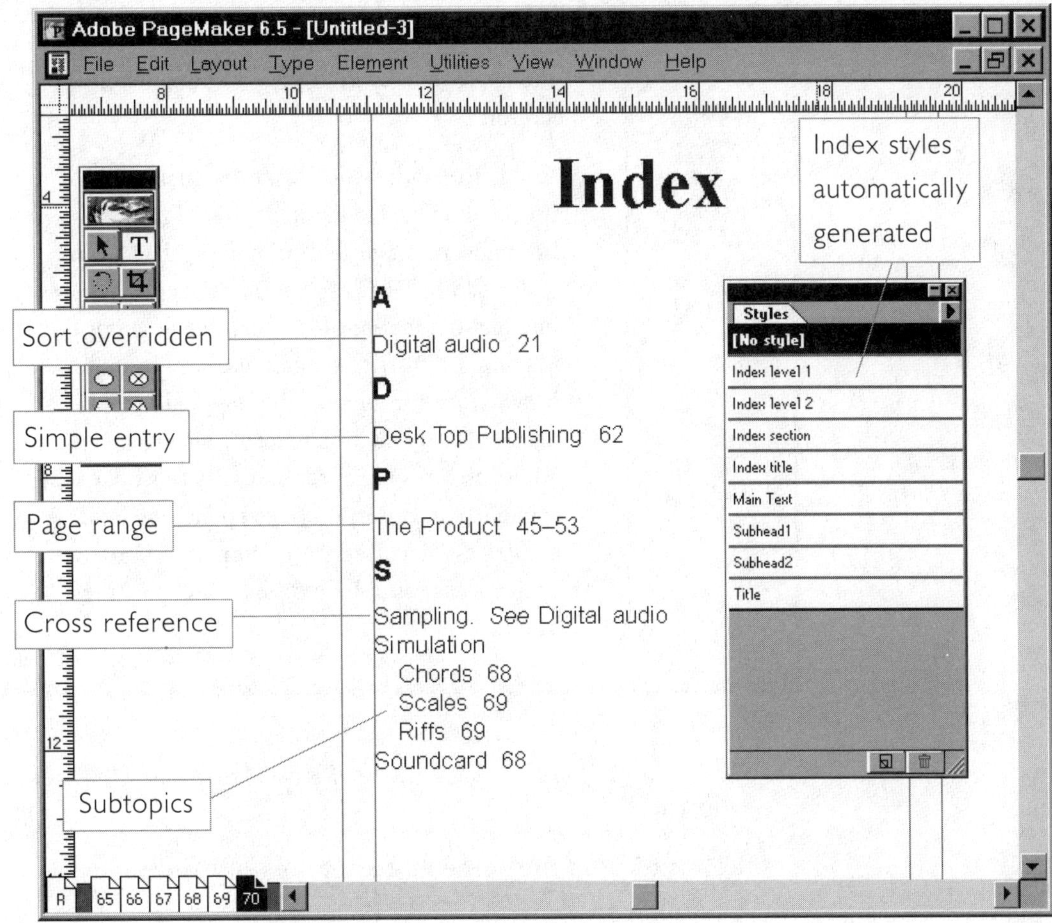

Indexing with the Story Editor

V4 and above

In the Story Editor, index markers show up as inverse diamond shapes.

You can search and replace using the index marker metacharacter (^;).

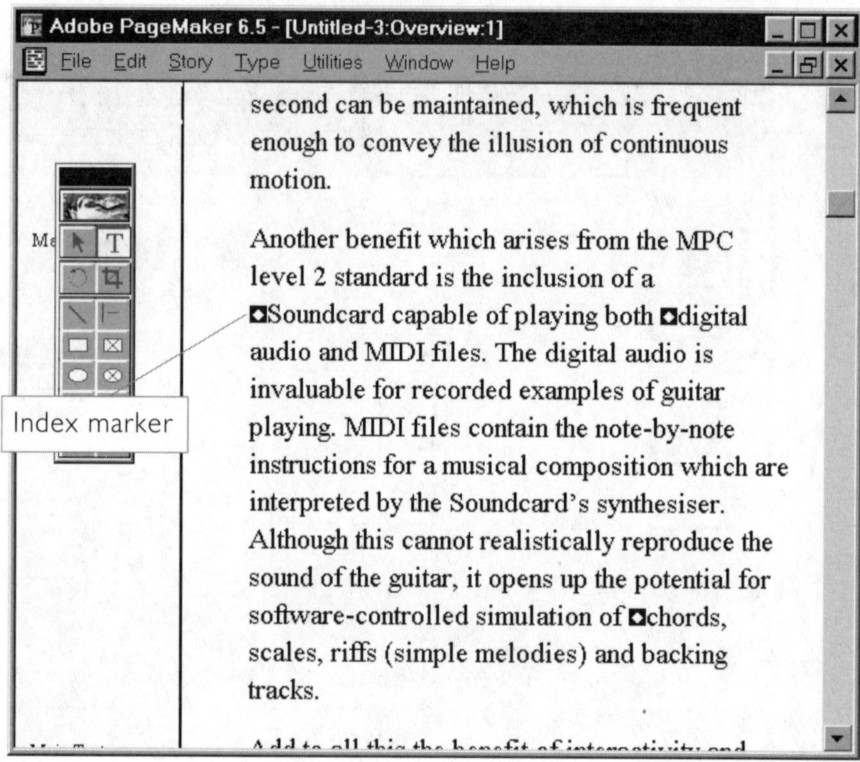

You can edit your index using **Show Index...** (Utilities menu).

Rebuilding is the same as for Tables of Contents.

The Colour Palette

1 Make sure the Colours palette is active (**Window** menu).

2 Select one or more elements whose colour you want to change.

Fill

Line

Both

Tint of selected colour

Defined colours

3 Choose line, fill or both from the Colour palette.

4 Select the colour.

Defining and Editing Colours

To edit an existing colour, hold down the Control key and click on its entry in the Colours palette.

To create and edit a new colour, Control-click on [None] in the Colour palette.

In either case the following dialog appears:

You can create, edit, delete and copy colours by choosing Define Colours... from the Utilities menu.

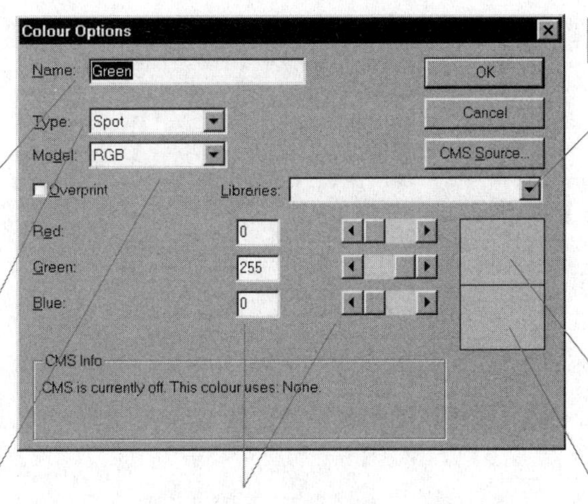

1 Pick a colour from the wide range of libraries in this pop-up menu, or follow steps 2-5.

2 Enter the colour name here.

3 Choose colour type from Spot, Process or Tint.

4 Select colour model from RGB, CMYK or HLS.

5 Edit the colour either numerically or by adjusting the slider bars.

Preview of the colour

Colour before editing

The Print Dialog

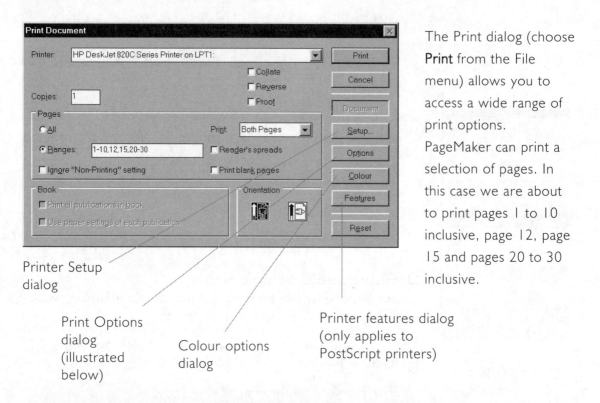

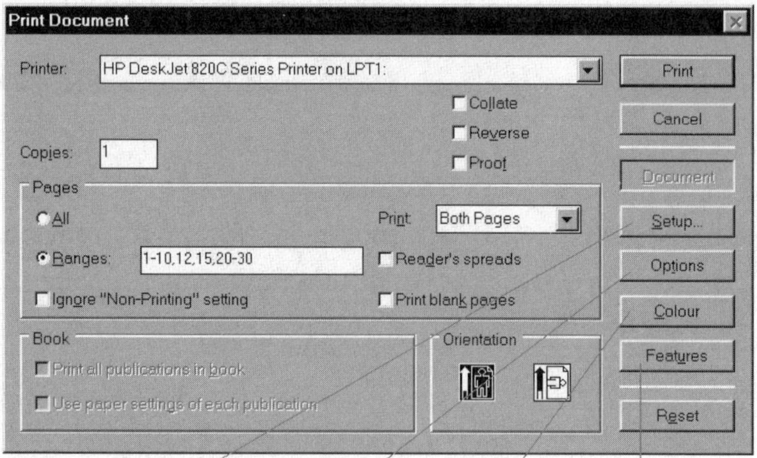

The Print dialog (choose **Print** from the File menu) allows you to access a wide range of print options. PageMaker can print a selection of pages. In this case we are about to print pages 1 to 10 inclusive, page 12, page 15 and pages 20 to 30 inclusive.

Printer Setup dialog

Print Options dialog (illustrated below)

Colour options dialog

Printer features dialog (only applies to PostScript printers)

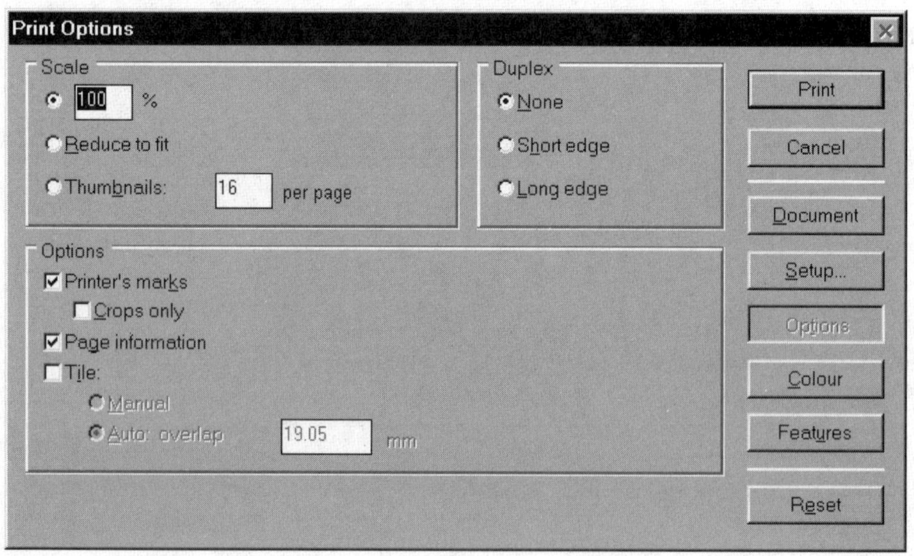

The Options dialog lets you control features such as print scaling, printer's marks and page information.

Chapter Thirteen

Links Management

V4 and above

PageMaker's Links features allow you to keep track of all your document's ingredients: imported text and graphic elements. This is invaluable when dealing with large complex projects, making use of corporate logos or working in teams with other people contibuting to your document content.

This chapter shows you how to monitor links, set automatic hot links or manually track changes made to original files.

Covers

The Links Dialog Box

The Links Manager gives you information about all items of text and graphics which have been placed into your document:

1 Choose **Links Manager** from the **File** menu.

The following dialog box appears.

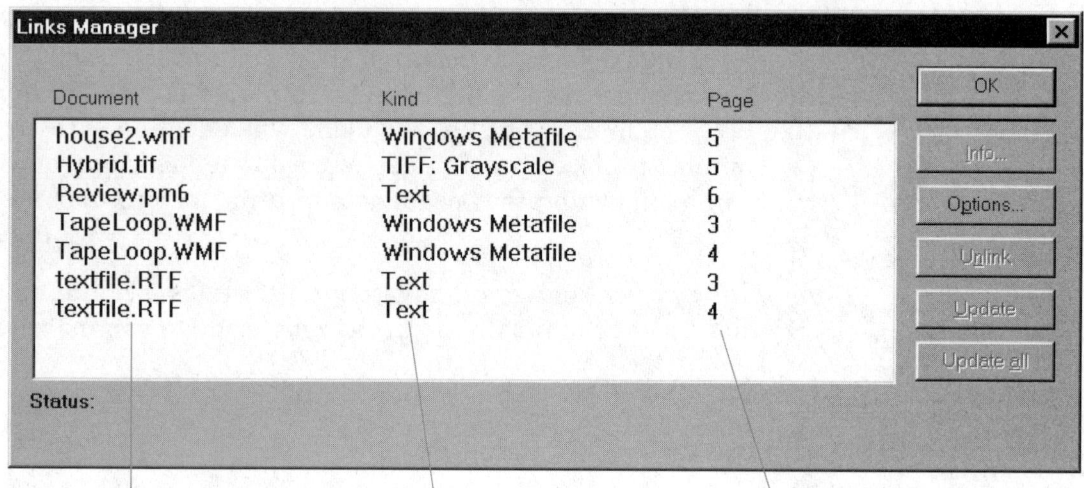

List of files imported into the current PageMaker document

Type of the originally imported file

Page on which the item appears. Note the same element may appear on more than one page

Note that the term Links Manager refers to tracking imported text and graphics. It has nothing to do with the Hyperlinks palette, or the HTML export feature.

PageMaker keeps track of all imported elements, remembering their file type, size, location and date modified.

2 Select an item from the list and click on the **Info** button.

Full details of the item appear:

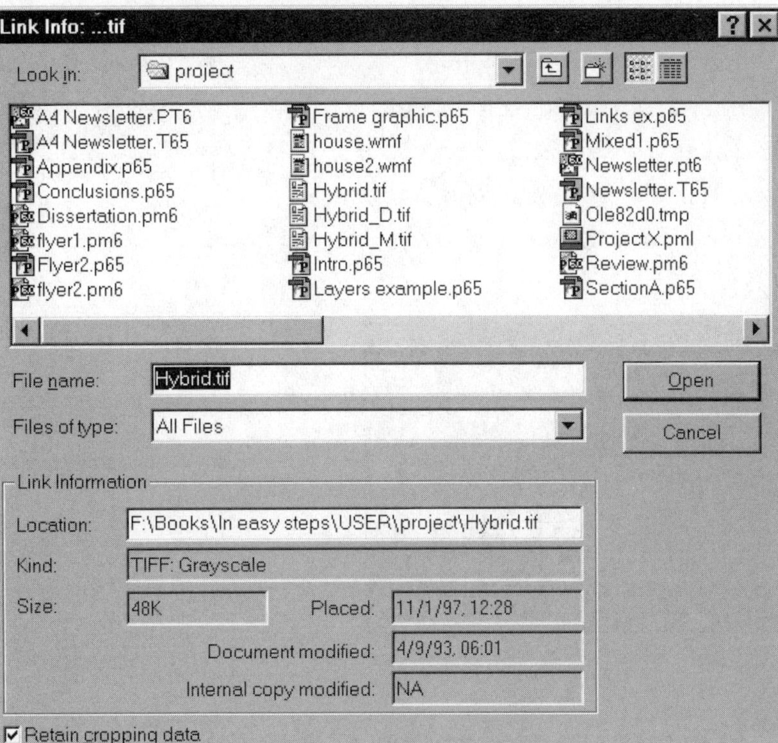

3 Click **Cancel** to return to the Links dialog box. Select another element and click on **Options**.

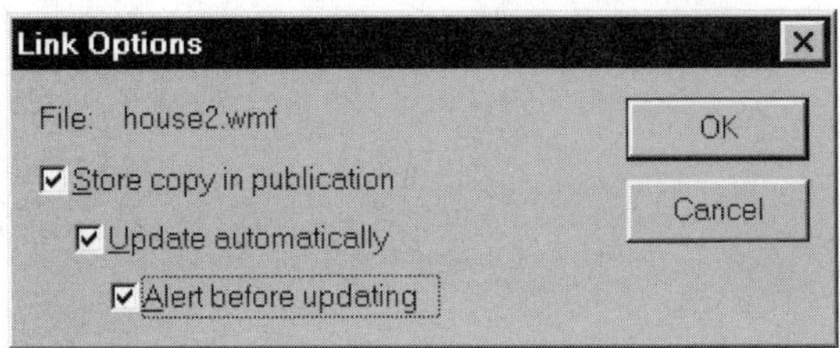

For graphic elements you have the choice to store a copy within the publication. This tends to make your document size large, but it also means that everything required for printing is available in this single file.

Automatic Updates

By setting automatic updates, you create a hot link. This means that whenever the source document is modified, PageMaker will re-import so that it always works with the most up-to-date version.

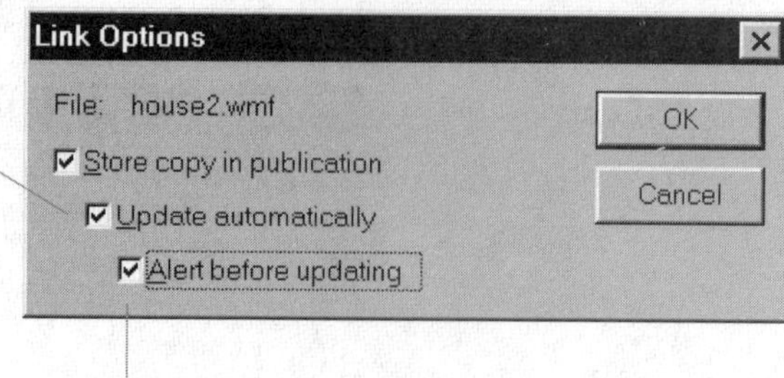

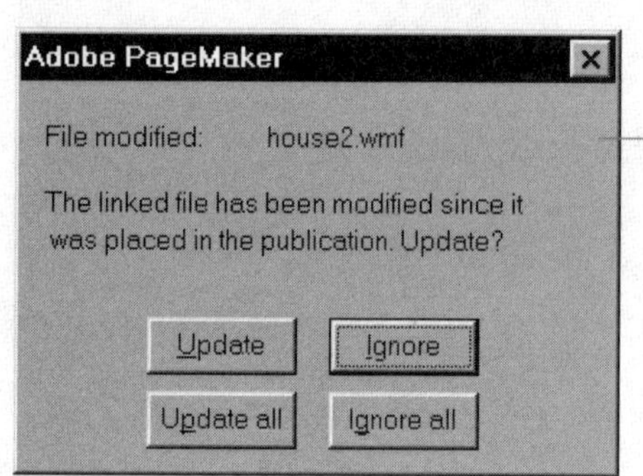

If you set the Alert before updating option, this message will appear whenever PageMaker attempts to update a link.

Checking Individual Objects

You can access Link info and Link options directly from your document:

1. Select the element with the Pointer tool.
2. Choose **Link info** or **Link options** from the **Element** menu.

Link Status

Sometimes a symbol appears before and/or after items in the Links dialog:

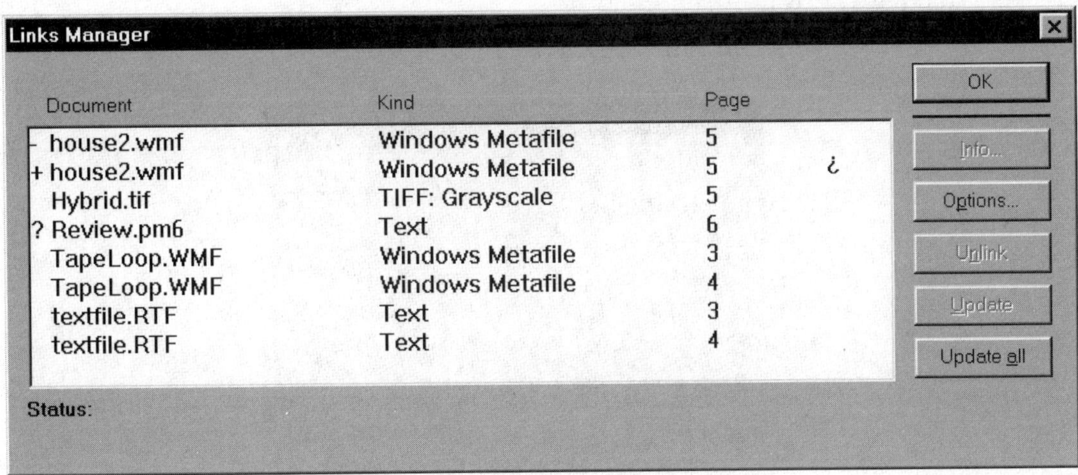

The hyphen (-) indicates that the item has been modified and that automatic updating was not requested. This means that the PageMaker version is now out of date. You can remedy this by clicking on **Update**.

The plus sign (+) means that, even though automatic update has been requested, the item is still out of date. This would normally be resolved when you first open the document, with PageMaker offering to update the link for you.

The question mark to the left of the item tells you that PageMaker can no longer locate the original file. You can reset the link by clicking on **Info**, or choose to clear the link completely by clicking on **Unlink**.

The upside-down question mark to the right of the item warns you that printing this element may produce unexpected results.

Global Link Options

Open the **Utilities** menu, **Plug-ins** submenu, and choose **Global Link Options**.

The following dialog box appears:

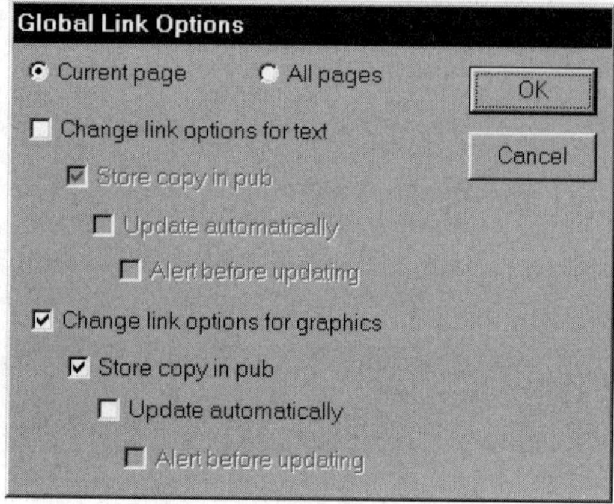

Here you can directly set options for all items on the current page, or even all items within the entire document.

There are separate controls to set the options for text and graphics. Note that text is normally stored within the publication, since it takes up little storage space. Whether or not you decide to store graphics within the document will depend more on the project in hand.

Object Linking and Embedding

When you choose **Insert Object** from the **Edit** menu, a slightly different system of linking is being used. Here you may import a Adobe Table object, for example, and then later invoke the Table Editor directly from within PageMaker.

Chapter Fourteen

Frames V6.5

PageMaker version 6.5 introduced Frames, a feature which gives you an alternative way to lay out and control both text and graphics. You can use frames to design a document, slotting in the actual content later on. This chapter shows you how to create Frames and use them in a productive way.

Covers

The Frame Tools

Box frame tool

Oval frame tool

Polygon frame tool

Frames are similar to normal toolbox objects. They can also be filled with either text or graphic content.

To Create a New Frame

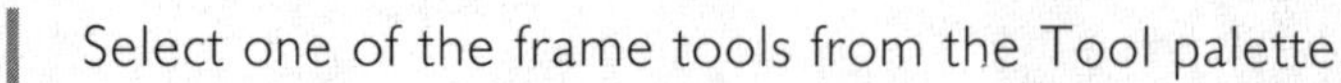

1 Select one of the frame tools from the Tool palette.

2 Click and drag over the page to create a Framed shape.

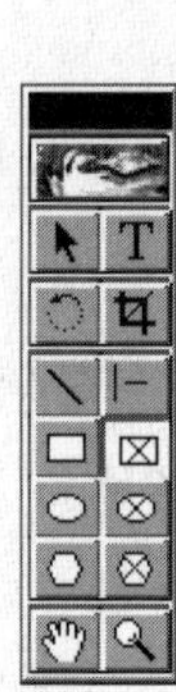

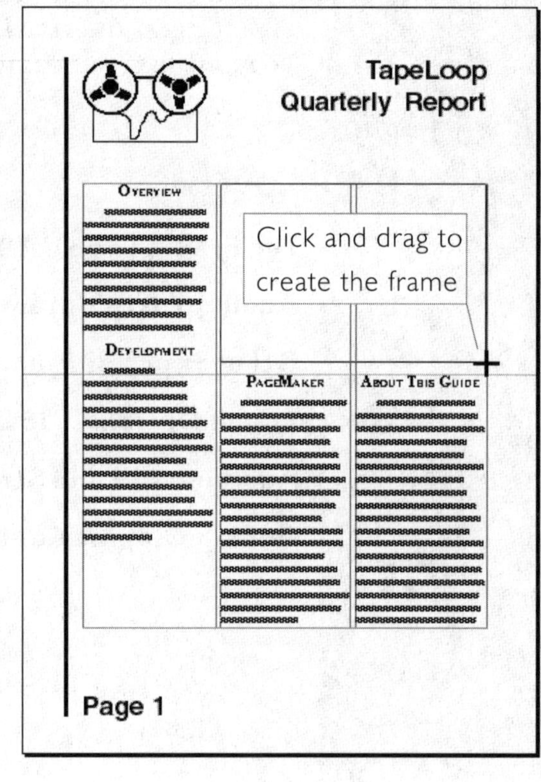

Note that the frame is initially empty. When selected it is characterised by a diagonal cross running from corner to corner.

If you're using the Polygon frame tool, you may want to double click on the normal Polygon tool first to access the Polygon settings dialog. (If you double click on a frame tool, PageMaker brings up a Frame Options dialog.)

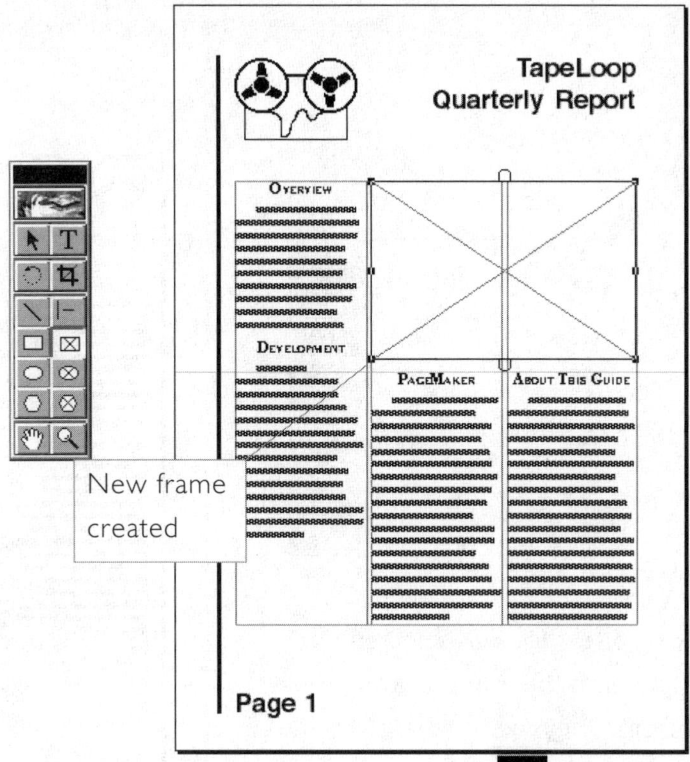

Adding Text Content to a Frame

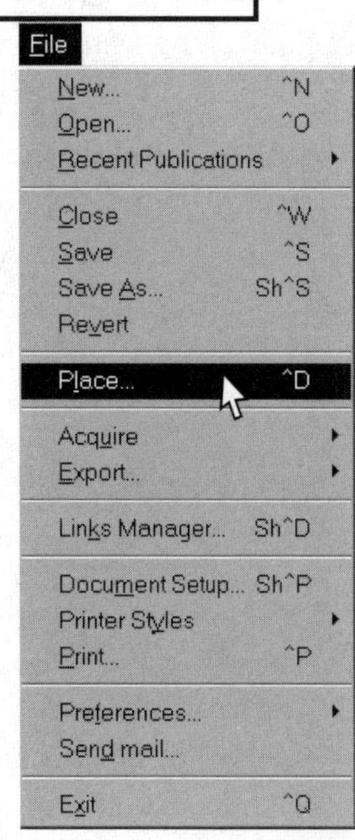

1. Select the empty frame with the Pointer tool.

2. Choose **Place** from the **File** menu.

3 Choose a file to import, and click **OK**.

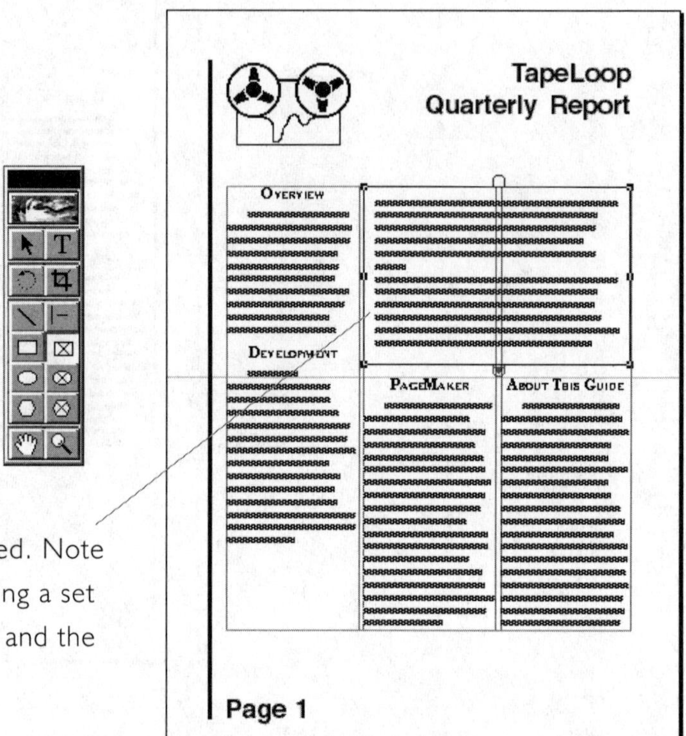

In this case a text file was selected. Note that it flows into the frame, leaving a set default margin between the text and the outline of the frame's box.

The frame is quite similar to a normal text box. There are corner handles for resizing the shape, and windowshade handles which let you know if there is more text to place.

By clicking on the red triangle, you can thread the text into another frame. Text can be threaded from one frame to another, or from one ordinary text box to another. However, it cannot be threaded from a frame to a normal text box, or vice versa.

Other Types of Frame

In this example we shall create an oval shaped frame, and then flow the text from the first frame into the second:

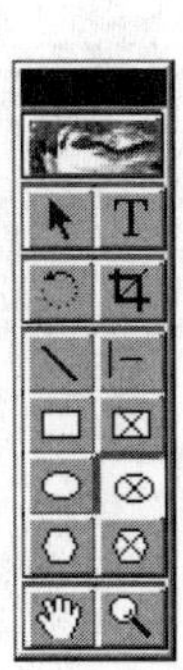

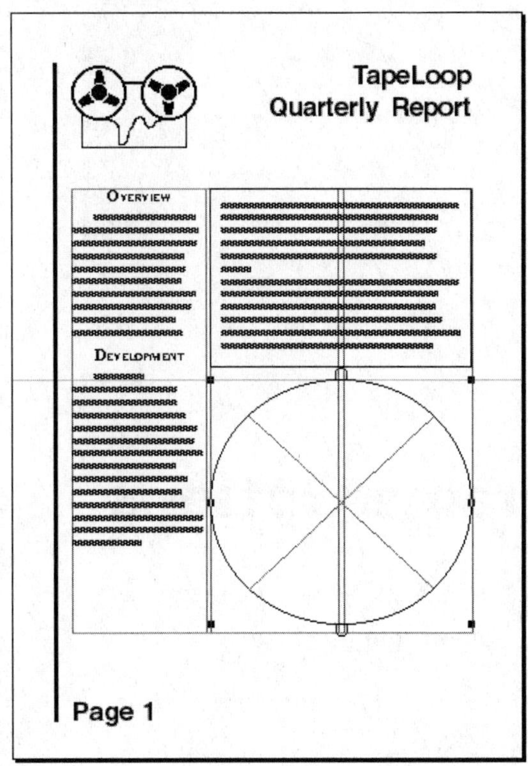

1. Select the oval frame tool.

2. Click and drag to create a new oval frame.

3. Now select the Pointer tool, and click directly on the red triangle in the bottom windowshade handle of the first frame.

4. A link icon will appear. Click inside the oval frame to thread the text into the new area.

The text flows into the new area...

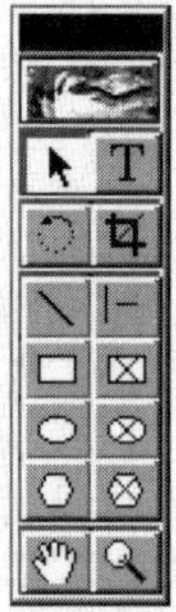

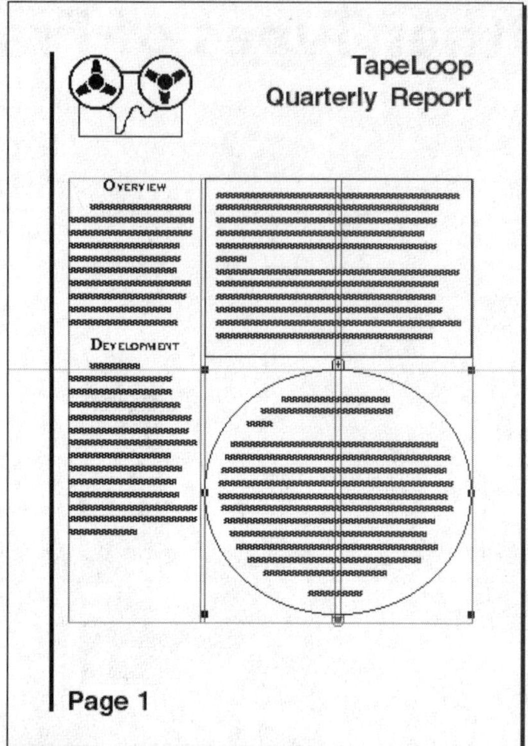

Frame Options

1 Select a frame which already has some contents.

2 Open the **Element** menu, **Frame** submenu, and choose **Options**.

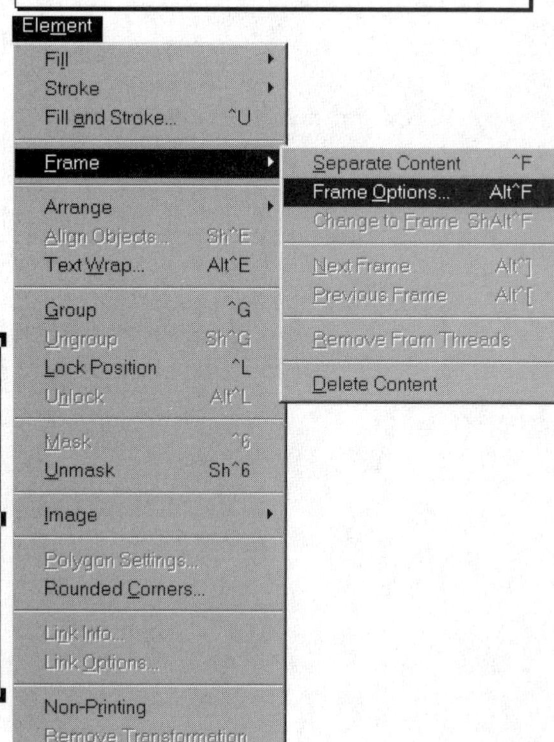

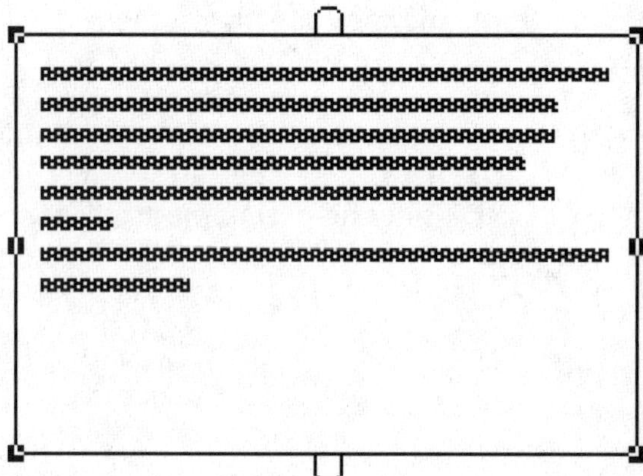

The following dialog box appears...

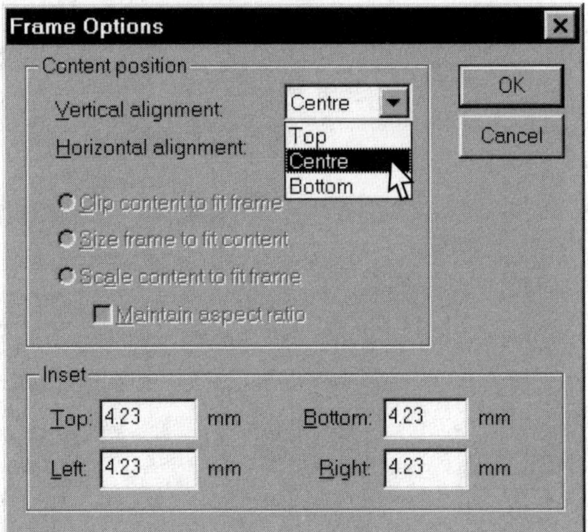

3 Choose the appropriate alignment and inset options.

4 Click **OK**.

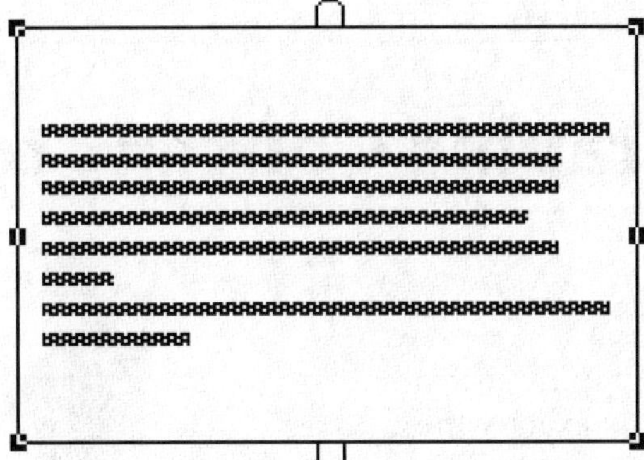

In this example the text contents are now vertically centred within the frame.

You may have noticed that the horizontal alignment option was greyed out in the Frame options dialog. This is because the frame contents consisted of text, and horizontal text alignment should be controlled from the Type menu or Paragraph dialog.

Applying Fill and Stroke

You can change the Fill and Stroke settings for a frame in the same way as for other Toolbox graphic objects:

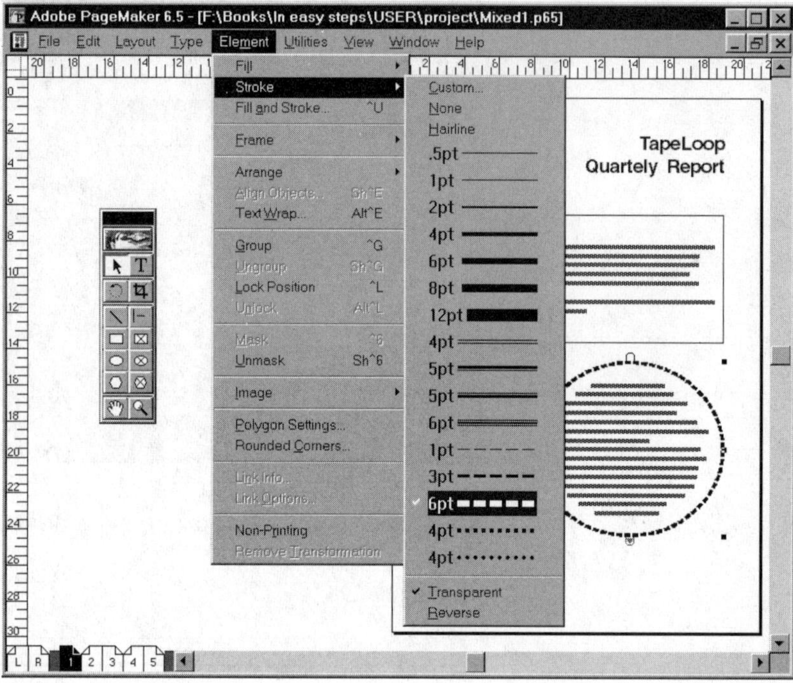

Adding Graphic Content to a Frame

You can also insert a graphic into a frame. The procedure is exactly the same: select the frame, choose **Place** from the File menu, and select the graphic to be imported.

In this case we placed a TIFF file inside a polygon frame.

Chapter Fifteen

Hyperlinks and HTML V6.5

Version 6.5 represents PageMaker's first serious foray into the world of Hypertext and Web publishing.

This chapter explains how to create and edit Hyperlinks within a document, and then how to use PageMaker as an efficient way of producing a wide range of Web pages – exported in HTML format.

Covers

Starting a Web Document

The World Wide Web displays pages built using HTML (hypertext markup language). Hypertext allows you to set up automatic links to another part of the page, or even other Web pages. In this example we'll set up hyperlinks and then create a series of Web pages.

There are two built-in Browser Dimensions settings. Choosing the 500x335 – small setting will ensure that your document page will be displayed on a single screen within most Web Browser application programs.

1. Choose **New** from the **File** menu,

2. In the Dimensions pop-up list, select an option which is suitable for display in a Web browser application.

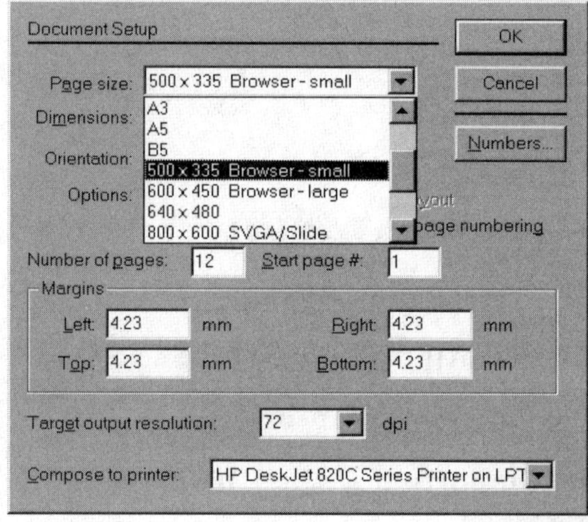

3. Make sure that the Hyperlinks palette is active (via the Window menu).

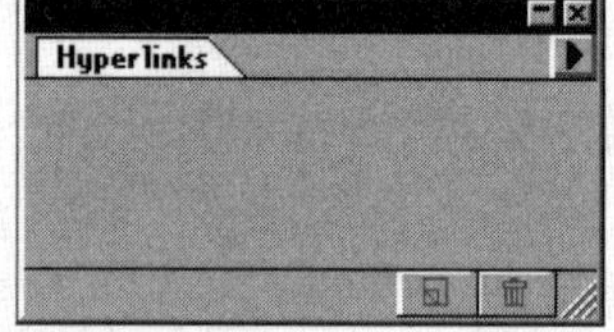

Initially the palette is empty. Once you have created the content for your document, you can start to select items of text or graphics as hyperlinks. This is done by defining a source and a destination for each link. A destination is sometimes referred to as an **Anchor**. There can be many links which share the same destination (anchor), but each source must be associated with one link only.

Creating an Anchor

1. Select the text or graphic item.
2. Open up the pop-up menu of the Hyperlinks palette and select **New Anchor**.

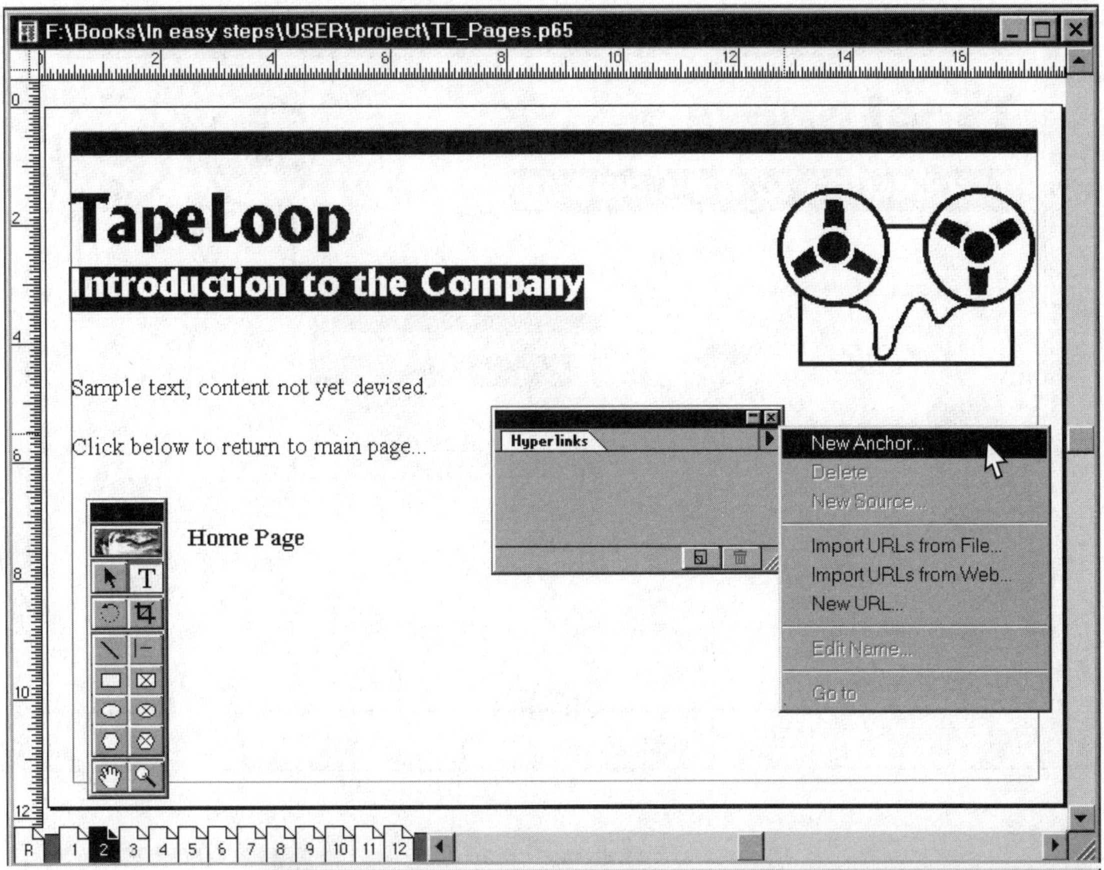

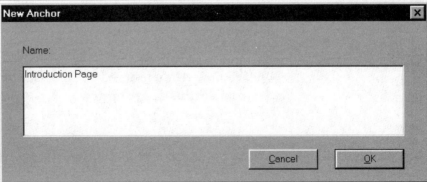

3. Type a name for the anchor in the dialog box which appears.

Now the Hyperlinks palette contains the new item.

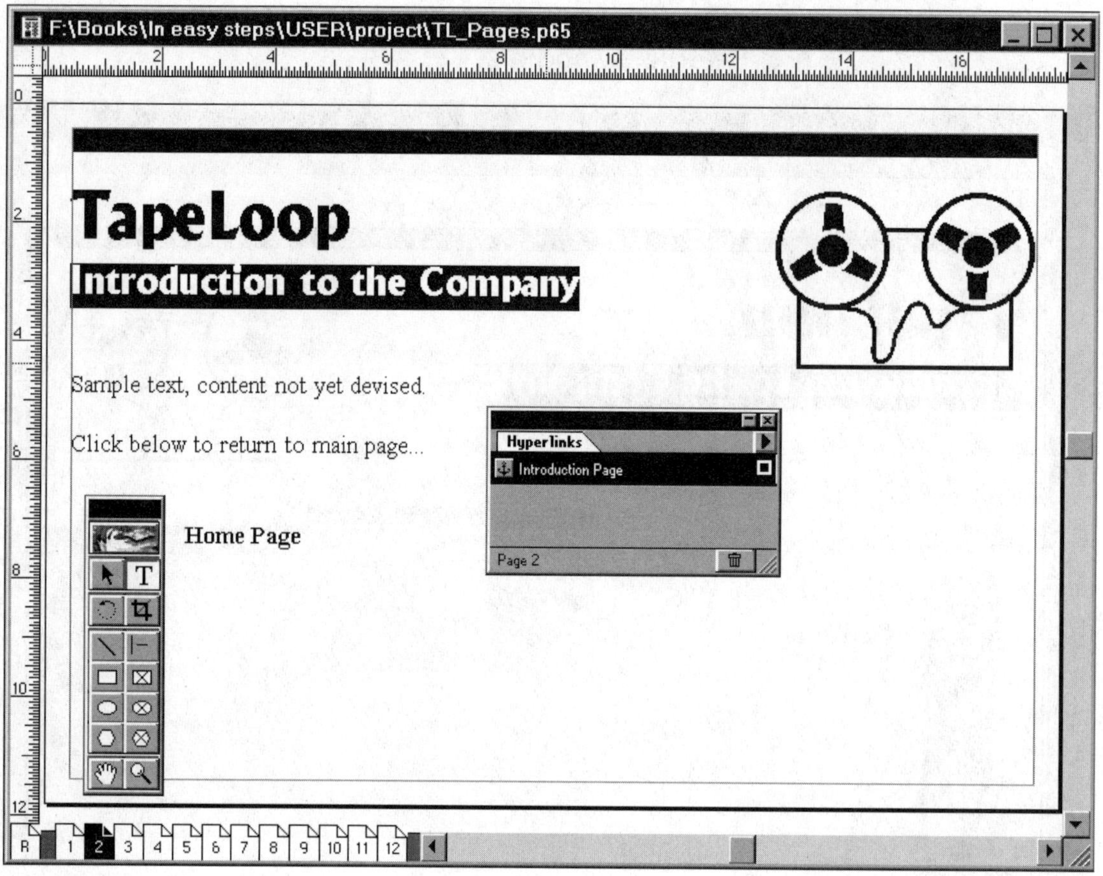

In this example we've added anchors for text items in each of the six pages within the document.

We are now ready to use these as destinations for new hyperlinks.

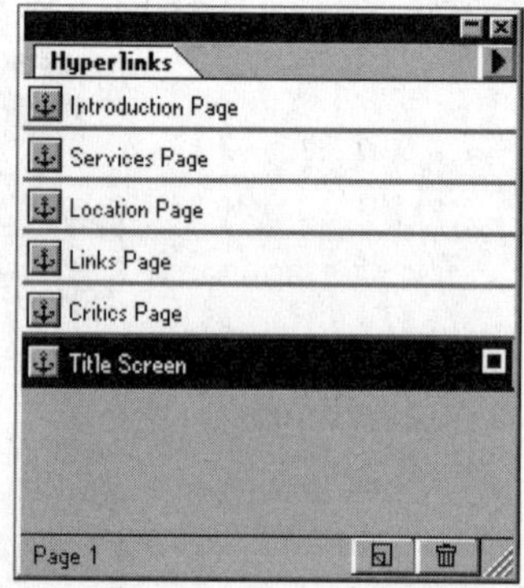

Creating a Link Source

1 Firstly select a target anchor in the Hyperlinks palette:

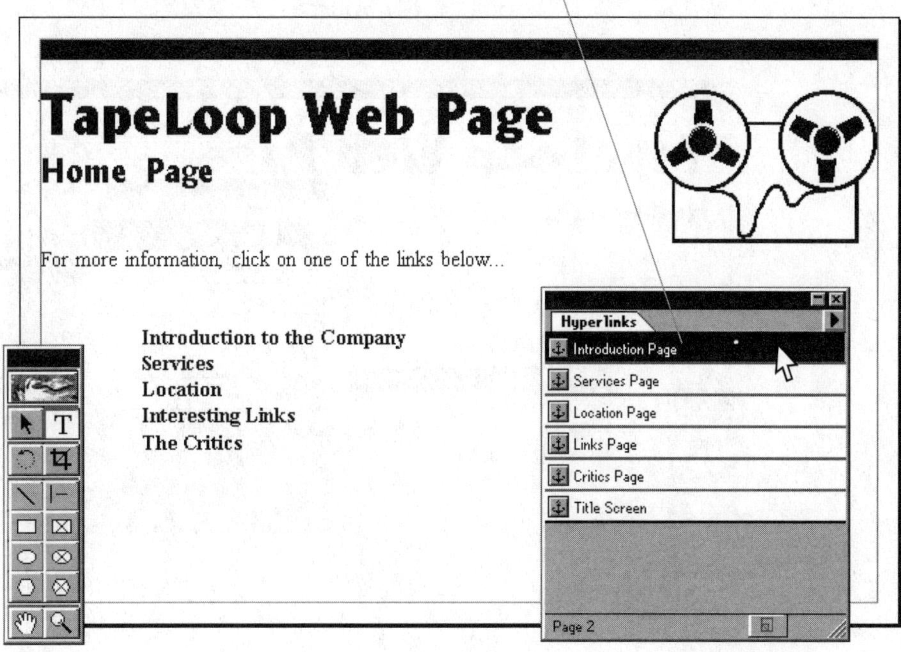

2 Next select the item (in this case some text) to be designated as the source.

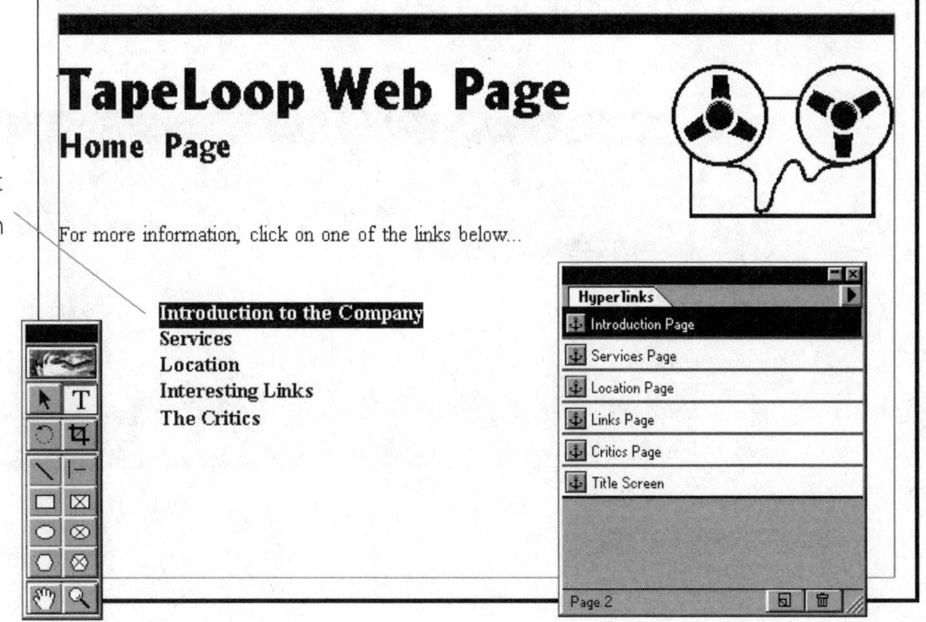

3 Open the pop-up menu in the Hyperlinks palette and choose **New Source**.

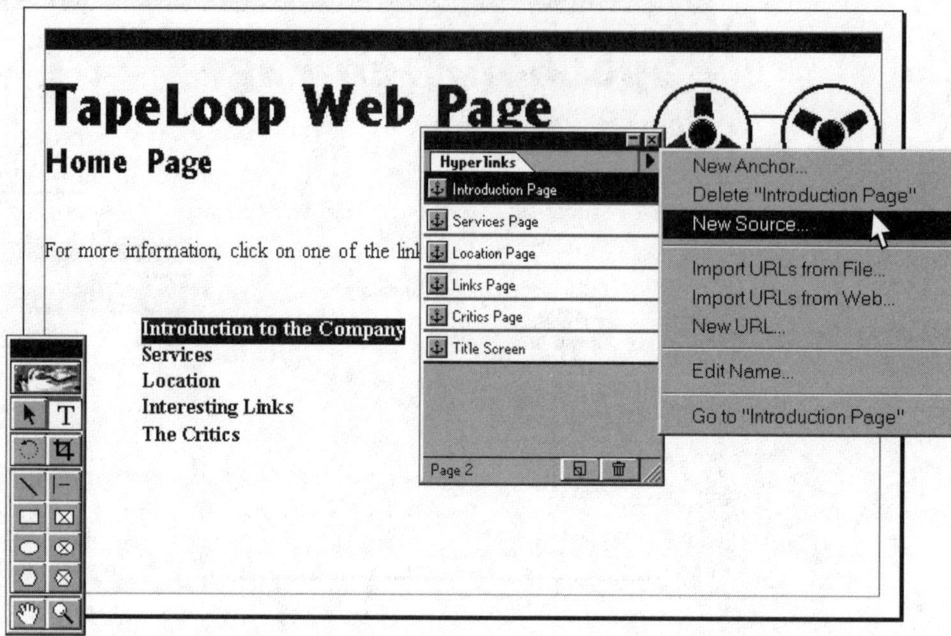

4 Enter a name for the link source in the dialog box which appears:

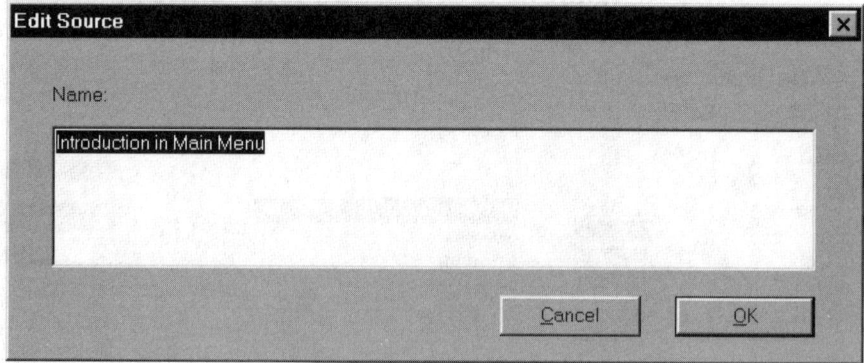

The new source appears underneath the target anchor:

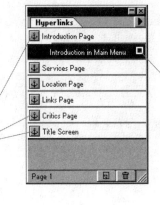

Note the anchor icons, indicating that these are destinations for hyperlinks.

This is a link source. The small box indicates that the currently selected item represents this source.

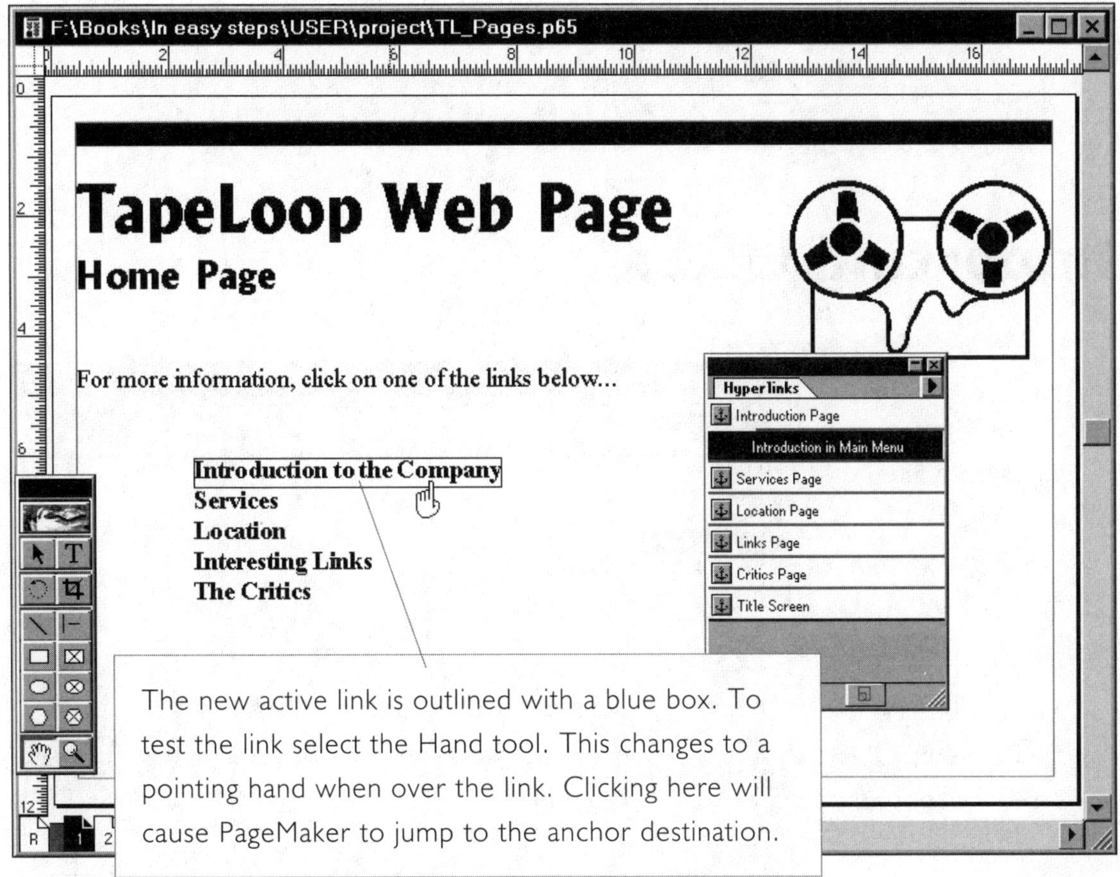

The new active link is outlined with a blue box. To test the link select the Hand tool. This changes to a pointing hand when over the link. Clicking here will cause PageMaker to jump to the anchor destination.

The Links Pop-up Menu

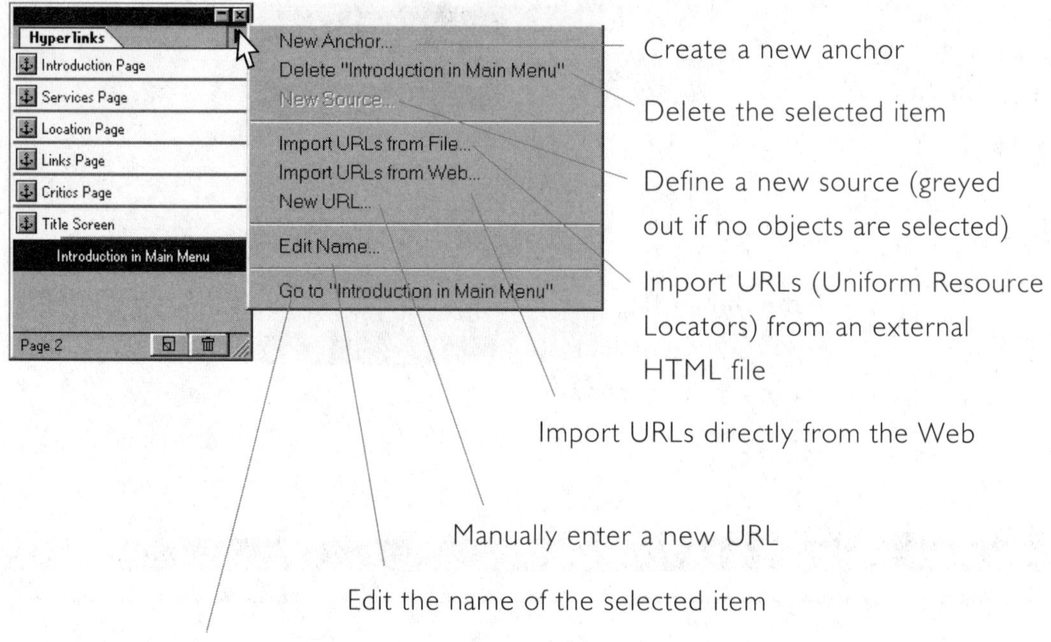

Importing URLs

1 Choose **Import URLs from File** from the Hyperlinks pop-up menu.

2 Locate and select the desired HTML file in the dialog box which appears.

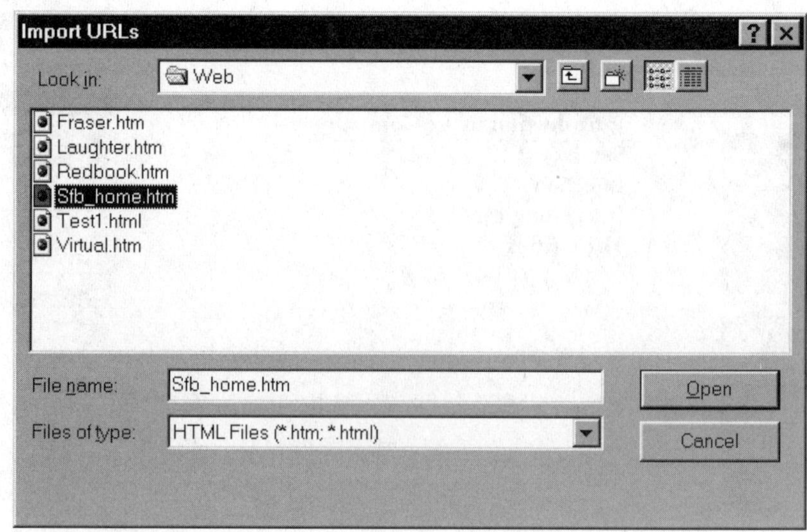

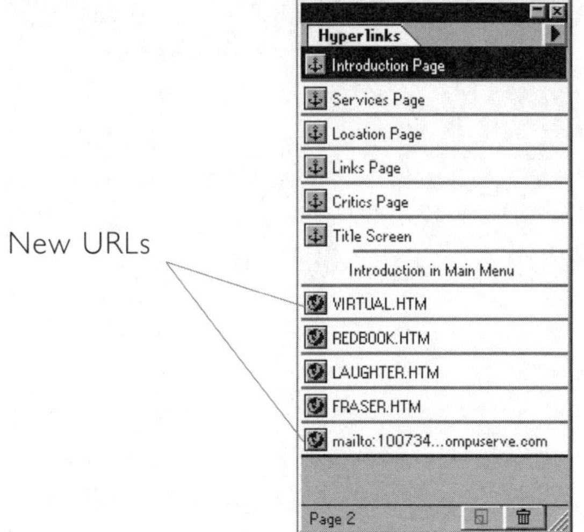

In this example five URL references were read from the HTML file. You can now use these in the same way as you would anchors, the difference being that they refer to Web pages resident somewhere on the Internet.

If you don't require any of these links destinations, then select the item and choose **Delete** from the pop-up menu.

Changing a Link Target

1. Select the appropriate source item within your document. Make sure that it is highlighted in the Hyperlinks palette.
2. Click on the anchor or URL icon for the new target. You must click on the icon rather than the target's name.
3. Click the **OK** button in the dialog box which appears. This confirms the new target.

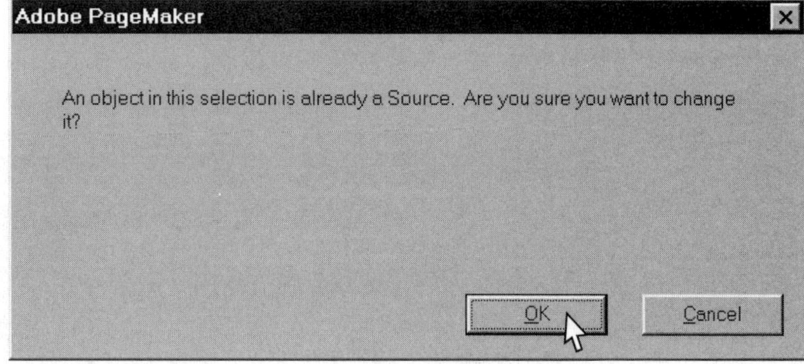

Exporting to HTML

When you are ready to create the HTML version of your document, open the **File menu**, choose the **Export** submenu, and then **HTML**.

The dialog box shown below appears.

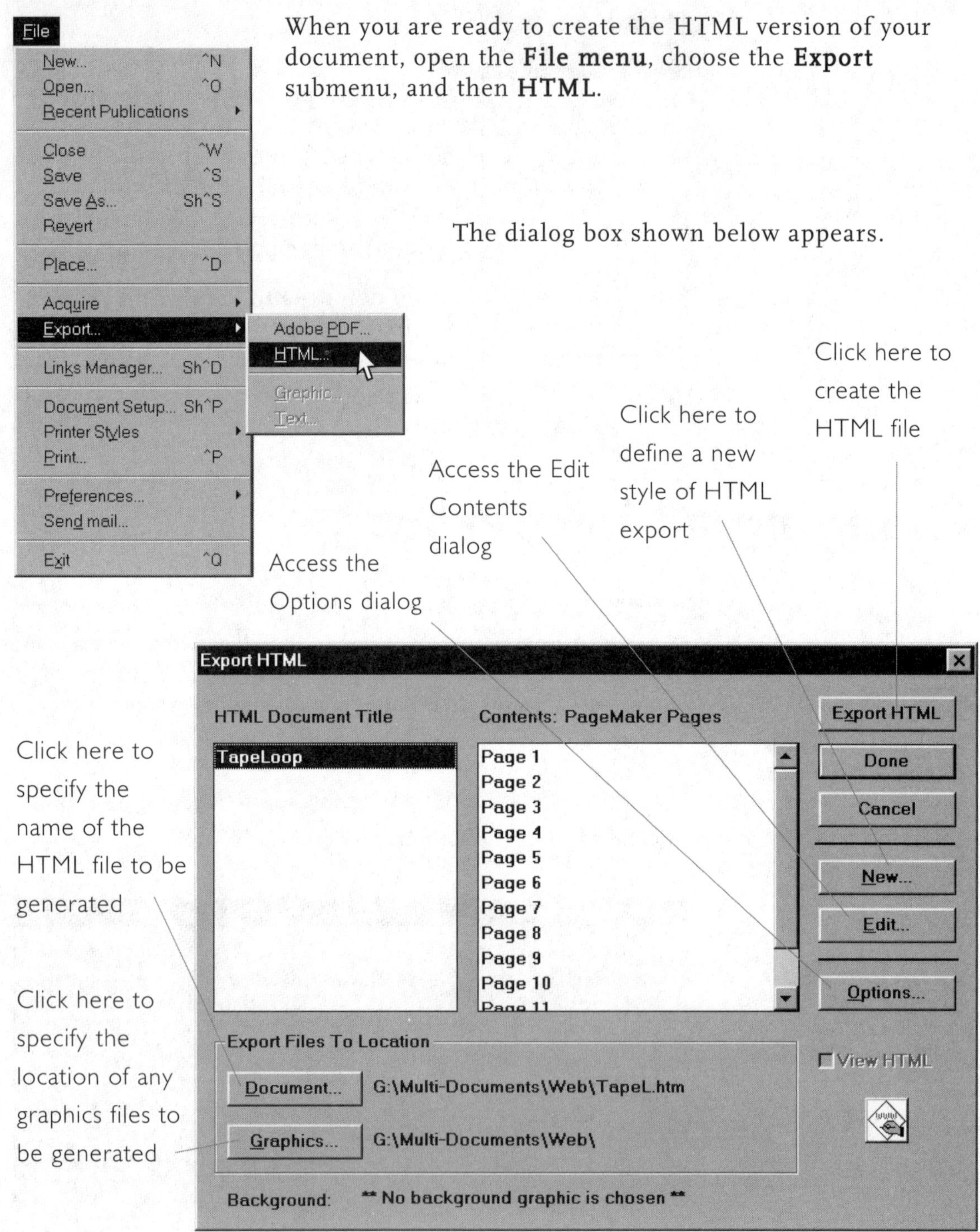

The Edit Contents Dialog

This dialog lets you give the document a title, assign pages within your document for export, and set a background graphic.

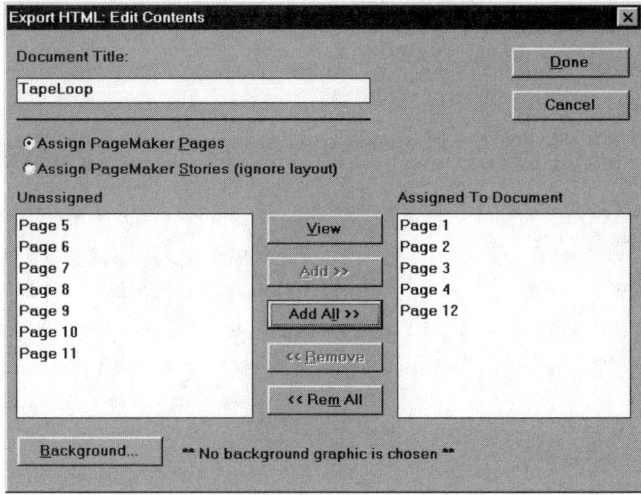

The Options Dialog

This dialog lets you set up a translation table between the styles used in your document, and the standard HTML styles which will be substituted when the Web pages are generated.

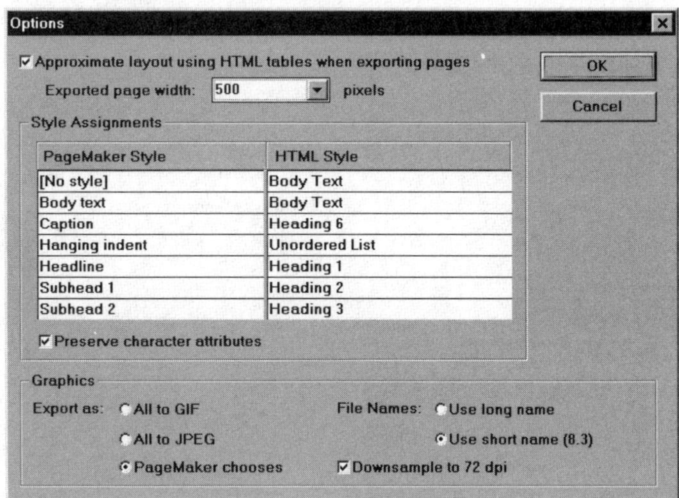

Online Preferences

1. Go to the **File menu**, open the **Preferences** submenu and choose **Online**.

The dialog box shown below appears.

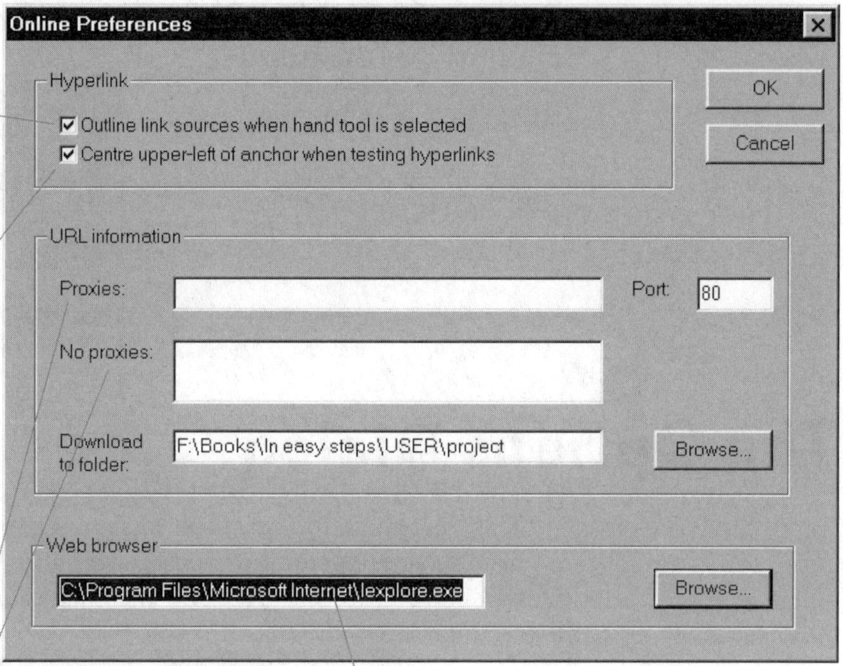

Here you can set PageMaker to highlight link sources as illustrated earlier in this chapter

This causes PageMaker to centre the page view on the top left corner of an anchor when activating a link

If filled in, these settings will depend on the setup of your Browser program

Using this box you can set up PageMaker to work with a Browser program resident within your system. If you cannot remember its name and path then click on the **Browse** button

Chapter Sixteen

Layers V6.5

In PageMaker 6.5 there is a Layers feature which is normally only found in high-end graphics packages. This allows you to organise your document into a series of overlapping layers, controlling their stacking order, appearance and locking preferences.

This chapter introduces the Layers palette, and uses visual examples to show you its range of features.

Covers

The Layers Palette

The Layers palette allows us to organise our document into a series of stacked layers. Initially there is only one layer in our document, so we'll use the Layers palette to add to this.

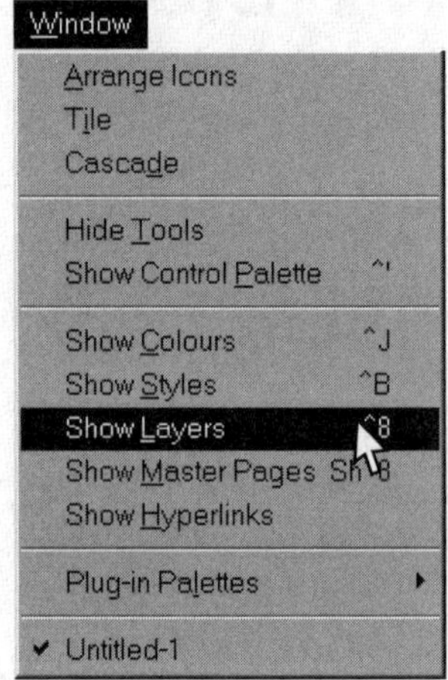

1. Make sure the Layers palette is visible (Window menu). Initially it appears with a single layer (called **Default**) present and active.

2. Prepare a document with a range of text and graphics objects on the first page. In this example we have used text, graphic illustrations and a horizontal and vertical ruled line.

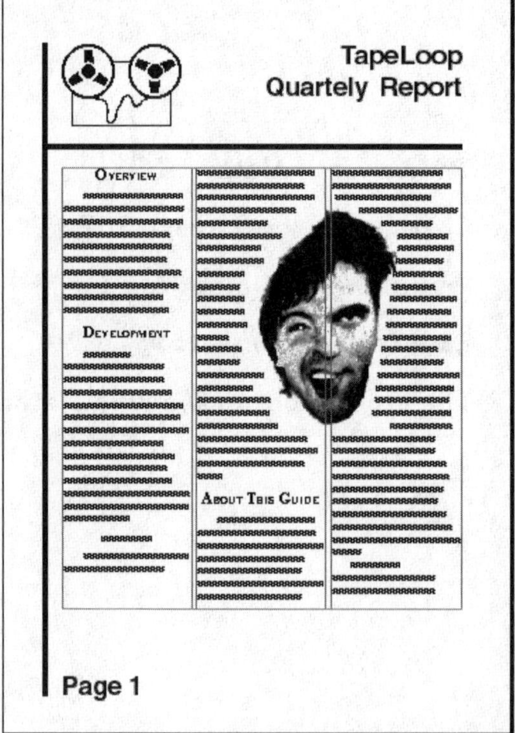

The layers palette

The pencil icon beside the default layer indicates that this is the drawing layer, where all newly created items will be placed.

Creating a New Layer

To help us to visually organise the document, we shall create a new layer specifically for the graphic illustrations. After we have assigned the graphics to that layer we will be able to control them independently of the rest of the page.

1 Open up the pop-up menu from the top right corner of the Layers palette.

2 Choose **New Layer**.

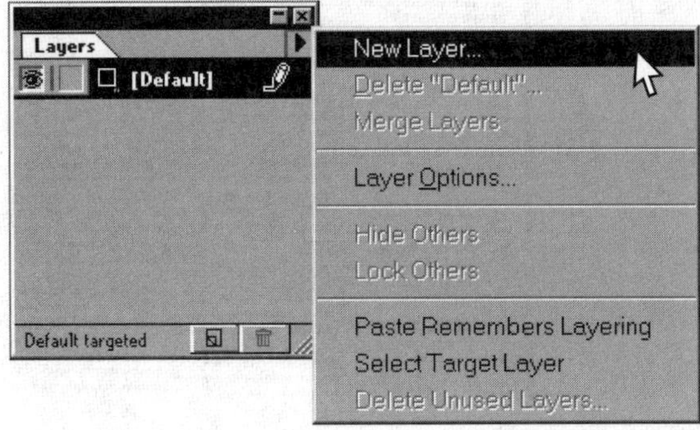

The dialog box shown below appears...

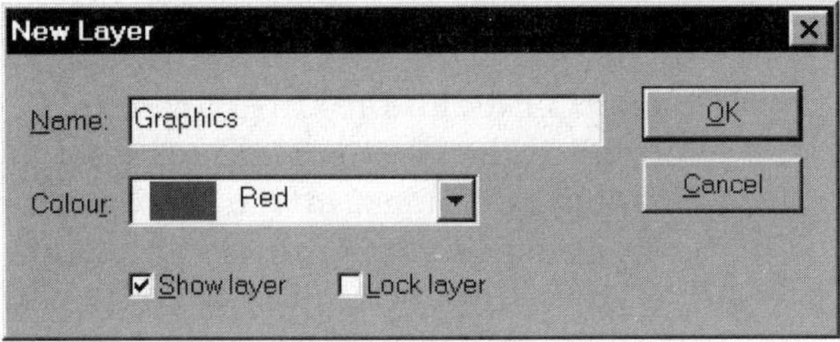

3 Enter a name for the new layer.

4 The colour you select from the Colour pop-up will determine how the layer appears in the Layer palette (it has nothing to do with printed colour). Select a colour then click **OK**.

Assigning an Object to a Layer

1 Select the appropriate object.

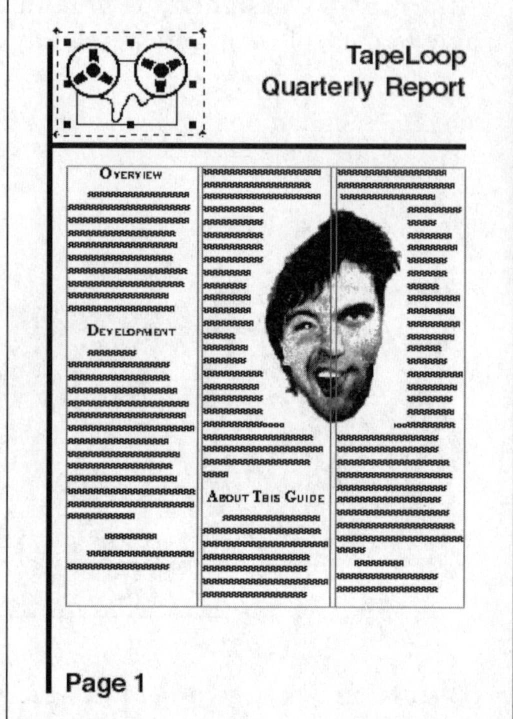

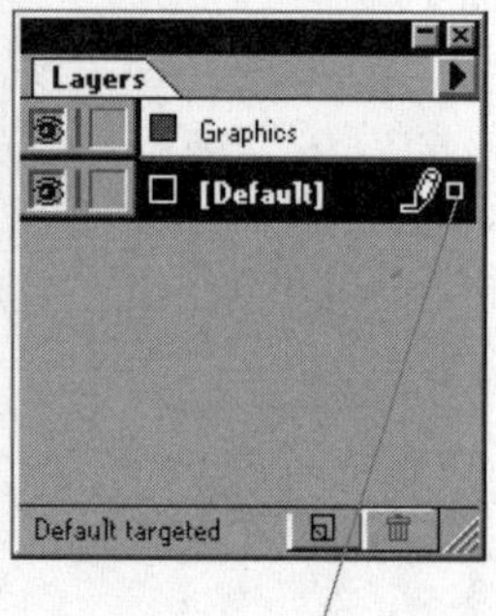

You can drag this icon from one layer to another

The object's current layer (in this case **Default**) is highlighted in the Layers palette. A small black box to the right of the layer's name represents the object(s) selected. Moving an object to another layer is simply a case of dragging this up or down to another layer entry.

3 Locate the small black box to the right of the layer's name. Drag this up onto the new Graphic layer.

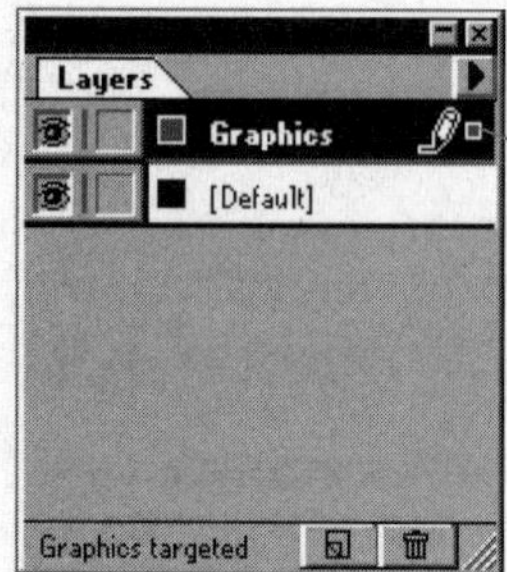

The selected item is now on the Graphics layer. Note that this has also become the new drawing layer, so all new elements will appear here initially.

Layers in Action

To take the example further, we've created separate layers for text, the horizontal/vertical lines, and some filled boxes which have been added.

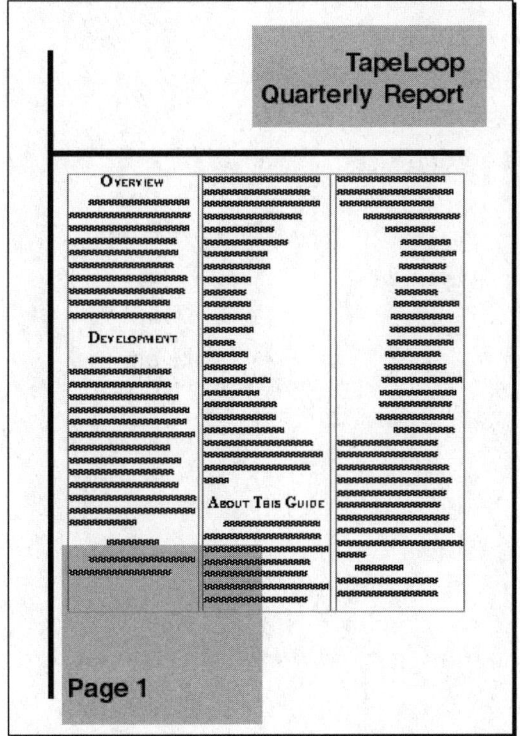

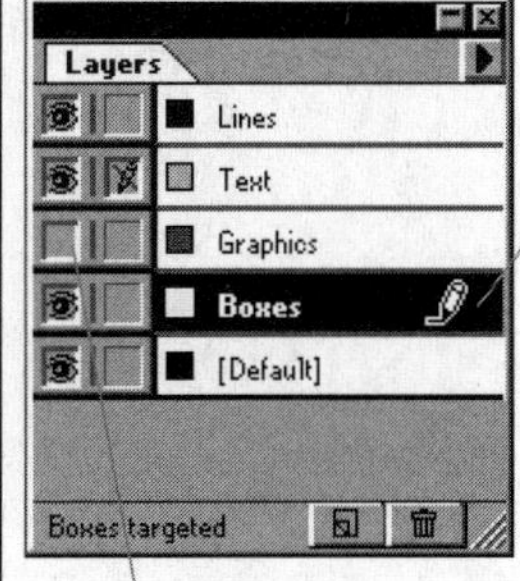

You can change the stacking order of layers simply by dragging them up or down within the palette. In this case we've moved the Boxes layer to make sure that it is below the text and graphics objects.

The eye-shaped icon can be used to toggle the layer on or off. Here we've temporarily switched off the display of the graphics elements.

It is useful to be able to switch layers off and on from time to time. Complex graphics can slow down your machine's screen redraw, and may prove to be a distraction when you're trying to edit other elements. It is much easier to make sure that all such graphics are assigned to their own layer, and then switched off when not required.

Layers can also be used to add annotations/notes to a document, then switched off prior to printing.

The Layer Pop-up Menu in Detail

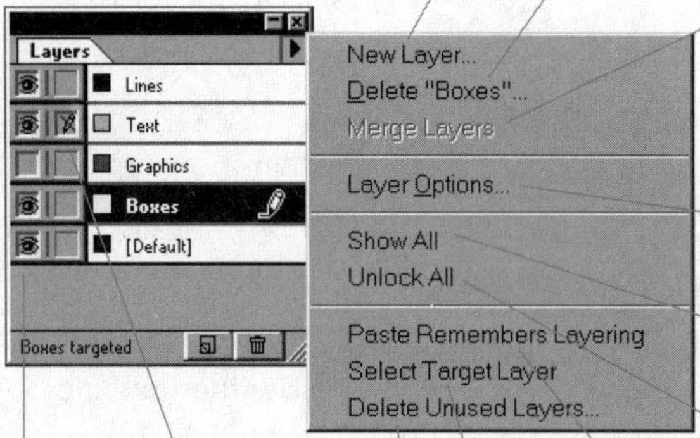

Create a new layer

Delete the selected layer

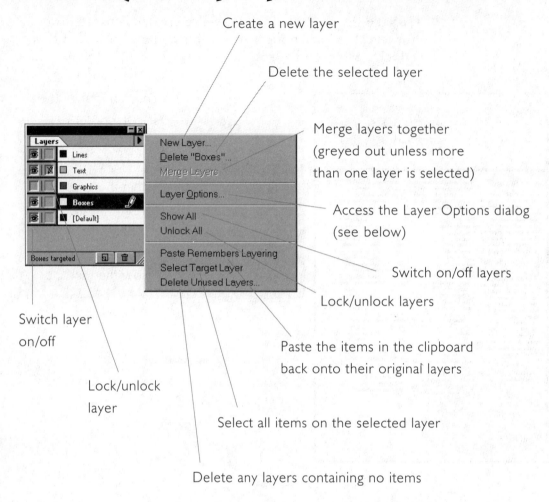

Merge layers together (greyed out unless more than one layer is selected)

Access the Layer Options dialog (see below)

Switch on/off layers

Lock/unlock layers

Switch layer on/off

Paste the items in the clipboard back onto their original layers

Lock/unlock layer

Select all items on the selected layer

Delete any layers containing no items

The Layer Options dialog allows you to rename the layer, select a different colour, show/hide and lock/ unlock the layer.

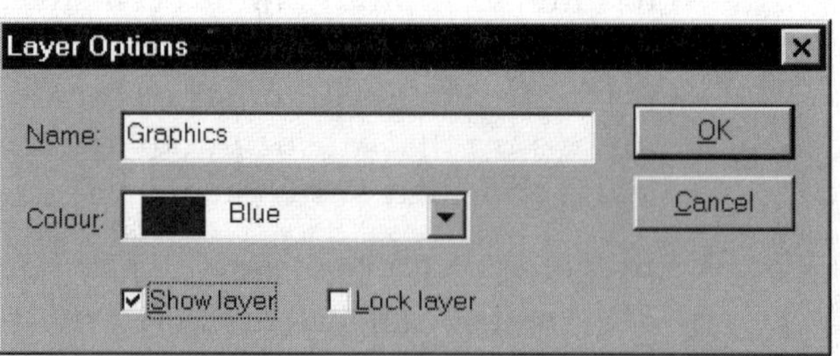

Chapter Seventeen

Utilities

PageMaker contains a wealth of utilities (many of which can be added to via the Plug-ins sub-menu). This chapter introduces you to a few of these, as well as some more integral features such as the Library palette and the facility to compress TIFF files.

Covers

The Table Editor V4 and above

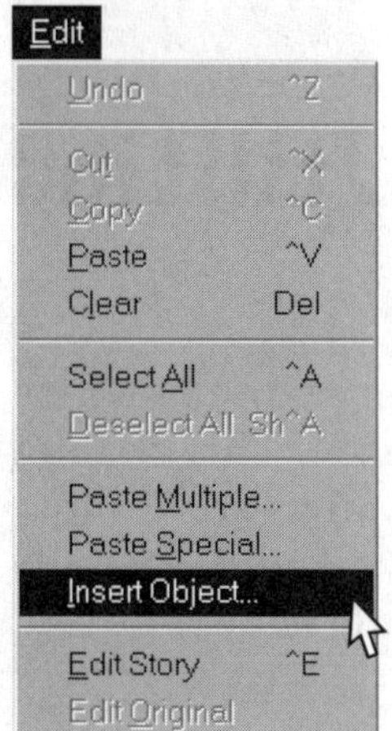

This is a separate Application program designed to help you create tables of text for use in PageMaker.

1. To activate the Table Editor from within PageMaker, choose **Insert Object** from the **Edit** menu.

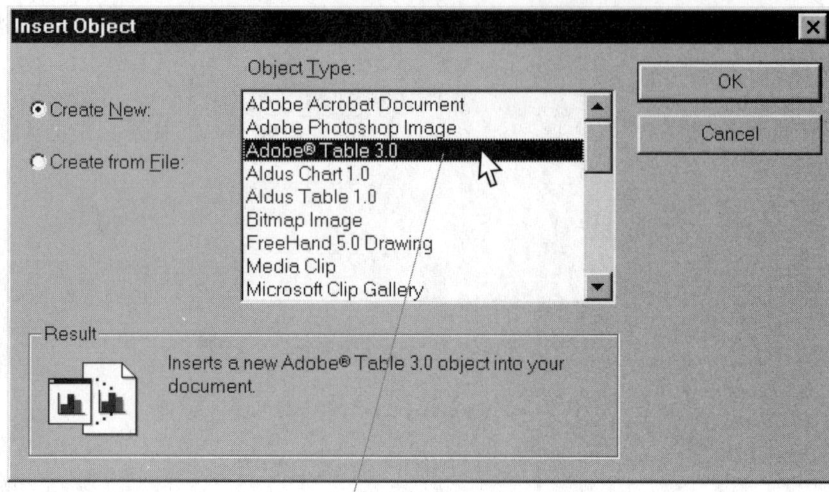

REMEMBER **You can also run the Table Editor program independently, from the Windows 95/98 Start menu, or the Windows 3.1 Program or File Manager.**

2. Select the **Adobe Table** object type and click **OK**.

3. Select the appropriate Table setup options, then click **OK**. You can return to this at any time from the Table Editor's File menu.

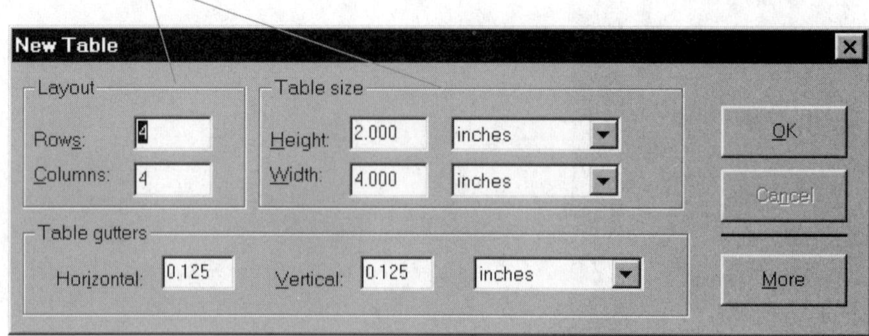

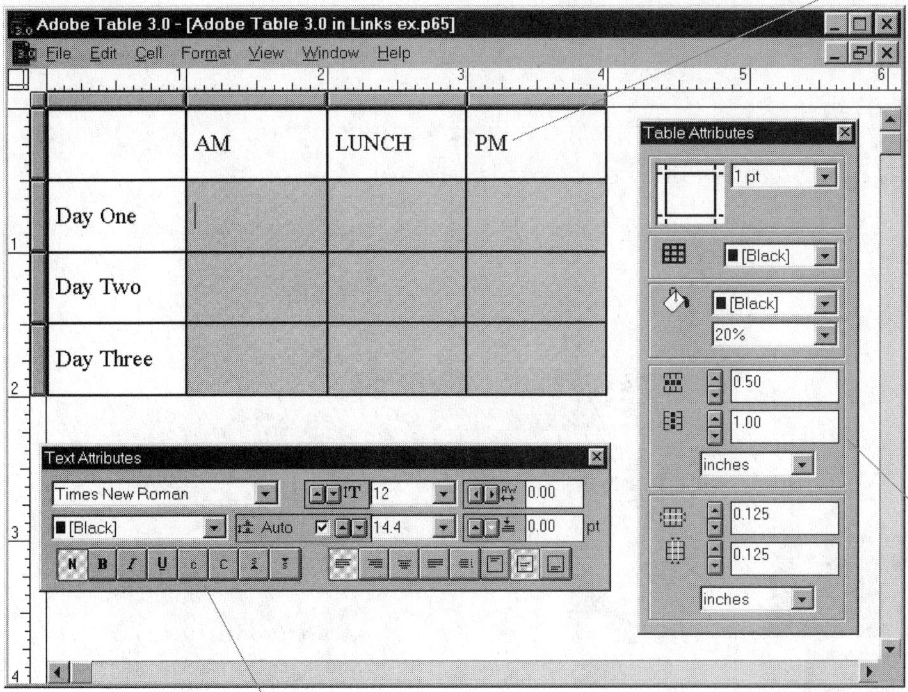

4 Enter the text of your table in the appropriate cells, just as you would in a spreadsheet package

You can use this palette to change cell attributes such as line, fill and dimensions

This palette controls text formatting. You can also choose Type and Paragraph Specs as menu options

5 When you are happy with your table, close the Table Editor by selecting the **Exit and Return** command from the **File** menu. You are returned to PageMaker, and the table appears in your document for you to position and resize.

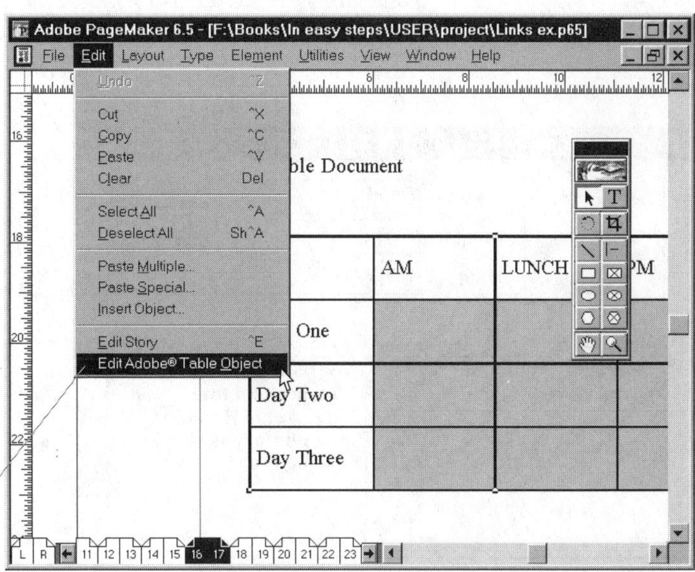

To edit the table subsequently, select it and then choose Edit Adobe® Table Object (Edit menu)

The Library Palette V5 and above

This palette can be used to store commonly required PageMaker elements.

REMEMBER **If there are no libraries to open, then enter a name to create a new library after attempting to activate the Library palette.**

1. Make sure that the **Library** palette option is active (**Window** menu). The current library will appear.

Click here to access the library options menu

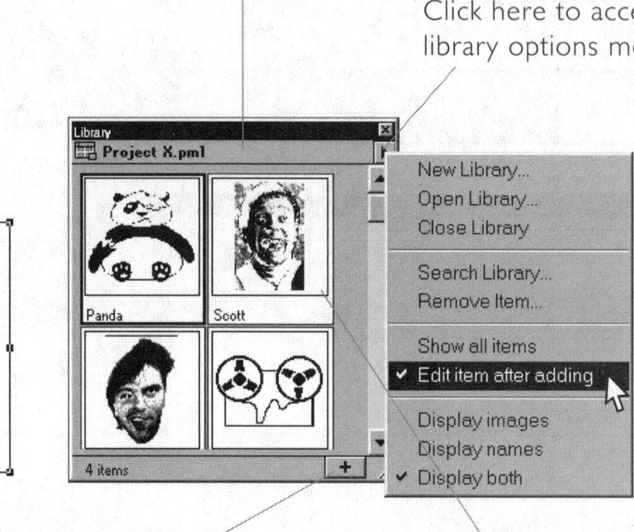

Click here to add the selected item to the current library

To retrieve a copy of an item from the library, simply drag it onto the page or Pasteboard

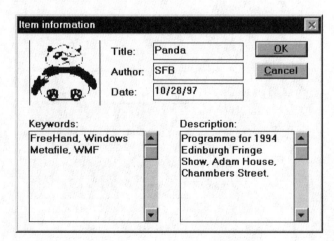

If you double-click on a library item you can enter information such as Title, Author, Date and Description.

Keywords can be used as a basis for a search operation activated from the library options menu.

Sorting Pages V5 and above

The **Sort Pages** feature, present as a plug-in Addition in PageMaker 5, can be accessed directly from the Layout menu in PageMaker 6 and above.

This allows you to easily re-order the pages in your document, simply by dragging the page thumbnail images around within the window.

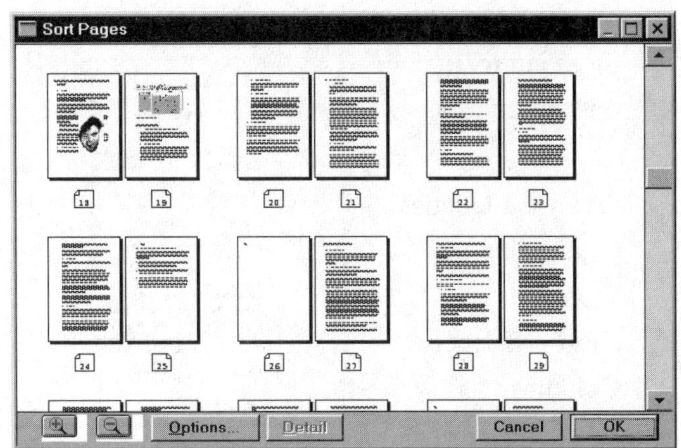

When re-ordering a publication, bear in mind any stories which run over several pages.

Create PDF V5 and above

PDF is Adobe's Portable Document Format, which allows the Adobe Acrobat reader to access PDF files with hyperlinks. The **Create Adobe PDF...** command allows you to export your PageMaker document in PDF form. To access this choose **File** menu, **Export** submenu then **Adobe PDF**.

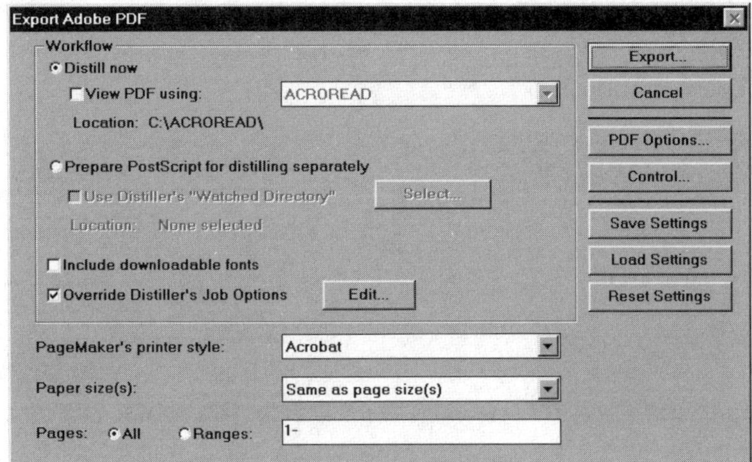

PDF files retain all formatting including fonts and graphics. With a freely available Plug-in utility, many Web browsers can display PDF files, providing true WYSIWYG (What You See Is What You Get) on the Internet.

Balancing Columns V5 and above

1. Select a number of columns of threaded text, all on the same page.

2. Open the **Utilities** menu, **Plug-ins** submenu, and choose **Balance Columns**.

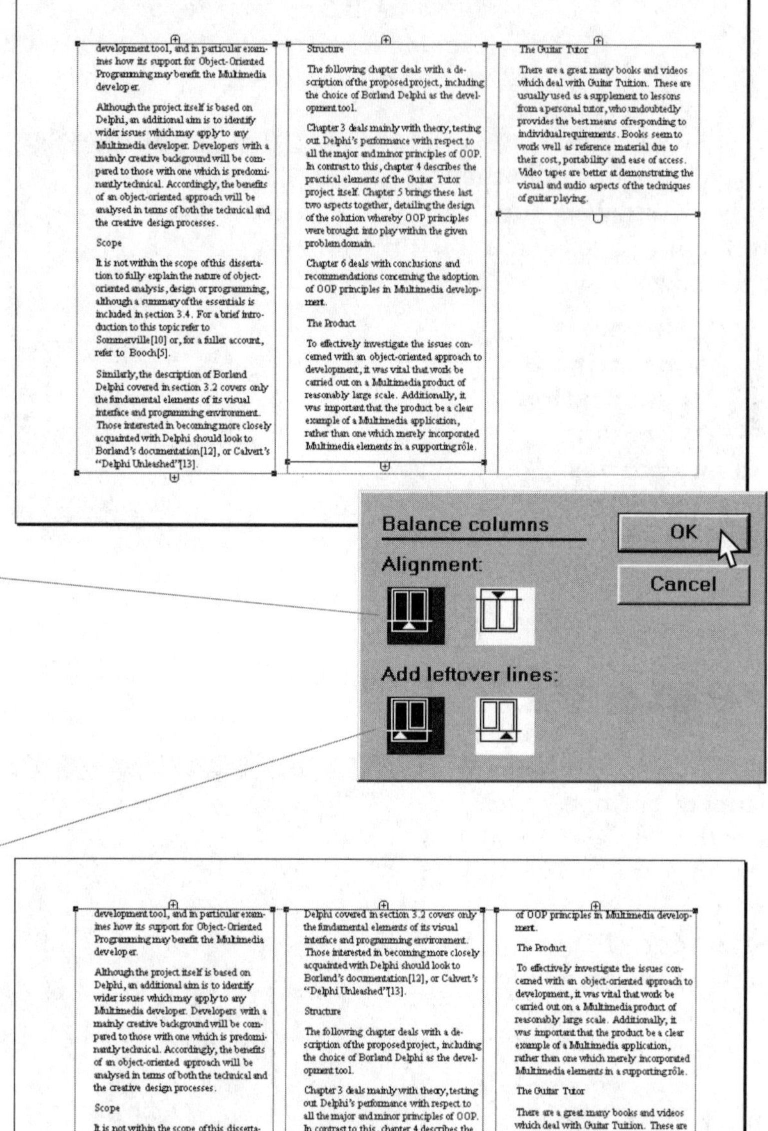

From this dialog you can choose to balance either the tops or bottoms of the selected columns

You can also specify where any additional left over lines will go

3. Click **OK**.

Create Keyline V5 and above

A keyline is usually an outline box which surrounds a text or graphic object. In PageMaker 6.5 you may wish to use the Frames feature to place an element within a frame which itself has a stroke (line) style. However, for other versions of PageMaker, and for smaller objects (e.g. icons), you can use the Create Keyline Plug-in.

1. Select the object.
2. Open the **Utilities** menu, **Plug-ins** submenu, and choose **Create Keyline** or **Keyline**.

The following dialog box appears:

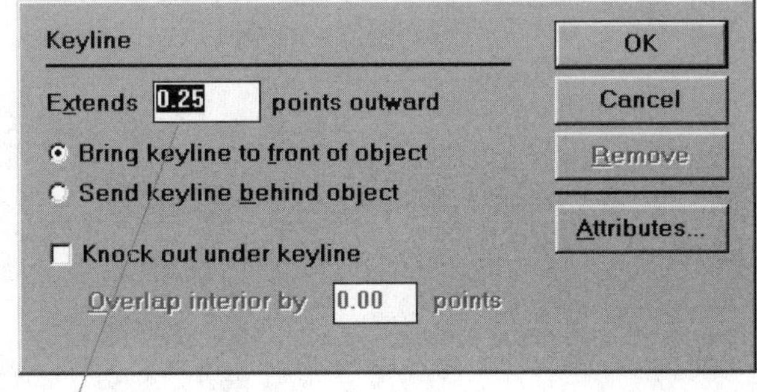

This figure represents how far away from each edge of the object the keyline will appear.

3. Choose the appropriate settings then click **OK**. The keyline appears. In PageMaker 6.5 the keyline is automatically grouped with its associated object.

Compressing TIFF Files

TIFF files can take up a lot of space on disk and within a document, depending on their size, resolution and number of colours/grey levels.

PageMaker has built-in LZW (Lempel-Ziv & Welch) TIFF compression, which works by making a compressed copy of the file without changing the original.

1. Choose **Place** from the **File** menu.

For moderate compression:

2. Select the file and then hold down **Control** and **Alt** as you click **OK**. Keep these keys held down for a few seconds afterwards.

To avoid name clashes PageMaker adds a suffix to the compressed copy it creates: (_P or _D for moderate compression, and _L or _M for maximum compression).

For maximum compression:

As above, but hold down **Control**, **Shift** and **Alt**.

Name	Size (bytes)
hybrid.tif	185520
hybrid_d.tif	37412
hybrid_m.tif	35322

The compression efficiency will depend on the contents of the graphic. In this example the original was compressed to about a fifth of its original size.

Chapter Eighteen

Tips and Techniques

As well as learning the features of PageMaker, it is important to spend time contemplating your general work methods. We have already seen that using Style Sheets can help you to work in a more organised and efficient fashion.

In this chapter we'll look at creating and using template documents, copying between documents, and general ways of improving your overall design skills. Finally, there are a few tips on how to use this book to its best effect if you have an Apple Macintosh.

Covers

Template Documents

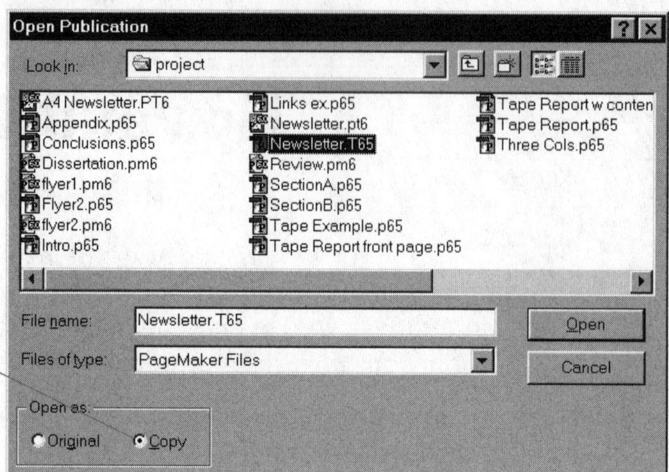

Note the default option to open an untitled copy. You can override this if you wish to edit the original file.

A PageMaker 6.5 template document has a T65 (PT6 for version 6, PT5 for version 5), rather than a P65 extension (or PM6, PM5, ...). PageMaker will by default open a copy (rather than the original) of a template when **Open** is chosen from the File menu.

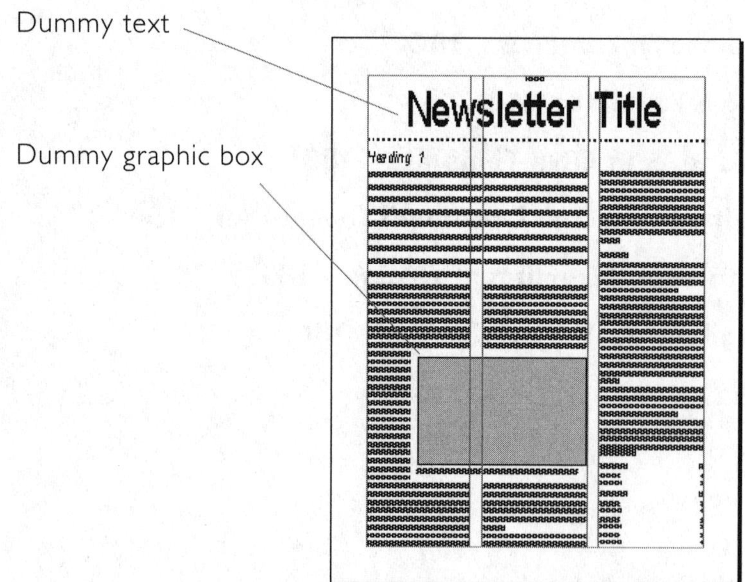

A template is actually an ordinary PageMaker document. It has normally been designed as a blueprint, a specimen for you to adapt to your own needs.

This template is a newsletter created using dummy text and FPO (for position only) graphic boxes.

Using a Template

Once you have opened a copy of a template, you can edit it just as you would a document you had created from scratch, replacing text and graphic objects as you see fit.

The original text was selected and then overtyped, retaining all of its original attributes.

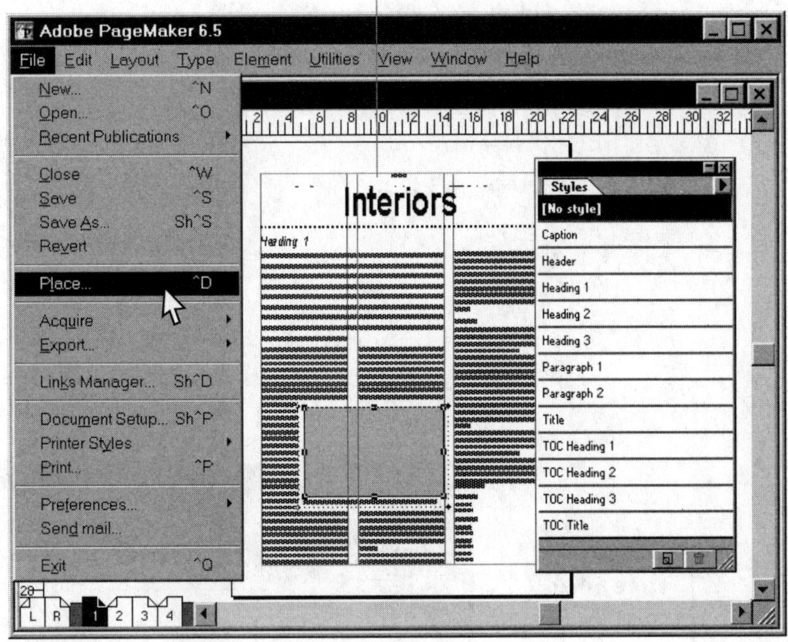

Retyping Text

Retype any small pieces of dummy text by selecting first with the text tool. The original text attributes will remain as you overtype.

Replacing Graphic Elements

1. Select a dummy graphic with the pointer tool.
2. Choose **Place** from the **File** menu.

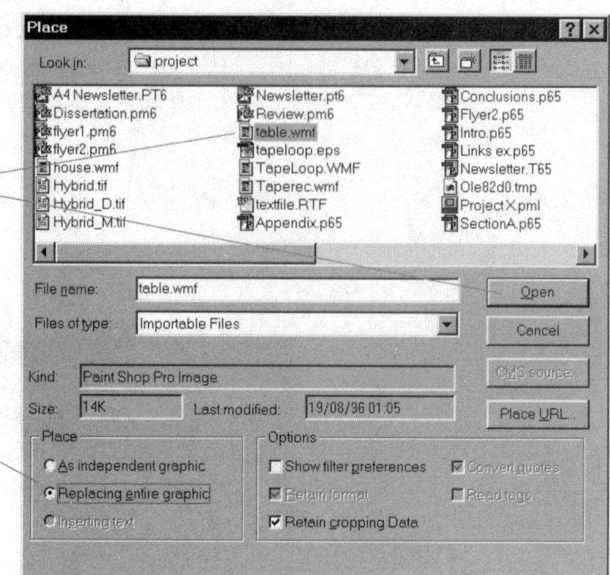

3 Select the new file and click **Open**.

4 From the Place dialog box, make sure that the **Replacing entire graphic** option is active. If it is greyed out then there is no element currently selected – click Cancel and repeat steps 1 and 2.

The imported element will replace the original, retaining its position, size and text wrap properties:

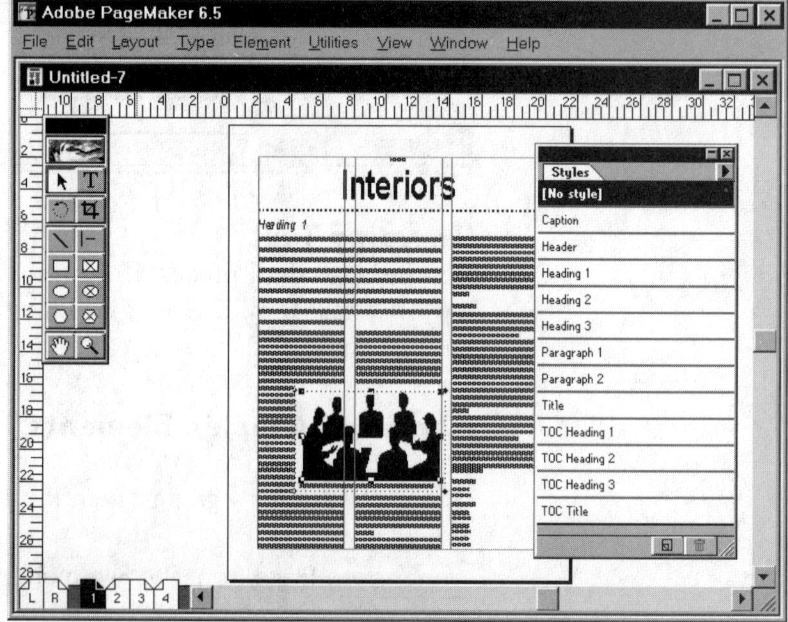

Single or threaded text blocks can also be replaced using this method.

Creating Your Own Template

If you need to produce a consistent series of documents (e.g. reports where the contents vary from month to month but the design remains the same), then it is a good idea to create a template:

1. Create the PageMaker document in the normal way. It is usual to use dummy text and grey boxes for graphics to be replaced.
2. Choose **Save** from the **File** menu.

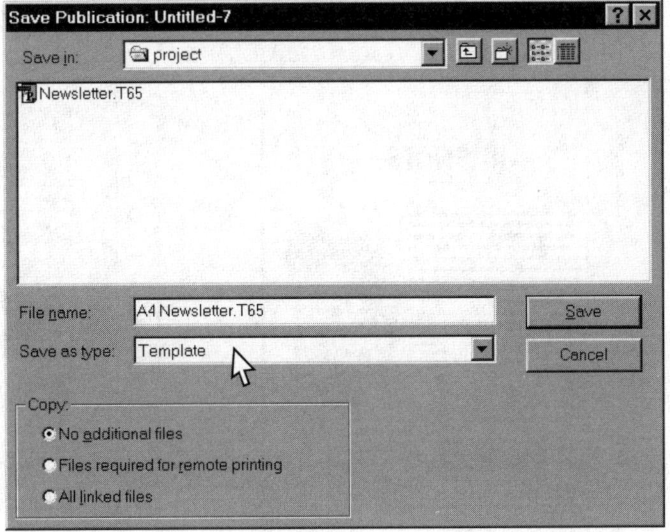

3. Select the **Template** option in the **Save as type** box.
4. Click **Save**.

A T65 document will be created. Another advantage of using templates is that they can be used by someone with minimal design/typography experience, since that part of the document-generation process has already been completed by the template designer.

Copying From One Document to Another

You can copy objects from one PageMaker document to another without using the Clipboard, simply by dragging an element over into an adjacent window:

1. Open both documents in turn (**File** menu).
2. Choose **Tile** from the **Window** menu:

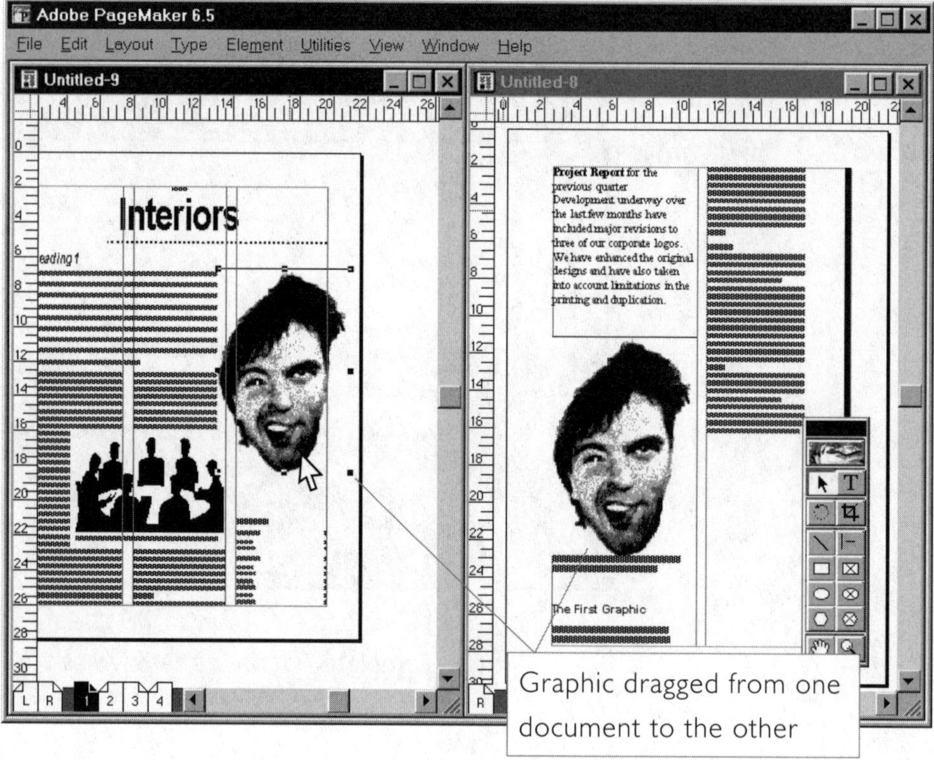

Graphic dragged from one document to the other

You will be able to view both publications side by side.

3. Locate the item to be copied in one document, then move to the proposed destination in the second.
4. Simply drag the element from one document to the other (the original will not be removed from the first document).

Tips for Good Document Design

- Use the Master pages as fully as possible to set up a consistent design which is carried throughout your document. Even if you use multiple Master pages, think about how you can make them visually consistent with each other.
- Use columns and guidelines to create a layout grid. If you keep your text and graphic elements aligned to this grid then your document will assume a clear structure. Remember that the Grid Manager (Utilities menu, Plug-ins submenu) can help with this.
- Try not to use too many fonts or text effects. Often good results can be gained from restricting yourself to two basic fonts, one for headings and one for body text.
- Allow yourself the use of white space. Surrounding white space is one of the most underused but most effective ways of emphasizing an element. It is usually not necessary to completely fill each page.
- Make sure that text is always readable. Too many characters to a line, or too little vertical space between lines (leading) can create a solid mass of text which is tiring to read.
- If your final output will be to an HTML file, bear in mind the limitations of the HTML standard. You have access to far fewer fonts and effects. Any precision layout work may not survive the translation to Web pages. Also note that people find it much more tiring to read large amounts of text from a computer screen compared with paper.
- Use paragraph styles as much as possible. This way you have the flexibility to make text-based design alterations in one simple manoeuvre at any time.
- Feel free to experiment with dummy text and graphics on the page during the early stages of design. Try to work out your document margins, text columns and general page structure right from the beginning.
- Keep your design as simple and consistent as possible.

Using PageMaker on the Mac

Although most screenshots in this book are taken from the Windows environment, Macintosh users should have little trouble in following the examples, since PageMaker is virtually identical on both platforms.

If you are a Macintosh user, bear in mind the following:

1. If a Windows keyboard command makes use of the **Control** key, use **Command** on the Macintosh, (the Control key on the Macintosh keyboard is rarely used).

2. Similarly, replace references to the Windows **Alt** key with **Option**.

3. Macintosh menus, windows and dialog boxes, whilst containing essentially the same information, have a different cosmetic look:

   Pop-up menus, indicated by a small downward-pointing arrow in Windows, sometimes appear as an option within a drop-shadow box on the Macintosh.

   Macintosh windows have a square Close box (in the top right corner) which is used to shut down the window.

   Unlike Windows, the file-type is not necessarily indicated using a three-letter suffix in its name.

   The Macintosh operating system has its own WIMP filing system which does the job of both the Windows 95/98 Desktop and Explorer, or the older Windows 3.1 File Manager and Program Manager.

Index

E

F

G

H

I

J

K

L

R

S

T

U

V

Z